Schooling in the Age of Austerity

New Frontiers in Education, Culture, and Politics

Edited by Kenneth J. Saltman

New Frontiers focuses on both topical educational issues and highly original works of educational policy and theory that are critical, publicly engaged, and interdisciplinary, drawing on contemporary philosophy and social theory. The books in the series aim to push the bounds of academic and public educational discourse while remaining largely accessible to an educated reading public. *New Frontiers* aims to contribute to thinking beyond the increasingly unified view of public education for narrow economic ends (economic mobility for the individual and global economic competition for the society) and in terms of efficacious delivery of education as akin to a consumable commodity. Books in the series provide both innovative and original criticism and offer visions for imagining educational theory, policy, and practice for radically different, egalitarian, and just social transformation.

Published by Palgrave Macmillan:

Education in the Age of Biocapitalism: Optimizing Educational Life for a Flat World
   By Clayton Pierce

Schooling in the Age of Austerity: Urban Education and the Struggle for Democratic Life
   By Alexander J. Means

Schooling in the Age of Austerity

Urban Education and the Struggle for Democratic Life

Alexander J. Means

KH

First published in 2013 by
PALGRAVE MACMILLAN®
in the United States—a division of St. Martin's Press LLC,
175 Fifth Avenue, New York, NY 10010.

Where this book is distributed in the UK, Europe and the rest of the world,
this is by Palgrave Macmillan, a division of Macmillan Publishers Limited,
registered in England, company number 785998, of Houndmills,
Basingstoke, Hampshire RG21 6XS.

Palgrave Macmillan is the global academic imprint of the above companies
and has companies and representatives throughout the world.

Palgrave® and Macmillan® are registered trademarks in the United States,
the United Kingdom, Europe and other countries.

ISBN: 978–1–137–03203–4 (hc)
ISBN: 978–1–137–03204–1 (pb)

Library of Congress Cataloging-in-Publication Data

Means, Alexander J., 1977–
    Schooling in the age of austerity : urban education and the struggle for
democratic life / Alexander J. Means.
        p. cm.
    ISBN 978–1–137–03203–4 (hardback)
    1. Urban schools—United States—Case studies. 2. Public schools—United
States—Case studies. 3. Children with social disabilities—Education—United
States—Case studies. 4. Education—Social aspects—United States—Case
studies. 5. Equality—United States—Case studies. 6. Neoliberalism—United
States—Case studies. I. Title.

LC5131.M37 2012
370.9173'2—dc23   2012033670

A catalogue record of the book is available from the British Library.

Design by Newgen Imaging Systems (P) Ltd., Chennai, India.

First edition: February 2013

10 9 8 7 6 5 4 3 2 1

10/6/14

Contents

Acknowledgments

Like all large projects, this book owes a debt to the kindness and generosity of many people. I should begin by thanking all of the educators, activists, and young people at Carter High School who took the time to talk with me and whose perspectives and experiences animate the text. Kathleen Gallagher needs to be singled out as well for supervising my PhD. Her passion and insight into ethnography and the study of culture and human beings has been a source of great inspiration. My gratitude also goes to Ken Saltman. His continued intellectual engagement and generosity have informed my thinking on a wide range of the issues taken up in this project, particularly around the relationship between security and neoliberalism. This project has also benefited from the support of many scholars who have provided opportunities and inspiration over the last several years. I would like to particularly thank Henry and Susan Giroux, Robin Truth Goodman, Roland Sintos Coloma, Megan Boler, Roger Simon, Pauline Lipman, Stephen Haymes, Michael Peters, Noah De Lissovoy, Chris Robbins, Tyson Lewis, Miles Weafer, Diane Uí Thonnaigh, Bryan Hoekstra, Kendall Taylor, and Josh Shepard. I owe special thanks to Kari Dehli, Caroline Fusco, and Alan Sears for serving on my PhD committee and for their support of my work. Special thanks also to those in the Critical Reading Group and the Society and Security Project at OISE, especially Shahrzad Mojab, Amir Hassanpour, Sara Carpenter, Tara Silver, Jesse Bazzul, and Chris Arthur. I also want to thank my friends Michael Conway and Paul Aitken. Paul Aitken, in particular, deserves being singled for gracefully accepting his role as my primary computer technician, document formatter, music collaborator, and sounding board for my various neurotic anxieties about academic life. Special thanks are also due to my family, especially to my sister Sarah for opening her home to me during the research phase of this project and also for providing continued inspiration through her talents as a teacher. Thanks also to Ken Berkey and to my twin nieces Cecelia and Caroline and nephew Jack for generally making things more interesting on my visits to Chicago. Thanks are also due to both my parents for their unconditional love and support over many years. My father's lifelong commitment to ideas and his enthusiasm for my work and our discussions on critical theory and politics continue to be deeply appreciated. And finally, and most importantly, to Anna Gelino, whose friendship, love, and support mean everything.

Introduction: Schooling in a Time of Crisis and Austerity

> Schools express the conflicts and limitations as well as the hopes of a divided and unequal society; and they continue to be both testing grounds and battlegrounds for building a more just and freer life for all.
>
> —*Samuel Bowles and Herbert Gintis,* Schooling in Capitalist America[1]

As we drift further into the second decade of the twenty-first century, public schooling in the United States has become a focal point of anxiety and a signpost of sobering challenges. In the dominant media and among the financial and political elite, a corporate consensus has emerged that has declared public schooling to be a failed experiment—an antiquated social institution incapable of meeting the demands and assorted crises of the global era.[2] The rhetoric of educational failure is most often invoked in relation to "urban education"—a not-so-subtle "race neutral" euphemism for public schools that serve primarily impoverished communities and mostly black and Latino youth. Dominant explanations for the perpetuation of "failure" in such schools—low test scores, dysfunctional environments, high dropout rates, and so on—have become increasingly predictable. Across a network of high-profile corporate reform advocates, right-wing think tanks, business groups, and corporate foundations the problem is said to be located in the inefficient and corrupt nature of the public sector itself and the supposed incompetence and greed of teachers and their unions. The future of the nation is said to depend on restructuring public school systems by subjecting them to commercial management and the private discipline of market forces. In order to save public education, it is argued, we must break-up the "public school monopoly" through the wholesale privatization of the educational commons. However, while the corporate reform movement has been framed in the progressive language of educational innovation and equity, the evidence continues to mount that free market experimentation has failed to improve public education in any meaningful sense while contributing to already staggering social and educational inequalities. In this light, the reforms appear to have more to do with political and economic expediency than with robust investment in the human development and the educational futures of all young people. How else to explain policies that continue to undermine the very public education system on which the future of the nation supposedly depends?[3]

Not unlike the spectacular failure of the global financial system in 2008, the problems that confront inner-city public schools today can be attributed largely to a systemic failure—a toxic mixture of global economic change and volatility, profiteering and corruption, stunted imagination, and misguided policies, values, and priorities. This has contributed to deepening poverty and inequality in the urban sphere and the evaporation of social commitments to public schools and young people, particularly the most historically disadvantaged and vulnerable. *Schooling in the Age of Austerity* examines this systemic failure "on the ground" through an ethnographic case study in a low-income and racially segregated community and public high school in the city of Chicago. Through the perspectives of those most affected, namely youth and their teachers, it documents the lived contradictions and myriad impacts of educational privatization, disinvestment, commercialization, and the rise of a militaristic culture of policing and containment in urban public schools and neighborhoods. It argues that these processes are indicative of a neoliberal culture and political economy that is eroding the educative and democratic purpose of urban public schools while making the daily lives and futures of young people ever more precarious and insecure. While the book offers no easy answers or quick fixes, at its core is a belief that a vibrant system of public education is a key ethical component in imagining and realizing a future worthy of our highest aspirations and ideals. As such, it advocates for an educational vision that locates public schooling not as a *commodity* valued primarily for its role in shoring-up narrow economic and national security imperatives, but as a *commons*—a site critical to developing human security, economic justice, and democratic life. Such an educational vision is already shared by scores of educators, parents, students, and community activists who are deeply skeptical and disillusioned with corporate management and market experimentation in education and who yearn for public schools responsive to the complex needs and desires of youth and their communities; schools that do not reduce learning to issues of market competition, punishment, and test scores; and schools designed to cultivate restorative and sustainable futures for all young people.

*   *   *

Over the last several years, I have had the good fortune of living in the city of Toronto, Ontario. As an American graduate student, living in Toronto has been valuable for observing issues concerning globalization and educational politics that have challenged and enriched my thinking not only about urban Canada but the United States as well. In 2007, during the first year of my doctoral studies at the University of Toronto, a 14-year-old student named Jordan Manners was shot and killed in the hallway of C. W. Jeffery's Collegiate Institute—a public high school in North Toronto. This rare and tragic event engendered an outpouring of public discussion in the Toronto media and prompted three major governmental commissions, one headed by attorney Julian Falconer at the behest of former Toronto mayor David Miller, another conducted by the Toronto District School Board (TDSB), and another provincial study undertaken by former Ontario minister Alvin Curling and former Ontario chief justice Roy McMurtry. Each of the investigations concluded that a variety of factors contribute to violence and insecurity in Toronto's schools, including concentrated poverty, racism, inadequate resources, and racial profiling of students by police.

Writing of the TDSB report in the *Toronto Star*, David Hulchanski (2008), director of the University of Toronto's Centre for Urban and Community Studies, has suggested that while the commissions rightly identified poverty and racism as central factors impacting schools and young people, they nonetheless fell short in sufficiently addressing the economic conditions and political decisions that serve to perpetuate and deepen inequality and exclusion in the city. His analysis points toward the systemic realities and effects of three decades of steep cuts to social services and the downward trajectory of income and job security within the city's postindustrial economy. Moreover, despite being relatively shielded from the most immediate and damaging effects of the global economic crisis—largely due to sane banking regulation and a western economic boom spurred by dirty tar sands oil—there has been a steady expansion of social inequality in Canada and a steady upward redistribution of wealth and power to the richest Canadians.[4] Hulchanski argues that amid these broader structural conditions, Toronto schools by themselves cannot be expected to provide substantive forms of security for students in a city that is increasingly divided by wealth and privilege. He concludes by asking "will 40 percent of Toronto be abandoned, as the research literature predicts, to become Toronto's vast 'ghetto of the excluded'?"

Hulchanksi's comments represent an attempt to make visible the economic, cultural, and political relations driving present experiences of insecurity and everyday violence across North American cities and beyond. They also raise basic questions about the meaning and limits of security within educational institutions and in the lives of youth at the margins of the new urban geography. Over the last three decades, cities across North America have become increasingly polarized along the lines of race, space, and class producing new patterns of social alienation, dispossession, and political contestation (Brenner & Theodore, 2002; Leitner, Sheppard, Sziato, & Maringanti, 2007; Wacquant, 2008). This has been driven by globalizing transformations in capital and labor, combined with the concurrent restructuring of state policy frameworks favoring privatization and market integration, financial deregulation, and the empowerment of transnational corporations at the expense of public and social investment. Further, amid the broader erosion of the social safety net accompanying the decline of the Keynesian welfare state and the emergence of the neoliberal state, a reactionary cultural logic and right-wing politics has emerged that asserts that issues of poverty, joblessness, and other forms of social deprivation and dislocation are largely individual failures as opposed to collective problems. In order to manage the contradictions and the consequences, we have witnessed the emergence of various punitive forms of enhanced urban policing and social control. This has included a racially predicated "war on drugs" and "imprisonment binge" responsible for generating a "new military urbanism" and the widespread "criminalization of poverty" (Graham, 2010; Wacquant, 2009).

While this book was conceived during my graduate studies at the University of Toronto, the ethnographic research was conducted in my former home of Chicago. As a former junior high school teacher in Chicago, I witnessed firsthand the systemic forces and everyday dilemmas that currently face urban schools and young people. The majority of my students, who were predominantly black and Latino, came from working-class homes. Many lived in poverty and many struggled to meet their basic needs. Some had one or both parents in prison, typically for nonviolent drug offenses, and many others had been victims of violence. My students often shared their sense of frustration at the insecurities permeating their lives and the very real existential dangers they faced navigating the city. Despite the fact that overall trends in crime and violence have declined since the early 1990s, each year dozens of Chicago youth continue to lose their lives in utterly senseless acts of violence.[5] Unlike in Toronto, these incidents typically do not inspire a great deal of public discussion, government commissions, and/or sustained social reflection. When the issue of violence is raised, the discussion tends to be much narrower such as in the aftermath of the tragic beating death of 16-year-old Chicago honors student Derrion Albert in the fall of 2009. Captured by a cell phone camera, Albert's death was run in full, sensationalized repetition on CNN and other corporate news outlets. Rather than seeking to understand and illuminate the historical inheritances and economic and political realities and decisions that perpetuate such violence, the media coverage tended to reaffirm reactionary narratives of urban youth as pathological and dangerous—legitimating further policies of disinvestment and containment rather than human development and restorative forms of justice.

As a teacher, it became clear to me that cultivating relationships through trust, mutual respect, compassion, humor, and socially relevant curricula provides the most powerful and empowering basis for promoting successful classrooms and ethical school cultures. Such commitments hold the potential to break down the walls of fear, violence, and insecurity that pervade the lives of so many of our students, enabling them to develop their moral, creative, and intellectual potential in safe and enlivening school environments. Unfortunately, many urban public schools across the United States are not presently organized in ways that facilitate this kind of climate. This is due to a variety of factors: extensive privatization and the drive to incorporate market forces into public governance leading to the further marginalization and defunding of public schools; deep cuts to social and educational services based on a neoconservative tax schema that serves the rich and deepens systemic inequalities; a deadening standardized test-based curricula that has laid waste to liberal arts and other socially relevant forms of pedagogy; attacks on teaching as a professional and intellectual endeavor; and, finally, the rise of a zero tolerance culture of metal detectors, surveillance cameras, lock-downs, contraband searches, drug sniffing dogs, and punitive law enforcement practices responsible for perpetuating a "school-to-prison pipeline" (AP, 2005, 2010). All of these factors present distinct challenges to the democratic purpose of public schooling and the livelihoods, dignities, and futures of young people in the inner-city and beyond.

*   *   *

Schooling in the Age of Austerity examines the unfolding drama of educational change and the human security of young people in the contemporary city.

Urban schools and communities find themselves subject to powerful destabilizing forces associated with globalization and neoliberal governance. The book analyzes these dynamics through an ethnographic study in a neighborhood and public high school in Chicago: Ellison Square and Carter High School (CHS).[6] It asks: What are the material and imaginative limits of security in urban education in a moment of escalating economic instability and social dislocation? Recent social science research has tended to examine questions of security in relation to the expansion of state security and global war in the post-9/11 period. In educational studies, the tendency has been to understand security primarily as a mode of educational risk management, violence prevention, and school discipline. While important, these perspectives have tended to occlude an adequate understanding of the *systemic and symbolic forms of violence* responsible for the *fragmentation of human security* in the lives of youth in their schools and communities. Specifically absent are empirical perspectives that chart the relationship between neoliberal transformations and precariousness in public schooling from the point of view of educators and youth themselves. My argument is that reading "security" both as a *form of governance* and as a *lived condition* offers essential insight into urban and educational change in relation to the present capacity of youth to secure their lives and futures. This approach enables insight not only into contemporary forms of systemic insecurity and violence, but also into how educators and youth strive for and imagine possibilities for change and transformation in urban schools and neighborhoods.

Central to this analysis is a critique of neoliberal political rationality—a mode of free market fundamentalism that has colonized state organization, culture, and public policy in matters of health care, education, labor law, taxes, financial regulation, and environmental protection over the last three decades. Despite having its central claims to greater shared prosperity and progress universally discredited by the global financial crisis in 2008 and its devastating aftermath, neoliberal ideology remains more powerful than ever. This is nowhere more visible than in the acceleration of public disinvestment and the turn to austerity in the wake of the Great Recession. Canadian political scientist David McNally (2012) observes:

> The Great Recession of 2008–9 represents a profound rupture in the neoliberal era, signaling the exhaustion of the accumulation regime that had emerged almost thirty years earlier. Rather than an ordinary recession, a short-lived downturn in the business cycle, it constituted a systemic crisis, a major contraction whose effects will be with us for many years to come. Among those effects are the extraordinary cuts to social programs, and the resultant impoverishment, announced as part of the Age of Austerity inaugurated by all major states. (p. 1)

As McNally and other analysts have noted, austerity is a strategic response by transnational capital markets, financial elites, and institutions to discipline nation states, particularly across Europe and North America, in order to socialize the costs of the economic crisis.[7] Concretely, this means that the toxic debt that accrued in the banking and financial system originating from the US subprime housing and securities markets has been converted into sovereign debt through massive government bailouts (an estimated $20 trillion in total). Rather than punishing those financial institutions whose excesses tanked the global economy, the costs, along with future financial risks, are being passed along to the public and to the poor through the intensification of neoliberal privatization, painful cuts to social services, and continued tax breaks for corporations and the already rich. What we have seen is spiraling levels of social inequality and insecurity—mass foreclosures; evaporating wages and savings; levels of unemployment, homelessness, and poverty not seen since the Great Depression; and an explosion of personal bankruptcy and debt. In this sense, austerity reflects both mutations in neoliberal governance and in its pauperizing consequences.

In the United States, calls for austerity represent commitments to the same failed supply-side, trickle-down ideology that emerged under Reagan in the early 1980s. Painfully demonstrative of what happens to a society when unfettered capitalism is mindlessly conflated with democracy, the United States now holds the ignoble status as the most unequal advanced nation with relative levels of inequality similar to many of the poorest nations in Africa and Latin America, and, despite a national presumption of meritocracy, the United States also has one of lowest rates of social mobility (Wilkinson & Pickett, 2009; Stiglitz, 2012). Despite three decades of economic growth (90% of which went to the top 10%) and despite record breaking corporate profits in the post-2008 period (the benefits of which have accrued mainly to the top 1%), 97.3 million Americans are now defined as "low income" or "near poverty" largely due to declining wages, reduced hours, job losses, and rising costs of living, while an additional 49 million struggle to survive below the federal poverty line. This means that 146 million, or 1 in 2 Americans, are now classified as either low-income or impoverished (Mishel, Bernstein, & Shierholz, 2009; Yen, 2011). Further, 28 million people are unemployed or underemployed (meaning they have a job that does not cover their needs); 45 million are relying on food assistance; and 50 million lack health insurance. Meanwhile, the United States continues to pour trillions of dollars into supporting the planet's largest and most costly military and prison industrial complexes (Alexander, 2010; Davis, 2005). According to the Pew Research Center, in the nation that brands itself as a global beacon of freedom and justice, 1 in 31 adults are currently under the direct control of the criminal justice system (either in prison, on parole, or probation) which is more than any other nation (PEW, 2009). These trends reflect three decades of institutionalized exploitation and the subversion and decay of public values and the democratic trust. What has emerged in the United States over this period is a hyperfragmented and punitive society where corporate forces and a fanatic right-wing stand openly determined to roll-back all vestiges of social progress made in the previous century.

The Great Recession and neoliberal austerity have taken an especially severe toll on young people and public schools. According to research conducted for Duke University's Child Well Being Index, "virtually all of the progress made in the family economic well-being domain since 1975 will be wiped out" as "families, schools, neighborhood, and community organizations, and governments continue to cope with budget cuts and the loss of jobs" (Land, 2010). Stanford University professor Linda Darling-Hammond (2011) elaborates on the condition of youth and the warped priorities that drive US policy:

> We live in a nation that is on the verge of forgetting its children. The United States now has a far higher poverty rate for children than any other industrialized country (25 percent, nearly double what it was thirty years ago); a more tattered safety net—more who are homeless, without healthcare and without food security; a more segregated and inequitable system of public education (a 10:1 ratio in spending across the country); a larger and more costly system of incarceration than any country in the world, including China (5 percent of the world's population and 25 percent of its inmates), one that is now directly cutting into the money we should be spending on education; a defense budget larger than that of the next twenty countries combined; and greater disparities in wealth than any other leading country. Our political leaders do not talk about these things. They simply say of poor children, 'Let them eat tests!'"

Alongside extensive cuts to social programs for the most vulnerable children, social disinvestment and austerity have been acutely felt in their impact on public education.[8] A report by the National Education Association titled *Starving America's Public Schools*, details how the spiraling costs of the Great Recession are being passed along to schools and communities through deep spending cuts (Bryant, 2011). Since 2008, states have laid off hundreds of thousands of teachers and staff, cut back curriculum and extracurricular programs, expanded class sizes, shortened school days and weeks, and even closed many schools altogether. For instance, Illinois has cut $152 million, New York $1.3 billion, Pennsylvania $422 million, Washington $1 billion, and Arizona $560 million in state funding to k-12 public schools, early childhood education, and child development services. Further, the report details that while educational budgets are being slashed, public money that would be going directly to schools is instead being redirected to corporate vendors mainly for expanding privatized commercial management, commercial curriculum contracts, commercial online "cyber-charter" school ventures, and commercial standardized testing services (a booming aspect of the $600 billion-per-year education market). Florida, as just one example, has cut $1 billion from its educational budget while it redirects roughly $299 million to corporate interests in the education market. These cuts are contributing to the erosion of the educative and civic mission of public schools by raising class sizes, narrowing the curriculum, and eliminating essential services (particularly in the poorest communities), while redirecting funding from the public to private interests (corporate lobbying for vast educational contracts has become a grand enterprise in the post-No Child Left Behind era).[9]

The impoverishment of young people and the institutions designed to protect and serve them not only raises disturbing questions about the status of public education as a fundamental right and basic social good, but also the status of youth as a key ethical and symbolic referent in a democratic society. This has led cultural critics like Henry Giroux (2009) to observe that youth, especially those marginalized by class and color, have become the primary collateral damage of the neoliberal era—a "disposable population" increasingly dispossessed of the means to secure their daily lives and future. He writes:

> Youth have become the all-important group onto which racial and class anxieties are projected. Their presence represents both the broken promise of capitalism in the age of deregulation and downsizing and a collective fear of the consequences wrought by systemic class inequalities, racism, and "infectious greed" that has created a generation of unskilled and displaced youth expelled from shrinking markets, blue collar jobs, and any viable hope in the future. (Giroux 2003, p. xvi)

Similarly to Giroux, I argue in this book that the precarious conditions facing young people in urban neighborhoods and schools in the age of austerity are expressive of the elevation of a market imperative and a military imperative over and above a social democratic imperative. Schools do not exist separately from the social contexts in which they are located. The hard realities of poverty combined with lack of access to living-wage job opportunities, basic health and human services, and affordable housing all create distinct barriers to successful urban communities and public schools. Rather than investing in young people and their communities, free market reforms combined with social disinvestments in neighborhoods and schools are exacerbating a historical legacy of race and class inequality while consigning marginalized young people to an attenuated future at the bottom of the postindustrial labor and consumer hierarchy. Perhaps most disconcertingly, as I outline in the following chapters, as public values and broader social commitments to young people and public schools have receded in the neoliberal era, there has been a stunning expansion of militarized zero tolerance enforcement and criminalizing punishment in urban public schools and neighborhoods. These developments present significant challenges to realizing the promise of public schooling as a commons oriented to social justice and authentic democracy.

*   *   *

The analysis that unfolds over the following chapters is a *critical ethnography of neoliberal schooling*. Critical ethnography is a post-positivist approach to social research that emerged in the 1960s and 1970s in the social sciences particularly within the fields of sociology, anthropology, and education (Anderson, 1989; Denzin & Lincoln, 2005; Yon, 2003). This diverse research perspective combines critical theory with traditional qualitative methods. It is both analytical and normative in orientation and seeks to study social processes, experiences, and human agency as they are produced and articulated in specific institutional and cultural contexts. Critical ethnography's *analytical dimension* is oriented to understanding the relation between values, understandings, and social practices in relation to the broader political, economic, and cultural forces in which they are located. In this sense, it attempts to make connections between the global and the local and the particular and the universal through a variety of empirical materials including document and data analysis, observations, and through dialogue with cultural insiders. As Denzin and Lincoln (2005) suggest, such an approach represents an effort to "make the world visible" by "attempting to make sense of, or interpret, phenomena in terms of the meanings people bring to them" (p. 3).

Critical ethnography relies centrally on critique as an analytic tool to not only bring knowledge to light but also to unsettle and challenge assumptions that reinforce and underlie dominant forms of knowledge and practice. Therefore, unlike positivist approaches to research, critical ethnography has an openly *normative dimension*. This is another way of saying that critical ethnography does not subtract ethical considerations from the research process. Rather than claiming value neutrality, it is driven by a sense of "ethical responsibility," which Soyini Madison (2012) describes as "a compelling sense of duty and commitment based on moral principles of human freedom and well-being, and hence a compassion for the suffering of living beings" (p. 5). Critical ethnography thus recognizes that research is a value-laden activity and therefore researcher positionality necessarily impacts interpretation. However, while critical ethnography seeks to remain critical of all knowledge claims including its own, it openly seeks to challenge injustice and to advocate for solutions to social problems in the interest of equity and democracy. The social sciences have a long history implicated in colonial and imperialist assumptions and practices including classism, racism, sexism, and homophobia (Clifford, 1983; Said, 1989). Against this historical legacy, critical ethnography is committed to unraveling and decolonizing relations of domination in the interest of promoting human development and social justice (Mohanty, 2003; Smith, 2005). Madison suggests that this entails probing "other possibilities that will challenge institutions, regimes of knowledge, and social practices that limit choices, constrain meaning, and denigrate identities and communities" (p. 5).

While much has been written on the relationship between neoliberalism and educational policy (Apple, 2006; Rizvi & Lingard, 2009; Lipman, 2003, 2011; Olssen, Codd, & O'Neil, 2004) relatively little research has been conducted that studies neoliberalism "on the ground" in urban communities and public schools. In this analysis, I theoretically situate neoliberalism as both a form of political economy (Harvey, 2003, 2005) and as a mode of governmentality (Brown, 2005; Foucault, 2008) in order to engage questions of educational policy and practice in Chicago's Ellison Square neighborhood and at CHS from the point of view of those living and working there, particularly young people and their teachers. Such an examination is thus intimately concerned with relations of space, place, and subjectivity. Geography and place are central in defining and maintaining relations of power, privilege, and security in late modern life (Bauman, 1998; Massey, 2005). They play a fundamental constitutive role in determining the uneven historical distribution of material and symbolic wealth along with access to transportation, housing, health care, quality schools, employment opportunities, and social mobility. Moreover, space and place are central components in the articulation and operation of capital, state policy and governance, and social relations across scales and institutional contexts (Harvey, 2006; Smith, 2008). Crucially, relations of policy, governance, and power are not simply imposed from the top down but also meet powerful local forms of cultural and individual agency and resistance. This means that neoliberal schooling is something

produced in a dialectical relationship between the global and the local and implicated in forging unique expressions of meaning, understanding, and identity in
specific institutional sites and everyday contexts.

Chicago is an ideal city to study the structural and political dimensions of
urban change and educational policy and governance (Lipman, 2003, 2011;
Wacquant, 2008). The city represents many of the contradictions of a "global city"
between significant corporate economic development in finance, real-estate, and
tourism, on the one hand, and profound economic insecurity and social polarization, on the other. While Chicago has become a powerful global financial center,
it also features some of the most impoverished, racially segregated, and heavily
policed neighborhoods and schools in the United States. Chicago has also consistently been at the forefront of adopting market forms of governance and management strategies in the educational sector such as privatization, centralized
mayoral control, accountability, scripted curriculum, and high-stakes testing. Its
1995 reform agenda, for instance, was a blueprint for the No Child Left Behind
Act. The Chicago Public Schools serve a population of over 400,000 students;
85 percent are visible minorities and 87 percent are considered low-income or
live below the federal poverty line. In recent years, the policies adopted by the
CPS, particularly under former Chicago schools' CEO and current secretary of
Education, Arne Duncan (2001–2009), have pushed for extensive privatization
and corporate integration in educational management. This has meant, among
other things, overseeing the closing of dozens of public schools and the opening of over 90 new deregulated charter and contract schools. These policies have
been highly controversial in Chicago and have increasingly come under intensive
community resistance due to their failure to make good on promises of improvement and because of their implication in deepening inequities and disinvestment
in traditional public schools.

The choice to focus on a single school and neighborhood at the margins of the
neoliberal city was a conscious decision. I wanted the opportunity to shine a light
on the human realities of a public school and a community too often rendered
invisible in the broader public sphere. Furthermore, when urban public schools
in high-poverty neighborhoods and the teachers and young people who inhabit
them are taken up in media and public debate, the narratives that emerge are too
often rooted in stereotypes and faulty assumptions in desperate need of empirical
clarification. Moreover, while the focus on a specific school and community may
present some challenges to generalizability as Chicago and its communities have
unique historical and cultural trajectories, it would perhaps allow me to acquire
deeper insight into the specific ways that educators and youth understand and
negotiate the broader processes of neoliberal schooling described throughout
this introduction and book.

After a difficult and lengthy access negotiation with the Chicago Public
Schools which I describe in some detail in chapter 2, I was granted permission
to conduct this research in Ellison Square and CHS on Chicago's South Side.
Ellison Square and CHS are broadly representative of public schools in Chicago
and many US cities. Ellison Square is a working-class and majority Latino neighborhood that has undergone significant economic and demographic changes

since the early 1970s. CHS draws its students from Ellison Square and also heavily from three neighboring historically African American communities. CHS thus serves a population that is approximately 50 percent Latino and 50 percent African American, roughly consistent demographically with the Chicago Public Schools as a whole. Ellison Square and its surrounding neighborhoods have experienced significant economic decline and instability particularly in the post-2008 context of mass foreclosures, disinvestment, and loss of jobs and working-class employment opportunities. These forces have had a substantial impact on social and educational life at CHS. The school has an official enrollment of just under 2,000 students, 97 percent of whom are considered "low-income" and/or "impoverished." It has a 55 percent dropout rate (close to the district average) and, like most of CPS schools, it is "on-probation" and subject to disciplinary measures due to inability to meet Average Yearly Progress on standardized tests as stipulated by the No Child Left Behind Act. The research for the study was conducted over the course of one semester during the academic year 2010–2011. The data collection and analysis included CPS policy documents, research reports and neighborhood data, media coverage, daily observation at CHS, and interviews with students, teachers, and youth workers in the community. I conducted 25 formal interviews with 10 teachers, 13 students, and 2 youth workers alongside scores of informal interviews with students, teachers, administrators, police, security guards, and parents.

The book is divided into two parts. Part I, Neoliberal Schooling and the Politics of Security, is composed of two theoretical and context setting chapters. Chapter 1 examines a crisis of human security in urban public schooling under neoliberalism. This analysis links the erosion of the public sector and social democratic commitments in the urban sphere to the extension of free market governance on the one hand, and the militarization of civil society and criminalization of the poor on the other. It then locates these processes within US educational policy and the governance of youth within economically and racially marginalized sectors of the contemporary city. In the concluding section of the chapter, I highlight historical tensions in the socializing functions of public schools from a concern primarily to train future workers and citizens under the Keynesian welfare state to a tendency toward warehousing and containment under the neoliberal state. I follow up this discussion in chapter 2 by examining the politics of conducting ethnography and social research within large urban school districts today. After profiling neoliberal development in Chicago and providing insight into educational policy and governance in the city, the chapter draws on descriptions from the field in order to discuss the ethical and logistical difficulties of gaining access and performing social research within urban school districts under current systems of market management and institutional cultures of risk and control. The chapter concludes by highlighting the importance of critical ethnography as a "public use of reason" in order to provide further methodological grounding for the case study in the following chapters.

Part II, Narratives of Enclosure and Possibility, features three chapters that form the heart of the ethnography in Chicago. Chapter 3 takes the reader to the Ellison Square neighborhood and CHS on Chicago's South Side. It utilizes Slavoj

Žižek's (2008) diagram of subjective, symbolic, and objective violence in order to think through the production of dispossession and precarious conditions in the neighborhood and school stemming from urban restructuring and the economic crisis. Through observations and analysis of interviews with educators and students, it details how specific processes of neoliberal governance have contributed to a climate of insecurity, alienation, and educational failure by limiting the capacity of public schools to provide meaningful security to youth in the form of social and holistic educational supports. It concludes by highlighting the production of conflict and the circulation of systemic violence in the school and the community. Extending this analysis, chapter 4 examines security culture at CHS. It profiles how ubiquitous surveillance and criminological authority and control produce a variety of inclusionary and exclusionary effects that criminalize student behaviors, identities, and interpersonal relations. It then highlights how youth and adults in the school perceive and make sense of these security practices in ways that are at once trenchantly critical and variously supportive. Drawing on Kathleen Gallagher's (2007) notion of the "occupied imagination," what emerges through these discussions is that criminological practices represent an image of militarized "security" that appears seemingly inevitable amid relations of entrenched poverty and everyday insecurity.

Chapter 5 takes up questions regarding the relation between human security, engagement, and civic and social agency at CHS. It proceeds by exploring tensions between various forms of enclosure (economic, social, curricular, spatial, political) and how students, educators, and youth workers at CHS imagine their own sense of social and ethical responsibility in relation to possibilities for educational change. The chapter also profiles two models of nontraditional education at CHS (the Junior Reserve Officers Training Corps and programs that promote social justice education) and examines how the assumptions and values that animate these programs point toward both new limitations and opportunities for alternative public school reform. Chapter 5 seeks to emphasize, in particular, that despite the challenges, conflicts, and insecurities that mark everyday life at CHS and schools like it, there is a wealth of local knowledge, desire for change, and positive social relations that point to the latent and too often subverted potential of public schools as sites of human development and democratic possibility.

In the conclusion, I discuss alternatives to neoliberal schooling. Specifically, I draw on perspectives in the social sciences and humanities on the global commons as a way of thinking with and beyond the social democratic reform tradition in education. I conclude by offering a series of broad and specific recommendations for transforming urban public schools in the interest of restorative justice and democratic development. While transforming urban public schooling in the interest of democracy and sustainability will not be easy, there presently exists a vast network of educators, activists, youth, and concerned parents in cities like Chicago that are committed to the task. The conclusions I draw from CHS and from Chicago are meant to contribute to this effort by advocating for a reinvigorated notion of the democratic commons within public life.

Part I

Neoliberal Schooling and the Politics of Security

1

Securing Precarious Urban Futures

Security reasoning entails an essential risk. A state which has security as its only task and source of legitimacy is a fragile organism; it can always be provoked by terrorism to turn itself terroristic...Nothing is therefore more important than a revision of the concept of security as the basic principle of state politics.

—*Giorgio Agamben*, "Security and Terror"

September 11, 2001 and the financial crisis of 2008 mark two transformative moments in the politics of security in the United States. On one hand, the terrorist attacks on the World Trade Center and the Pentagon on 9/11 ushered in a stunning expansion of state security. We saw this in the passage of the USA Patriot Act; the creation of the Department of Homeland Security; the pursuit of the global War on Terrorism in Iraq, Afghanistan, and beyond; and the diversion of trillions of public dollars into the war industry and projects of domestic surveillance and policing. On the other hand, ongoing instabilities in global capitalism and continued fallout from the 2008 economic crisis have made visible a stark erosion of social and material security in contemporary life. While Wall Street and the corporate sector have resumed minting new billionaires and posting record profits (the top 1% now has a higher net worth than the bottom 90%), millions have been left with foreclosed homes, debilitating debt, vanishing jobs, and stagnating wages. Concurrently, a regressive politics of disinvestment and austerity continues to hollow-out commitments to public infrastructure, health care, child development, education, and labor and environmental protections further eroding the basis for securing human well-being and the future.

These developments signal an erosion of human security in late modern life that Feldman, Geisler, and Menon (2011) have identified as a crisis of social reproduction—that is, those "historically contingent processes by which we reproduce the conditions and relations of economic and social security" (p.2). This concerns not only "the physical integrity of our bodies, but also the methods by which we reproduce ourselves as political subjects—that is, the relations of rule we legitimate" (p. 2). As primary sites of social reproduction, schools have played a formative historical role in socializing and sorting young people into their future adult roles as workers and citizens. This process has always been contingent upon the demands of the market, property, and power relations immanent to a capitalist society (Bowles & Gintis, 2011). It has also always been a highly contradictory and contested process. Public school systems and schools themselves have historically operated to discipline and track youth disadvantaged by class and color toward the lower end of the employment structure or out of the formal economy altogether. However, while imperfect and at times oppressive, public schools have also functioned as sites where all young people, regardless of their social position, might develop their human potential and civic awareness in ways that prepare them for social and democratic engagement and ultimately unpredictable futures.

In this chapter, I examine the traffic between present articulations of security and urban educational change under neoliberal governance. I argue that expansionary processes of marketization, state security, and social control are eroding social democratic commitments and contributing to a crisis of human security in urban schooling. First, I discuss how neoliberal political economy and governance reframe questions of security from a social democratic paradigm to a market paradigm.[1] Second, I highlight extant patterns of social polarization, precariousness, aggressive policing, and criminalization in the neoliberal city. In the following sections, I bring these ideas into conversation with educational policy in the United States since the 1980s and explore the transformation of urban public schooling alongside current social conditions facing youth. In the final section, I highlight tensions in the historic socializing functions of public schooling in relation to the security of young people and their future.

Neoliberalism and Security Politics

> The problem of neoliberalism is how the overall exercise of political power can be modeled on the principles of the market economy. So it is not a question of freeing an empty space, but of taking the formal principles of a market economy and referring and relating them to, and projecting them onto a general art of government.
>
> —*Michel Foucault*, The Birth of Biopolitics[2]

Neoliberalism is a term widely used in the social sciences to describe recent transformations in state restructuring and social life under globalization and advanced capitalism. It has been associated with the rejection of Keynesian economics and social democratic policy; the generalization of market logics and the commodity-form to all aspects of governance and daily life; and the deregulation of national economies and global trade under transnational institutions like the World Bank, International Monetary Fund, and World Trade Organization. With the elections of Ronald Reagan in the United States and Margaret Thatcher in the United Kingdom in the early 1980s, neoliberal ideology—a revamped form of classical economic liberalism—emerged out of neoconservative think tanks, corporate foundations, and academic departments such as the Chicago school of economics to become the driving intellectual and political force of the emergent global era. After the fall of the Soviet Union and "actually existing socialism" in 1989, Margaret Thatcher's dictum that "There is No Alternative" was broadly enshrined as accepted wisdom.

The political economy of neoliberal development is often associated with the crisis of Fordism in the early 1970s (Duminél & Lévy, 2004, 2011 Harvey, 2003, 2005). Fordism (1914–1973) is typically characterized as a mode of political economic organization that peaked in the post–World War II era. It was defined by national systems of standardized industrial production, the Keynesian mediation of labor conflicts and business cycles by the state, and social democratic commitments to public institutions and social investments within nationally bound projects of social and civic identification. In the late 1960s and early 1970s, Fordism entered a period of structural crisis due to growth stagnation, spiking energy costs, and falling profits. This was aggravated by widespread discontent over entrenched inequality and a wave of social unrest—civil rights, labor, feminist, and transnational anti-imperialist movements. These economic and social tensions provided rationale and context for the turn to post-Fordism, or what Harvey (1990) has referred to as "flexible accumulation"—a series of capitalist class strategies meant to offset the crisis under Fordism and return the system to profitability and growth, principally via market and labor deregulation along with opening up and colonizing new sites for profit-making across global space and time.

The shift to post-Fordism thus signals the emergence of the current phase of world capitalist development, or *neoliberal globalization*. This has been defined by the enhanced global mobility of production and capital across borders; extensive deregulation and the dismantling of welfare state protections; the reorganization and cheapening of labor on a global scale (outsourcing, automation, free trade/labor zones, reliance on temporary "flexible" contracting); and vast innovations in communications technologies and speculative finance. Over the last three decades, these economic and state transformations have opened up new spheres for capital largely through new deregulatory regimes and the privatization of public infrastructures signaling a new round of *enclosures of the global commons* in areas like health and education, utilities, transportation, communications, land, and natural resources (Mansfield, 2008).[3] This has produced extensive *uneven development* marked by historic concentrations of wealth and power at the top of the global class structure and deepening social inequality across the global division of labor (today the richest 50 individuals in the world have a combined income greater than the poorest 416 million; 2.5 billion people—or 40% of the world's population—live on less than $2 a day, while 54% of global income goes to the richest 10% of the world's population). Further, the global economic crisis and recession have revealed new systemic instabilities for capitalism and a crisis of legitimation for the neoliberal project. This is visible in an eruption of protests from Cairo to London, Athens to New York, Santiago to Montreal, that have opposed the continued degradation of publics, people, and the environment across the Global North and South while advocating for a more just and democratic vision for the future (McNally, 2011).

Neoliberalism can be situated as the intellectual and political architecture that has underpinned much of this broader political economic landscape. In his lectures at the *Collège de France* in the late 1970s, Michel Foucault (2008) identified the emergent free market discourse as a distinct form of *governmentality* by which he meant an ensemble of institutional, legal, cultural, and political practices and rationalities marking out the broader terrain of governance.[4] For Foucault, governmentality is both material, in the sense that it works within and through concrete activities (production, finance, trade, law, education, policing, etc.), and symbolic, in the sense that it is derived from as well as influences perceptions, values, and the social production of meaning and understanding. As a form of governmentality, neoliberalism can be understood as implicated not only in global processes but in variable local transformations in everyday life including senses of self, ways of being, and the organization of sociality and community.

In his 1978–1979 lectures entitled "The Birth of Biopolitics," Foucault traced the development of neoliberal governmentality from the classical liberalism of Adam Smith and Adam Ferguson in the eighteenth century, through the postwar German Ordoliberals, to thinkers associated with the Chicago school of economics such as Milton Freidman and Friedrich von Hayek. In short, neoliberal rationalities take as given the natural efficiency and ethical neutrality of the market and the supposed inefficiency and corruption of the public sector. Here, all social relations from environmental protection, education, health and child care, to conceptions of democratic and civic engagement can and should be brought under the competitive domain of the market and the supposedly rational economic decision-making capacity of the individual citizen, who is recast as an entrepreneurial-consumer citizen. While neoliberalism rejects the Keynesian era diagram of a social democratic state operating to regulate capitalism and provide a modicum of security against its most destructive tendencies, it actively recruits the state to restructure society along economic lines. It does so by incorporating market logic into all aspects of governance and by creating markets where they previously did not exist. Synthesizing Foucault's approach, Wendy Brown (2005) has suggested that neoliberalism represents a normative and constructivist political project that has emerged as a powerful form of "commonsense" across the political spectrum informing policy, culture, and everyday lived experience: "a mode of governance encompassing but not limited to the state, and one that produces subjects, forms of citizenship and behavior, and a new organization of the social" (p. 37).

This brief analysis concerning the intersection of neoliberal political economy and governance has profound repercussions for how we understand relations of security and human insecurity in the contemporary moment. For Foucault (2007), security was an essential element in the art of liberal government as it developed in the seventeenth and eighteenth centuries. While sovereignty is concerned primarily with the rule of law, security is concerned with the management and regulation of populations—or what Foucault referred to as *biopolitics*—processes whereby some lives and forms of life are made more or less valuable than others.[5] Under neoliberalism, security is privatized and desocialized. This means that risk and responsibility are increasingly transferred from the state and the public sphere onto individuals and communities as social provisions are cut and public infrastructures are deregulated and commodified. If security was once primarily imagined within a set of public values containing certain economic and social rights, protections, and responsibilities under Keynesian liberalism (however inadequate or problematic this may have been in practice), under neoliberalism, it is conceived largely in terms of market values, the privatization of risk and responsibility, and the criminalization of poverty and social insecurity.

Within this atomized vision of the social, what Ulrich Beck (1991) has referred to as the "risk society," citizens are positioned primarily as entrepreneurial consumers who are held solely responsible and morally culpable for their own security and well-being regardless of the circumstances. Zygmunt Bauman (1999, 2001) has noted that as social democratic referents of security recede in the neoliberal consumer society, individuals must engage in hypercompetitive strategies of acquiring private security such as pursuing constant educational retraining, consumer lifestyle distinctions, and various forms of self-help so as to maximize personal fitness and market value while effectively outcompeting their rivals in an increasingly precarious and transient employment structure. This is reinforced by an array of cultural phenomena in mass media that celebrates market values and consumer identifications such as Oprah-inflected pop-psychology (*If I just believe in me, I will prosper!*), to Darwinian "reality" television shows, mass corporate advertising, and 24/7 news cycles. The inability of individuals and communities to meet normative criteria for entrepreneurial and consumer engagement can lead to the further withdrawal of state and social supports as they are viewed in neoconservative discourse as moral failings that breed "pathology" and "dependency" (Fraser & Gordon, 1996). In turn, social insecurity and abjection, particularly for economically and racially marginalized populations, become viewed as the private problems of failed individuals and communities as opposed to public problems and broader social concerns. This marks out divisions between *affiliated consumers* and dishonored populations of *suspicion and criminality* (Rose, 1996). Such divisions signal authoritarian tendencies inherent to neoliberal governance, where forms of social dislocation give way to state interventions aimed at policing those zones and identities perceived as threatening and/or as redundant to the global economic order (Dean, 2007).

Despite rhetorical commitments to "small government," neoliberal governance has been marked by a significant expansion of state power. Pierre Bourdieu (1999) describes this as the simultaneous erosion of the state's "left arm," or social functions, and the expansion of its "right arm"—those capacities concerned with security, punishment, and policing. While the Keynesian state operated to regulate the market, under neoliberalism the market becomes the internal regulator of the state, reducing its role in social reproduction while expanding its security and disciplinary capacities. Harvey (2003, 2005) details how neoliberal formations have thus been inseparable from neoconservative politics and the new imperialism. For instance, in structural adjustment policies imposed by the World Bank, WTO, and IMF, where nations across the Global South have been made subject to coercive debt arrangements that enable greater transnational corporate control over their markets and natural resources. It is also visible in the Bush and Obama administrations' efforts to retrench civil liberties, skirt the Geneva Conventions, engage in torture, and pursue extralegal detentions and drone-strike executions outside the rule of law as part of the global war on terrorism. Furthermore, as demonstrated by the 2008 financial crisis and subsequent Wall Street bailouts and turn to austerity, neoliberal capitalism relies on a strong state in order to ameliorate market failure while downwardly distributing fiscal austerity, debt, and risk onto an insecure and fragmented public sphere. Lastly, neoliberal governance has signaled an oppressive domestic law and order turn based on aggressive policing and mass incarceration as primary state strategies of social regulation of the poor and disenfranchised (Wacquant, 2009). As Harvey (2006) observes, "public-private partnerships are favored in which the public sector bears all of the risk and the corporate sector reaps all of the profit. Business interests get to write legislation and to determine public policies... if necessary the state will resort to coercive legislation... surveillance and policing multiply" (p. 26).

Securing the Revanchist City

As I have outlined above, the emergence of neoliberalism as a dominant political rationality has come to frame issues of security in specific kinds of ways. On one hand, individuals are increasingly made personally responsible and culpable for their own private security regardless of their social condition. On the other hand, as public values and social commitments fade in the neoliberal consumer society, the state has limited its involvement in social reproduction and extended its role in social control and policing. The contemporary city is a key staging ground for these trends. The urban sphere plays an increasingly central role in managing the flows of finance, technology, information, and labor that are the lifeblood of globalization. It is also a prime site for the implementation of neoliberal logic. Moreover, cities are also contested sites where the global and local coalesce in the everyday and where dominant sociopolitical processes intersect with various forms of cultural agency, identity formation, and democratic contestation. In this section, I outline the extension of market governance, social polarization, and the production of criminalized spaces of social insecurity and securitized containment in the urban sphere.

Neoliberal urbanism can be characterized as a general trend toward the "rolling back" of social democratic policy regimes and the "rolling out" of entrepreneurial and market-based governance (Cronin & Hetherington, 2008; Peck & Tickel, 2002). Liberal urban policy of the 1950s and 1960s was defined by strong commitments to public management, public oversight over capital and the rights of labor, and basic redistributive aims designed to promote economic development and ameliorate urban blight and poverty through investments in welfare programs, job training, and urban renewal. While this social democratic paradigm remained rooted in racial, gender, and class inequality and often contributed to the very problems it attempted to address, it nevertheless provided a set of referents for conceiving an urban social contract defined by commitments to collective security and human welfare. In contrast, Brenner and Theodore (2002) note that neoliberal policies have been characterized by:

> the deregulation of state control over major industries, assaults on organized labor, the reduction of corporate taxes, the shrinking and/or privatization of public services, the dismantling of welfare programs, the enhancement of international capital mobility, the intensification of interlocality competition, and the criminalization of the urban poor. (p. 3)

Brenner and Theodore observe that "actually existing neoliberalism"—neoliberalism in practice as opposed to its rhetorical and/or doctrinal assertions—represents a contradictory process that manifests in uneven ways in specific geographical, institutional, and social contexts. On one hand, this has involved efforts to transform urban space and the urban economy through privatization, deregulatory regimes, corporate tax breaks and incentives, and the construction of tourist and entertainment districts and other gentrification and real estate projects (Sassen, 2006 Smith 1996, 2002). On the other hand, neoliberal urbanism has produced new experiences of urban sociality as public values, social engagement, and civic identification are replaced by entrepreneurial norms, consumer identifications, and market imaginaries (Isin, 2000).

Market governance in the city has coincided with deepening inequality and social polarization (Brenner & Theodore, 2002; Wacquant, 2008). From New York, Chicago, Toronto, to Paris, neoliberal urbanism has been implicated in the increased bifurcation between urban spaces of consumption and corporate development and increasingly marginalized sectors of concentrated poverty and sociopolitical alienation. In the context of US urbanism, this has been traced to historical patterns of racial segregation, suburbanization and deindustrialization, and the emergence of a stratified postindustrial labor market (Massey & Denton, 1993; Sugrue, 1996; Wilson, 1996). Since the 1970s, the enhanced global mobility of capital and production combined with the rise of financial and consumer service sectors has led to extensive labor segmentation: the formation of a small, highly mobile professional class of corporate managers, executives, and information workers; a declining middle class sector marked by the erosion of wages, long-term contracts, benefits, and union representation; and an expanding pool of precarious laborers, the majority of whom are women, immigrants, and people of color.[6] Millions of people in this bottom tier of "disposable workers" often work full time in low-wage jobs that do not meet their needs. Millions more are unemployed and/or underemployed (an estimated 28 million total in the United States, not counting those who have permanently exited the formal labor market) (Magdoff, 2011). The presence of a mass "reserve army" of workers is certainly nothing new to the historical geographies of capitalism (Marx, 1977). However, as production has given way to debt-fueled consumption and speculative finance as the principle drivers of economic growth, and as individualized consumer norms replace public values and universal norms of citizenship, economically alienated populations are less likely to be viewed as needing to be reincorporated by the state into productive economic and civic roles (Feldman et al., 2011). Thus, rather than thought deserving of collective investment in their security and welfare, they are imagined as security threats— surplus populations haunting the peripheries of the city. This includes many young people and young graduates as they struggle to enter the labor market in the post-2008 context.

Class polarization in the urban sphere is complicated by the racial politics of neoliberal culture where social inequality is positioned as the moral failings of communities and individuals as opposed to effects of political and historical conditions. This allows histories of racial oppression and exclusion to disappear behind what David Theo Goldberg (2002) has described as "colorblind" or "race-less racism," the seductive idea that in a post–civil rights era where racial minorities have achieved limited entry to the middle class (although this has begun to reverse itself in the last decade) and even high-profile positions of wealth and power (most notably the US presidency under Barack Obama) race is no longer a salient factor in determining one's life chances within the supposedly universal and equitable opportunities provided by the market. If racism does exist, it is thought to linger only as a private prejudice as opposed to a structural reality. Assertions of a postracial society are belied, however, by a deepening chasm in wealth and opportunity in the United States. According to the Pew Research Center, in the wake of the 2008 recession and collapse of the subprime housing market, which disproportionally impacted minority communities, the median wealth of white households has increased to 20 times that of black and 18 times that of Hispanic households, while unemployment rates in minority communities persistently remain double and triple the national average (Kochhar, Fry & Taylor, 2011). Furthermore, in light of embedded economic and social dislocation and four decades of the disastrous "war on drugs," a racially predicated imprisonment binge has emerged that legal scholar Michelle Alexander (2010) has evocatively referred to as the "New Jim Crow." Today, visible minorities make up 70 percent of the roughly 2.3 million people incarcerated in US prisons, the majority for nonviolent drug offenses, even though racial minorities constitute only 24 percent of the overall population and a small percentage of illegal drug users (PEW, 2009).[7]

The retrenchment of race and class inequality has dovetailed with what Mike Davis (1990) has referred to as the "fortress city": an urban landscape defined by the expansion of militarized surveillance and security from gated communities, CCTV cameras, to SWAT and paramilitary antidrug police units ostensibly deployed to make the city "safe" for capital development, for tourism and consumer activities, as well as for upper-income professionals and their families. While efforts to regulate the poor have always been a fixture of urban governance, Davis notes that under present formations:

> the defense of luxury life-styles is translated into a proliferation of new repressions in space and movement, undergirded by the ubiquitous 'armed response.' This obsession with physical security systems, and, collaterally, with the architectural policing of social boundaries, has become a zeitgeist of urban restructuring, a master narrative in the emerging built environment. (p. 223)

Fueled by a cultural politics that has long played upon racialized depictions of the urban poor, and urban "Others," as undeserving and dangerous, the city becomes a site of heightened contradictions and contested geographies: new commercial areas and gentrified residential zones stand as corridors of investment, order, and civility while efforts are made to contain the poor and other problem populations within disinvested spaces of perceived disorder, incivility, and danger via mechanisms of surveillance and state repression (Macek, 2006; Parenti, 1999; Wacquant, 2008, 2009).

Neil Smith (1996, 2002) has utilized the metaphor of "revanchism" in order to describe how the erosion of social democratic commitments to the public has contributed to the violent return to late-nineteenth century conservative attitudes toward the poor and the indigent. Smith takes revanchism from the French word *revanche* which literally means "revenge"—a term proudly mobilized by reactionary bourgeois movements in Second Empire Paris as a rallying cry for hunting down and eliminating their working-class enemies from the city.[8] Smith locates the roots of contemporary revanchist urbanism in 1990s New York, where under the authoritarian zeal of Rudolph Giuliani, new strategies of policing and social control were developed to reclaim public space from the homeless, racialized youth, panhandlers, graffiti artists, squeegee cleaners, protestors, and other dishonored populations that had become the primary and most visible scapegoats for urban decay and the failures of urban policy in post-Reagan America. The revanchist approach to urban social control, which quickly spread to cities across North America and Western Europe, has included zero tolerance "quality of life" policing, new civility and antitrespass laws, modifications in the built environment such as "bum proof" benches and the proliferation of CCTV surveillance cameras, harsh mandatory minimum sentences for nonviolent drug offenses, and a turn to historic levels of mass incarceration (Beckett & Herbert, 2008). Loïc Wacquant (2009) has argued that revanchist politics and the turn to authoritarian policing is directed primarily at managing the racialized poor and other devalued populations in an era of public downsizing, the erosion of stable employment, and globalized labor surpluses. He describes this as the neoliberal government of social insecurity—"that applies the doctrine of 'laissez-faire' upstream, when it comes to social inequalities and the mechanisms that generate them (the free play of capital, deregulation of labor law and deregulation of employment, retraction or removal of collective protections), but turns out to be brutally paternalistic and punitive downstream, when it comes to coping with their consequences on a daily level" (p. 43).

The Erosion of Public Schooling

We have seen how the city becomes an arena for neoliberal restructuring and the production of precarious conditions particularly for economically and racially marginalized and criminalized populations. I now want to bring these ideas into conversation with educational policy in the United States. Over the last three decades, educational reform and policy has been largely redefined from a social democratic orientation to a neoliberal one. In what follows, I discuss the triumph of market forces in US education since the 1980s, specifically in relation to issues of social inequality and the human security of young people. Second, I discuss the trend toward marketization in relation to urban schooling. Finally, I examine how the traffic between marketization and the decline of human security under neoliberalism has coincided with the securitization of school environments and the criminalization of urban youth.

Unleashing the Market:
From the Great Society to No Child Left Behind

Since the late nineteenth and early twentieth centuries, business and political leaders have attempted to influence educational processes in ways favorable to capital and labor market demands (Bowles & Gintis, 2011). Many of the contemporary reform policies such as increased use of testing and teacher accountability practices resemble older factory-based efficiency models championed by twentieth century reformers like Elwood Cubberly, Franklin Bobbitt, and David Snedden to integrate Taylorist "scientific management" principles into schooling. What makes neoliberal education policies different from this earlier efficiency movement, however, is that not only are they geared toward promoting the forms of management, knowledge, and discipline necessary for workforce preparation, which today is said to be predicated on developing "twenty-first century skills" and globally competitive "entrepreneurial" citizens, but they also take the market itself as the very basis for educational organization. In other words, neoliberal policies not only conflate the democratic and ethical purpose of education with economic rationalities, but also project economic principles onto a general art of educational governance. This has contributed to profoundly changing the dynamics of educational practice and experiences of equity.

In the United States, the New Deal legacy and the postwar Keynesian consensus were defined by a substantive federal commitment to a social contract that included basic public protection for the most vulnerable, including expanded investment and access to health care, public housing, child welfare, and education. Extensive pressures from the civil rights movement culminated in the early 1960s with Lyndon Johnson's Great Society and the Civil Rights Act in 1964 along with the Elementary and Secondary Education Act (ESEA) in 1965. The latter supported desegregation of public schools and provided significant federal commitments to educational funding directed toward ameliorating poverty and providing equality of opportunity to low-income urban and rural youth with the greatest need. The social democratic policies of this era should not be overly romanticized. They often proved to be obsessively bureaucratic and paternalistic and ultimately fell short in fundamentally altering the mechanisms that maintained economic injustice and exclusions of women and racial and sexual minorities from the benefits of full citizenship. Further, educational reforms during the 1960s were predicated on deficit models of racial inequality based on a "culture of poverty" discourse, signified perhaps most famously by Daniel Patrick Moynihan's (1965) description of a "tangle of pathology" in reference to impoverished black families, which tended to reinforce rather than uproot racist stereotypes and practices in public schools. However, despite these limitations and contrary to neoconservative assertions regarding the failures of "big government," the social welfare and educational policies in the 1960s and 1970s led to the near equalization of school funding between urban and suburban districts; cut the black-white achievement gap in half over 15 years; reduced child poverty rates by 60 percent of where they are today; significantly expanded access to health care for poor families; invested heavily in hiring and retaining high quality teachers in underserved schools; and achieved college enrollment for minority youth at rates comparable to whites for the only time either before or since (Darling-Hammond, 2010). Perhaps most importantly, these hard-won social democratic gains were rooted in public values and commitments to equity that benefited not only disadvantaged young people and their communities, but also the broader shape of democratic life and culture (Judt, 2009).

Over the last three decades, there has been a profound retrenchment in educational equity, achievement, and access leading to the evaporation of gains made in the 1960s and 1970s. Today in the wake of the Great Recession and three decades of neoliberal and neoconservative attacks on the public and the social state, the United States has one of the highest rates of child poverty ranking ahead only of Romania on a scale of 35 developed nations (UNICEF, 2012). Children under 18 are the largest group living in poverty in the United States. 15 million or 21 percent of US children live in poverty (nearly double what it was 25 years ago), while 31 million, or 42 percent of all children, now live at the edge of the federal poverty rate ($22,500 a year for a family of four) (Land, 2010). Slipping into poverty even for a brief period of time has been shown to impede the educational, health, and social development of young people. Furthermore, the United States maintains one of the worst records of advanced nations in providing health and human services to youth and women with children while maintaining shameful inequalities in educational investment (Wilkinson & Pickett, 2009). As Darling-Hammond notes (2010), in contrast to Canada, Europe, and Asia where educational funding tends to be centralized and equitably distributed, the wealthiest school districts in the United States spend up to 10 times more than the poorest.[9] This reinforces a highly stratified and racially segregated education system particularly in the inner-city where class sizes have grown, achievement gaps have widened, and dropout rates have stagnated. Combined with soaring poverty and generalized insecurity, youth with the greatest needs are being denied the substantive investments necessary to secure their future economic and social well-being.[10] It is no coincidence that spending on criminal corrections since the 1980s has mushroomed by 300 percent (growing at a rate that is three times faster than the rate of investment in public education over the same period) (PEW, 2009).

Since the Reagan era report *A Nation at Risk*, which worked to stoke national anxieties over educational performance in the emergent global economy, a neoliberal market ethos has become a broadly shared form of "commonsense" in educational reform. Part of this story can be traced to concerted attempts to discredit the public sector and equate public investment with the racialized and gendered "dependencies" and "pathologies" of the urban poor (Fraser & Gordon, 1996). Ronald Reagan's anecdotes of the mythical African American "Welfare Queen" cruising in style in her "Pink Cadillac," with her "30 addresses," "80 names," and "12 social security cards" to "defraud the system" in order to collect welfare checks is a case in point (Cowen & Siciliano, 2011a). The narrative tactfully played upon white working-class resentment (even though whites have always been and continue to be the majority of welfare recipients) against the gains of the civil rights and feminist movements and worked to build support for Bill Clinton's "third way" postwelfare politics. Michael Apple (2005) has referred to this as the "long-term creative ideological work" of "devaluing of public goods and services" where "anything that is public is 'bad' and anything that is private is 'good'" (p.15). Following this logic, the Reagan administration cut taxes on the rich and corporations, poured money into a Cold War military buildup, all while slashing funds for public education at all levels including a 50 percent cut in Title 1 funds to low-income schools (Bellamy Foster, 2011).

The market vision in education has been promoted by both the Democratic and Republican parties; an extensive network of well-funded neoliberal and neoconservative think tanks like the Heritage Foundation and the Fordham and Hoover institutes; corporate philanthropic organizations like the Gates, Broad, and Walton foundations; business groups like the Business Roundtable and Chamber of Commerce; and through corporate media such as in recent films like *Waiting for Superman* and *The Lottery* (Apple, 2006; Saltman, 2009). The stated aims of the new educational reform alliance are to break down the "public school monopoly" by supporting privatization, dismantle the teachers' unions, and to impose a system of corporate management. In terms of policy, this has meant the promotion of school voucher and market-based choice initiatives, the proliferation of publicly funded but privately run charter and contract schools, as well as experiments in direct for-profit secondary education. Second, it has meant efforts to bring market-based strategies of accountability and institutional "efficiency" modeled on the corporation into schooling at all levels—standardization, auditing and accountability mechanisms, and emphasis on the rote learning of "basic skills" conjoined with mandatory high-stakes testing. These reform strategies were codified into law with the passage of George W. Bush's No Child Left Behind (NCLB) legislation in 2001.

The logic driving the NCLB assumes that education, by itself, can provide equality of opportunity through markets and school choice and by holding schools and teachers accountable for test scores. However, as Harvey Kantor and Robert Lowe (2006) detail, the law has been more likely to deepen race and class inequality than ameliorate it. They note that the law has further stigmatized and legitimated disinvestment in low-income schools by holding them to unrealistic performance benchmarks and then labeling them failures and punishing them for the resulting low-test scores (80% of all US public schools are slated to be labeled failing by 2014). It has also significantly narrowed curriculum as more than 70 percent of the nation's school districts have responded to testing requirements by reducing instruction in liberal arts subjects and focusing almost exclusively on drilling for the tests. This has been most intensive in schools serving high-poverty students. Most significantly, Kantor and Lowe point out that while the law rightly rejects the language of cultural deficits that blame achievement gaps on the deficiencies of the poor and racial minorities, its exclusive focus on markets and testing fails to address structural economic barriers and the cumulative effects of historical racial exclusion and discrimination. They state:

> The Great Society fore-fronted the connection between race, poverty, and education, although it framed that connection in terms that were as likely to reproduce racial and class inequality as ameliorate it. For good reason, the NCLB rejects that language. In doing so, however, it also rejects the idea that there is any connection between class and racial inequality and school achievement at all, or to put it more broadly, that the "problem of schooling" is somehow unconnected to the larger structures of inequality in which schools exist…Not merely absent but precluded are discussions about the connections between schooling and unequal access to labor markets, income, adequate housing and health care, as well as educational resources, though the "problem of schooling" cannot be addressed without attention to all of them. (p. 485)

Rather than working to improve the overall quality of the public educational system, the NCLB shifts responsibility for educational success and failure to schools, teachers, and localities. It does so by encouraging privatization and school choice arrangements that position families as consumers and schools as commercial entities that are required to compete over students and scarce resources. Child poverty, homelessness, home and neighborhood instability, and racism become "excuses," while low educational performance is blamed on supposedly incompetent teachers and their unions. Instead of attempting to mitigate the effects of economic and social dislocation, the law favors market competition and "get tough" disciplinary sanctions designed to hold schools and teachers accountable for student performance on standardized tests. The Obama administration has broadly continued and intensified NCLB style market, test, and punish reforms through policies such as Race to the Top where, as Ken Saltman (2010) has noted, "billions in public dollars are being dangled in front of cash strapped states in order to induce them to expand privatized and managerialist school reform…that imagine historically neglected schools as private enterprises that need to be subject to the 'creative destruction' of private markets" (p. 4).

Capitalizing on Failure and Transforming Urban Schools

Market reforms have been particularly prevalent in the urban context. As Pauline Lipman (2003, 2011) has documented, large urban districts like Chicago, New

York, and Los Angeles have become "laboratories" for neoliberal reform experiments. This has foremost meant significant efforts to privatize schools and educational services. Under systems of centralized mayoral control, public-private partnerships with the corporate sector, as well as direct corporate management, large and small urban school districts have widely attempted to create competitive market systems in education through school closures, voucher programs, and the integration of charter, contract, and direct for-profit schools. Charter schools, which are publicly funded but privately operated, are the most common and celebrated type of alternative school option. They were conceived in the 1980s by reformers like Al Shanker, former president of the American Federation of Teachers, to be small, public, teacher-run schools serving struggling students outside many of the constraints of the formal system. In some cases, charter schools have opened up possibilities for desperately needed experimentation and opportunities for progressive pedagogy outside the bureaucratic structures of large urban school systems. However, over the past ten years, charters have become part of a broader policy agenda to defund and privatize urban public schools, break up the teachers' unions, and move traditional secondary education toward a for-profit model (Saltman, 2012). As Naomi Klein (2007) has pointed out, the strategic devaluing of the public sector presents business opportunities to institute reforms that enable the transfer of public resources like schools from the public trust to private interests. For example, in the wake of Hurricane Katrina, market reformers presented the storm as a "golden opportunity" to "clean the slate" to privatize the historically neglected New Orleans Public Schools—today 60 percent of New Orleans youth attend charter schools run largely by corporate educational management companies (Saltman, 2007). There are numerous projects across North American cities that have seized on decades of neglect in order to privatize schools, utilities, transportation systems, and various other public entities. Such projects relinquish public control to private interests, funded, of course, through public revenue, representing a stark imbalance between public and private wealth and power.

The second pillar of urban educational restructuring has been the reframing of educational focus in line with the demands of the new economy. This has meant extensive emphasis on basic skills curricula and high-stakes testing. While educational reform rhetoric focuses on preparing students with the twenty-first century skills needed for college and work in the global knowledge economy, the reality is that the vast majority of jobs in the coming decades are projected to be low-wage service jobs that will not require advanced knowledge and/or college degrees. Very few jobs will be in information or STEM fields (science, technology, engineering, mathematics). According to the Bureau of Labor Statistics, 22 out of the top 30, and 7 out of the top 10, fast growing employment niches over the next decade will be in "low-wage" and "very low-wage" sectors including in-home health workers, food service (including fast food), security guards, retail sales, and customer service representatives (Bureau of Labor Statistics [BLS], 2012). Standardized testing and scripted curricula work to shore up and discipline a low-wage, service-oriented workforce by emphasizing rudimentary skills and knowledge (Aronowitz, 2008; Lipman, 2003). Rather than promoting a broad liberal arts or progressive curriculum that enables youth to develop their intellectual capacities and human potential in common with others, test-based curricula reduces knowledge to an individualized, competitive, and technical process. Within this context, African American and Latino youth are thought to require the mechanistic discipline of "skill and drill" forms of learning, while in contrast their more affluent peers in the suburbs and selective enrollment and magnet schools are provided with elite academic tracks, arts and culture programs, sports facilities, and clean modern buildings replete with new science labs, technology, and supplementary resources and services. With smaller class sizes and greater emphasis on student-centered curriculum, these schools exist in stark contrast to many of their urban counterparts, what Jonathan Kozol (2005) has referred to as "apartheid schools"—disinvested and segregated schools that underserve the racialized poor in substandard buildings, large class sizes, and narrow curriculum. This places limits on innovative pedagogy and creative learning while sorting disadvantaged youth into low-wage service sector labor tracks or out the formal economy altogether.

Under neoliberal discourse, the "failures" of urban public schools are blamed largely on public schools, teachers, and localities as opposed to the effects of concentrated poverty and disinvestment in communities and public schools. However, the record of privatization, accountability, and testing has largely been one of failure rather than success (Saltman, 2012). For instance, according to a nation-wide Stanford University study, the majority of charter schools perform either worse or no better than their traditional public school counterparts (CREDO, 2009). The small percentage that have succeeded, like those celebrated in the film *Waiting for Superman*, have been highly selective of their students while receiving hundreds of millions of dollars in supplementary funding from corporate philanthropies. Further, research studies from the United States and United Kingdom have noted (Ball, 2003; Gerwitz, Ball, & Bowe, 1995; Raey & Helen, 2003) that privatization and school "choice" initiatives have tended to benefit families with the cultural capital to acquire seats in the best schools over low-income families and youth with disabilities and/or low test-scores. Whereas public schools, at least in theory if not always in practice, operate to serve all young people equitably under public oversight—privately run charter, contract, and for-profit schools often have selective enrollment, lack public accountability, are hostile to unions, and operate under a commercial value structure often at odds with noncommercial democratic values. What has emerged in urban school districts is a deeply inequitable system with a top tier of options for the elite, a middle tier of semipublic options for a beleaguered and shrinking middle class, and a large bottom tier of disinvested public schools sorting low-income and racialized youth into a low-wage and no-wage future. Entrenched economic insecurity and the turn to austerity are intensifying these educational inequities contributing to a precarious future of instability and uncertainty for young people in the neoliberal city.

Securitizing Schools and Criminalizing Youth

> While all youth are now suspect, poor minority youth have become especially
> targeted by modes of social regulation, crime control, and disposability that
> have become the major prisms that now define many of the public institutions
> and spheres that govern their lives.
>
> —*Henry Giroux*, Youth in a Suspect Society[11]

Alongside the retrenchment of educational inequality, schools have become
implicated in the broader criminalization of youth. With the waning of social
democratic policy and the emergence of neoliberal governance, social commitments to schools and to youth have evaporated at the bottom of the race and class
structure while the state has broadly expanded various punitive forms of social
control. This has meant that in the post-Columbine and post-9/11 context, public
schools have broadly experimented with new systems of risk management, security, and surveillance rooted in the symbolic and material practices of the criminal justice system. However, while all schools have to some degree experienced
heightened security arrangements over the last ten years, these practices have
been much more prevalent and intensive in urban public schools serving high
concentrations of low-income minority students. Paul Hirschfield (2008) thus
observes that "the gated community may be a more apt metaphor to describe
the security transformation of affluent schools, while the prison metaphor better
suits that of inner-city schools" (p. 84).

The atmosphere of criminological control in urban public schools serving
high concentrations of low-income and racialized youth is defined by various
interlocking technologies and practices imported from the corporate security sector and law enforcement. First, urban districts, large and small, have
broadly integrated metal detectors, CCTV cameras, access control screening
technologies, new spatial designs and architectural arrangements, and uniformed security officers into the everyday security and disciplinary infrastructures and procedures of schools. Second, there has been a vast expansion of
direct law enforcement into public schools. For example, as of 2008, the New
York City Public Schools had 5,000 "school safety agents" supervised directly
by the NYPD, along with an additional 200 armed officers, patrolling school
hallways. This means that the NYPD's school safety division is now larger
than the entire police forces of Washington DC, Detroit, Boston, or Las Vegas
(NCLU). Police presence has broadly transformed how public schools imagine
and handle issues relating to security and student regulation and discipline
(Kupchik, 2010; Lyons & Drew, 2006; Nolan, 2011). Schools now rely on procedures imported from the prison system such as "lockdowns" and invasive
searches, where police perform drug and weapon sweeps in schools through
random locker checks, bag searches, and frisking—for instance, nationwide, 41
percent of middle schools and 61 percent of high schools used drug sniffing dogs
for such purposes during the 2005–2006 school year (Kupchik, 2010). Students
are now routinely arrested for offenses that used to be handled by teachers and
administrators (Advancement Project [AP], 2005, 2010). For instance, in 2003

alone 8,539 students were arrested in the Chicago Public Schools for various offenses, the vast majority of which did not involve injuries, weapons, or serious crimes (AP, 2005).

These trends have been supported by the sociolegal framework of "zero tolerance" which came into US public education via the Gun Free Schools Act of 1994. The law tied increased Federal funding for schools to the adoption of new practices for dealing with and neutralizing crime on campuses. By applying mandatory across-the-board penalties for rule violations by students, zero tolerance was designed to eliminate bias and strengthen consistency in punishments. However, research indicates that the policies have undermined the discretion of teachers and administrators for handling rule violations by students (AP, 2005, 2010). This has tended to shift responsibility for dealing with student misbehavior from a rehabilitative model guided by social and professional norms of child development, to a punitive one modeled on law enforcement policing (Robbins, 2009). As a result, studies indicate that the integration of zero tolerance has led to the rapid inflation of the number of students suspended, arrested, and expelled in public schools each year and that this has had a significantly disproportionate impact on minority students (AP, 2005, 2010). The research also notes that this racial bias in punishment is largely unreflective of behavioral differences across geographical and racial lines, for instance, in the use and sale of illegal drugs in schools which is as prevalent in the suburbs as in the city (Simon, 2007). Uneven distributions of punishments have, however, mirrored the broader racial dimensions of imprisonment contributing to a "school-to-prison pipeline" (Nogeura, 2003; Johnson, Boyden & Pittz, 2001).

The expansion of a crime control paradigm in urban schools must be understood alongside broader political and economic transformations. In reaction to fiscal crisis, deindustrialization, capital flight, and unemployment in the mid-1970s, US urban policy has focused public resources and attention to aggressive policing as a central way of containing social dislocation and unrest. Jonathan Simon (2007) has coined the phrase "governing through crime" to describe how, out of the ashes of the New Deal consensus and Johnson's Great Society, the "war on drugs" came to replace the "war on poverty" as the central plank in the state management of the poor. He argues that since the passage of Richard Nixon's Omnibus Crime Control Act in 1968, the logic of "governing through crime" has emerged as a dominant framework particularly in public schools serving disadvantaged young people where law enforcement and school organization have become ever more coextensive. He states:

> The merging of school and penal system has speeded the collapse of the progressive project of education and tilted the administration of schools toward a highly authoritarian and mechanistic model. This model collapses all the normal/expected/predictable vulnerabilities of youth into variations of the categories of criminal violence. This transformation is especially problematic since when the generally preferred "solution"—the tight policing of everyone—fails, as it inevitably will, the response is to shift responsibility onto everyone but the incumbent regime, primarily through such emotionally satisfying, but substantively empty, slogans such as "accountability" and "zero tolerance." (p. 9)

In this milieu, education policies have turned toward privatization, account-ability initiatives, testing, exclusionary discipline, and militarized security as cost-saving alternatives to investment in the universal modernization of public school buildings, well-rounded curriculum, small class sizes, and other robust ameliorative support services for youth such as restorative approaches to violence prevention and other social work services that could uplift and improve strug-gling public schools (Hirschfield, 2008). Instead, a militaristic crime control par-adigm in public schooling—of metal detectors, screening technologies, CCTV cameras, and extensive law enforcement presence—has meant that many urban public schools, particularly those at the margins of the neoliberal city that serve economically precarious communities, appear less invested in socializing youth for economic and civic engagement than in warehousing and control (Ibid).

The emergence of criminological security and surveillance practices in schools also reflects shifting cultural attitudes and contemporary "moral panics" over youth (Grossberg, 2005). Popular concerns over young people are certainly noth-ing new. As Nancy Lesko (2001) has detailed, since its invention in the nineteenth century, "youth" as a social category marking a population in between childhood and adulthood, has been associated with hope as well as profound social anxiety. In her study of the racial politics of youth and neoliberalism in the city of Oakland, Jennifer Tilton (2010) has suggested that "youth today call to mind a troubling set of images: kids failing school or falling behind, 'babies having babies,' gang mem-bers, and school shooters" (p. 3). These moral panics "have distorted our image of youth and our public policy responses at the turn of the 21st century. We are afraid for 'our own kids' but deeply fearful of 'other people's children'" (p. 3). Therefore, urban youth tend to be positioned as either "endangered" or "dangerous," while social problems are increasingly framed in terms of the supposed criminal pathol-ogy of young people. This has contributed to the development of punitive school climates that situate disadvantaged youth primarily as either potential victims or criminals as opposed to future workers or democratic citizens, while doing little to address the systemic violence that permeates their lives. Such a punitive climate also socializes youth to accept a diminished future marked by uncertainty and daily engagements with repressive forms of authority. As Henry Giroux (2009) has suggested, in this punitive framework, where social control becomes more impor-tant than social investment, urban youth are increasingly treated as a "generation of suspects" rather than a vital source of hope for the future.

Conclusion:
Public Schooling and Precarious Reproduction

Schools have long been the central public institution charged with directing young people into their future roles in a democratic society (Durkheim, 1961; Dewey, 1944). Since the inception of the common school movement in the nine-teenth century, the socializing functions of schooling have been directed to workforce preparation and acculturating both immigrant and nonimmigrant youth into national identification and citizenship (Tyack, 1974). As my analysis in this chapter has implied, with new economic realities and the fading of social democratic commitments and the triumph of deregulated market governance, tensions and contradictions have emerged that have rendered the social reproductive functions of urban schooling ever more precarious and repressive. This is particularly salient for those schools at the margins of the contemporary urban geography. In this concluding section, I want to raise some critical questions concerning these transformations in urban education in relation to the security of young people.

There is a long tradition of critical sociology that has linked educational processes to the sorting of youth for their future roles in the workforce. In their classic study, *Schooling in Capitalist America*, Samuel Bowles and Herbert Gintis (2011) analyzed the history of school reform since the late nineteenth century in order to demonstrate a "correspondence principle" between schooling and the economic and social relations of production and accumulation. Bowles and Gintis argued that contrary to operating on a meritocratic basis, schools mirror and reproduce the hierarchical divisions of labor and inequality immanent to "the market, property, and power relationships which define the capitalist system" (p. 11). They do so by sorting students according to socioeconomic class, race, gender, and ability into different hierarchical educational opportunities, academic tracks, and fields of study. Bowles and Gintis observed that bottom tier schools and academic tracks tend to emphasize rudimentary skills and rule following behavior suitable for low-wage factory and manual labor, while affluent schools and elite tracks encourage the forms of thinking and skills necessary for college readiness and future positions as managers and professionals. Schools also train and socialize students into the rationalized processes of the modern workplace by teaching punctuality, deference to authority, and individual competition and accountability through various methods of external rewards and punishments such as individualized grading, schedules, and competitive examinations. Lastly, schools manage reserve armies of workers both by warehousing youth who would otherwise be entering the labor market and by "creating surpluses of skilled labor sufficiently extensive to render effective the prime weapon of the employer in disciplining labor—the power to hire and fire" (p. 11).

Political economic perspectives have offered an incisive lens to understand the role of schools in reproducing inequality. Rather than situating inequality as derived from some inherent characteristic of students, they have crucially alerted us to the ways in which inequality is internal to the normal functioning of the market, property, and power relations that define capitalist systems. However, these perspectives have also rightly been criticized as being overly deterministic and blind to the dynamics of culture, contestation, and agency in educational contexts. Sociologists Pierre Bourdieu and Jean-Claude Passeron (1977), for instance, have linked social reproduction processes in schools to the negotiation of cultural capital—that is, those embodied forms of speech, style, and physical comportment that demarcate the subtle markers of symbolic status and distinction. Schools tend to reinforce and reward upper- and middle-class forms of cultural capital within daily school interactions, thereby serving to exclude and silence the experiences, identities, and knowledge of working-class, racial, and sexual minority students. Importantly, however, these struggles over cultural capital and school knowledge are far from static or one-sided relations of domination. Rather, they represent contradictory and contested processes. Scholars such as Paul Willis (1977), Henry Giroux (1983), and Angela McRobbie (1978), for instance, have provided essential insight into how young people across the lines of race, class, gender, ability, and sexuality exercise their own agency and talk back to structures of authority and resist oppressive conditions. Furthermore, schools are not institutions that simply reproduce and/or legitimate inequality. Educational spheres have also functioned historically as key sites for what John Dewey (1944) described as the "realization of democratic ideals" where working people, communities, and youth might develop and exercise the capacities necessary to attain greater social recognition, material security, and push for democratic change and possibility.

Any sophisticated theory of neoliberal urban schooling has to take all of these dynamics into account. Schools reflect broader contradictions and relations of power and inequality in the economic and social sphere while providing a potential site for developing the democratic capacities, values, and consciousness necessary to alter these relations in the interest of the common good. However, the perspectives of Bowles and Gintis, Bourdieu and Passeron, Willis, McRobbie, and others, were largely developed under a Fordist paradigm where the factory occupied a central referent in the organization of society and when social democratic policies broadly supported a social contract rooted in collective security and investment. Writing in the 1960s and 1970s, Michel Foucault's (1977) historical analysis suggests that Fordist social regulation found its apex under the postwar Keynesian welfare state, where institutions such as the school, prison, family, trade union, factory, and army barrack were tightly bound to national systems of industrial production and social and civic identification. In contrast, under post-Fordism, these institutions are said to be in a state of crisis (Deleuze, 1995; Hardt & Negri, 2001). This is expressed by dysfunctional schools; the splintering of the nuclear family; the erosion of unions and stable employment; the transition from social citizenship to consumer citizenship; and the decline of a rehabilitative ideal and the extension of repressive state power in the realm of policing, punishment, and social control. Nancy Fraser (2003) has written that Fordist social regulation was "totalizing, socially concentrated within a national frame, and oriented to self-regulation...mobilizing 'useful [if not wholly docile] bodies' in nationally bounded societies of mass production and mass consumption" (p. 164–165). In contrast, post-Fordism and neoliberal culture have reshaped social relations and governance toward something increasingly "multilayered as opposed to nationally bounded, dispersed and marketized as opposed to socially concentrated, increasingly repressive as opposed to self-regulating" (p. 166–167).

Questions thus emerge as to how we are to understand the socializing and sorting processes of schools amid these transformations. As I have tried to highlight throughout this chapter, the erosion of social democratic commitments and the interweaving of market governance and criminological discipline introduces tensions in contemporary educational policy and the social reproductive functions of schools. Public schools in the United States that serve high proportions of impoverished urban youth have been socially devalued, neglected, and subjected to privatization and market management. Such schools are populated by young people living in precarious conditions facing highly unstable economic futures in the stratified global economy pointing toward a crisis of human security in urban educational contexts. How are we then to understand the social reproductive function of urban public schools today when the corporation and the prison have seemingly eclipsed the factory as the primary institutional referents in schools? How do we imagine security in public schools when the consumer and the criminal have emerged as the primary categories marking youth as deserving or undeserving of social recognition and protection? Most importantly, for the interests of the narrative analysis that will unfold in the following chapters, as processes of socialization become more precarious and repressive under neoliberal governance, how do young people and educators understand and negotiate these realities within everyday schooling?

The perspectives I have outlined throughout this chapter suggest that security has tended to become both privatized and militarized. On one hand, security is imagined as an individual responsibility to be managed through the market as opposed to a collectively lived and democratically mediated condition. On the other hand, security has become conceived through the lens of crime control and the creeping diffusion of militarized responses to social problems across institutional sectors and circulations of everyday urban and educational life. We can see how this operates within the context of educational policy where, in the name of security, public schools are subject to market governance and the extension of criminalizing practices which have contributed to altering the educative and civic operation and mission of school systems and environments. I have argued that this signals a crisis of human security and a moment of precarious social reproduction in urban schooling particularly for already disadvantaged young people. This crisis of security speaks directly to the fraying of the material conditions and public values and social commitments necessary to secure the daily lives and futures of young people. My concern moving forward to my case study of Chicago school policy and the Ellison Square neighborhood and Carter High School is to examine how these phenomena manifest in urban and educational contexts in ways that delimit social relations and future pathways for youth. In what comes next, I turn my attention to the Chicago context and the politics of social research in urban districts.

2

Chicago and the Management of Social Research

For positivism, which has assumed the judicial office of enlightened reason, to speculate about intelligible worlds is no longer merely forbidden but senseless prattle.

—*Max Horkheimer and Theodore Adorno*, The Dialectic of Enlightenment[1]

A light rain was falling as I made my way from the bus stop toward Romero High School on Chicago's West Side. As I approached the school, the first thing I noticed was the police vehicle parked in front—a boxy, truck-like paddy wagon. There was an additional police cruiser across the street. The school itself is a massive red brick building featuring about 20 different front doors that were all closed and locked except for one at the far right hand side. I noticed the unmistakable black plastic eye of a surveillance camera above the open door. As I entered the school, I was immediately met by a male African American security guard dressed in a blue uniform. Not official police, I realized, despite the fact that he had a pair of shiny steel handcuffs attached to his belt. I was then asked to put my bag through an airport-like security screener and another similarly dressed female security guard examined its contents via a closed circuit monitor. As I stepped through the metal detector I raised my arms and the male guard gave me a halfhearted pat down. Next, I signed in at the security desk and made my way up the stairs to the main office. On the stairwell, I passed by a large brightly painted mural—a monument to military service featuring a proud-looking Latina in camouflage fatigues set against an American flag background. In the office, I was asked to take a seat and wait for the principal who I came to see regarding potential access for my research. On the wall above the administrative assistant's desk were four mounted closed circuit television monitors scrolling through images from the school's many surveillance cameras. From my seat, I had an unobstructed view of the hallway. A white, middle aged, male cop proceeded to walk by the office. He had a semiautomatic pistol in his belt and his hands were tucked nonchalantly into the sides of his bullet proof vest. Above a row of red metallic lockers on the other side of the hallway was another surveillance camera. Disconcertingly, it appeared to be pointed in my direction. I looked to the CCTV monitors on the wall. Sure enough, after a few sequences of scattered images beamed in from cameras throughout the school, an image of me sitting in the office appeared on one of the screens. Surreal, I thought to myself, welcome to the postindustrial school where everyone, including researchers, are regarded as potential security threats.

I begin with this reflection from a visit to Romero High School in order highlight a couple of tendencies regarding educational environments and social research in urban districts today. First, like students, teachers, and other adults, researchers are becoming subject to enhanced institutional risk management and security protocols. Second, I want to suggest that this description of my visit to Romero High School prefigures how an everyday aesthetic of fear and security within urban public schools intersects with a more generalized form of corporate managerialism that has contributed to altering the dynamics of qualitative educational research in urban schools. This has occurred in a broader political context that has produced renewed efforts to domesticate social research under a neo-positivist framework which favors market-oriented technical rationality and risk management over social and ethical engagement at the level of policy, research, and governance. These processes are placing new restrictions on social research in urban schools that limit inquiry, access, and opportunities for informed criticism of policies.

This chapter discusses the Chicago context and the politics of critical social research within neoliberal schooling. Much has been written about Chicago as a postindustrial city and recent scholarship has also provided insightful analysis of the restructuring of the Chicago Public Schools (CPS) (Koval, 2006; Lipman, 2003, 2011). I focus here mainly on linkages between recent transformations in Chicago and patterns of austerity and social insecurity in the shadow of the Great Recession. I further situate these developments in relation to the last two decades of educational policy and school reform in Chicago. Next, I turn to reflecting on the research process within the CPS and how my difficulties in gaining access to the field highlight emergent challenges to research in relation to the new managerialism and security culture.

Chicago as Context:
From Global City to City of Austerity

When you're starving and your back is up against the wall and you see no other option, then what are you supposed to do?

—*Community college student in Chicago*[2]

Since the late 1960s and early 1970s, Chicago has been broadly reshaped by processes associated with globalization and neoliberal urbanism. Unlike many of its "rustbelt" counterparts, such as Detroit and Cleveland, Chicago has been largely successful in making the transition from an industrial model to a service, tourism, and finance-based model of economic development. Under the direction of former mayor Richard M. Daley (1989–2011) and now under current mayor, Rahm Emmanuel, Chicago's political and business elite have followed a neoliberal path in order to make the city a strategic site for capital and a competitive force in global markets. Currently, the Chicago region is home to 19 billionaires; dozens of transnational corporations including 20 in the fortune 500 such as Kraft, Motorola, United Airlines, and McDonalds; and the third largest stock exchange in the United States.

Chicago's postindustrial transition has been highly uneven. This is marked by a significant downtown proximate economic boom visible in the construction of new corporate office towers, trendy retail and entertainment complexes, and upscale condos and residential housing. However, while gentrified commercial areas have flourished, large sections of Chicago's historically neglected and racially segregated residential zones have continued to decline under the combined weight of concentrated poverty, social disinvestment, and generalized social insecurity (Street, 2007; Wacquant, 2008). As Loïc Wacquant (2008) documents, patterns of economic dislocation and racial isolation in Chicago can be attributed to multiple factors including deindustrialization and the evaporation of living-wage employment opportunities, historical patterns of exclusionary residential segregation, and the "planned shrinkage" of public institutions in disinvested communities (pp. 69–88). These patterns reflect deep historical and political divisions and Chicago's long held status as the most ethnoracially segregated city in the United States. Currently, Chicago is a triethnic city that is roughly 34 percent black, 33 percent white, and 27 percent Latino. Two-thirds of the city's nearly one million African Americans live in neighborhoods that are 80 percent black, while over half live in hypersegregated and impoverished communities that are over 96 percent black (Bogira, 2011). The city's growing Latino population also experiences significant residential segregation. Further, the dismantling and privatization of public housing combined with real estate speculation and extensive gentrification has contributed to pushing/pricing-out many low-income and working people into economically declining neighborhoods or out of the city altogether (Ibid).

John Koval (2006) uses the metaphor of an "hourglass economy" to describe the erosion of the middle class and the polarization of wealth and opportunity in Chicago. This divergence has been inflected by neoliberal policy. During the 1990s and 2000s, the Daley administration presided over extensive privatization and public downsizing. Highlights include selling off the Chicago Skyway and the Chicago Parking Services to Morgan Stanley and the sovereign wealth fund of Abu Dhabi—decisions that were made to patch short-term budget gaps but are now slated to deprive the city of billions in crucial future revenue (Taibbi, 2010). At the federal level, conservative tax cuts since the Reagan era (Bush's tax cuts alone cost $3 trillion in federal revenue between 2001 and 2011), profligate spending on militarism and foreign wars (roughly $7.6 trillion over the same 10-year period), have dovetailed with extensive reductions in federal, state, and local investments in cities (Harrar, 2011). At the state level, a report put out by the Center for Tax and Budget Accountability reports that in the period between 2002 and 2013, Illinois will have cut $1.64 billion from human services,

$2.8 billion from K-12 and higher education, and $277 million from health care (Center for Tax and Budget Accountability, 2012). This is experienced at the local level in cuts to libraries, schools, health services, and public housing alongside public sector layoffs (including thousands of teachers) and steep wage and benefit concessions from city workers. Public disinvestment has been found to have a greater impact on low- and middle-income residents. For example, gains made by an emergent black middle class in the 1990s have eroded during the Great Recession as African Americans are disproportionally impacted by public sector job loss (Williams, 2011).

The erosion of the public sphere in Chicago is one element in the broader erosion of human security that began well before the economic crisis in 2008 and has accelerated in its aftermath. The Heartland Alliance (2010) reports that in Illinois, "the Great Recession has crumbled economic stability for millions of families in the form of massive job loss, cut backs in hours, the elimination of work benefits, skyrocketing foreclosures and bankruptcies, and the eroding value of retirement investments" (p. 1). Their data (2010–2011) paint a stunning picture of hardship in Chicago and across the state of Illinois:

- As of 2011, there were nearly 1 million Illinoisans unemployed or underemployed (working fewer hours than they would like) and many more have stopped looking for work altogether. Workers in the lowest income group in Illinois had a 1930's-like unemployment rate of 27.0 percent in the fourth quarter of 2009.
- Almost 100,000 workers in Illinois who work full time, year round, still fall below the poverty line. Byron Dickens, a Chicago resident, describes his situation: "Working 40 hours a week in a minimum wage job I don't earn enough to cover my housing, food, transportation, and all my medical expenses. And I don't even have a family."
- Between 2008 and 2009, unemployment claims in the Chicago region increased by a staggering 30 percent; there were 128,049 new foreclosure filings; and 253,000 more people in the Chicago region (including 87,000 children) fell into poverty ($22,050 for a family of four).
- As of 2011, there were 1.1 million (13.6%) residents in the Chicago region living in poverty with 482,297 classified as living in "extreme poverty," while an additional 1.4 million had low incomes (17.3%).
- In addition to those living in poverty, around 40 percent of households in the Chicago region have annual incomes below $50,000, which is near the amount it takes for a one-parent family with two kids to make ends meet.
- Currently, children under 18 are the largest group of people living in poverty in the Chicago region.
- Unemployment among youth has increased 34 percent in the Chicago region since 2007 and is much higher than rates for older workers. Unemployment for black and Latino youth is now over 40 percent.
- The average amount of student loan debt among recent graduates from Illinois colleges is now $23,885.

- In more than half of Illinois counties, at least one out of every four kids experiences food insecurity. In the Chicago region, there were 1,202,180 people experiencing food insecurity, including 488,740 children.
- In 2008, an additional 10,600 CPS students were reported as homeless, an increase of 32 percent over five years.

These statistics point to deep systemic problems and a profound crisis of human security, especially for young people. There are simply not enough jobs that pay a living wage to go around. Slashing social investment only adds more pain, making it harder for working people to meet their basic needs. Moreover, as economists have noted, this combination of austerity and escalating inequality is not only toxic to human dignity and the social fabric but that it is also bad for a capitalist economy—widespread loss of jobs and low wages for workers stifle demand for goods and services while decaying public infrastructure and frayed safety nets diminish the capacity of cities and regions to create jobs, invest in people, and spur economic development (Stiglitz, 2012). Given this stark assessment, the Heartland Alliance concludes that:

> long-term economic shifts, which have left millions in low-wage jobs that do not pay family-supporting wages, point to the need for a constant and responsive safety net to help families bridge the gap between what they are paid and what it takes to make ends meet. Yet years of disinvestment in Illinois' safety net, combined with the effects of the recession and an antiquated state revenue system, have resulted in an erosion of human services across the state. The implications of massive service cuts to those experiencing poverty—many of whom rely on state-funded services in their communities literally for survival, particularly those in extreme poverty—will be nothing short of devastating. (2010, p. 1)

Meanwhile, as the systemic violence deepens, the United States continues seemingly limitless investment in militarism and domestic security and policing. Total spending on defense and homeland security in the United States in 2013 is slated to be roughly $1 trillion, which vastly exceeds that of all other nations. As a point of comparison, federal funding for education in 2013 is expected to be only $64 billion (Hellman & Kramer, 2012). Chicago's budget is no exception. Over the last twenty years, Chicago has spent hundreds of millions on its militarized surveillance and policing capacities under the rubric of the drug war and the war on terror. This includes the construction of a high-tech Homeland Security Grid that includes over 10,000 interconnected surveillance cameras, new computer systems of data tracking and risk management, zero tolerance enforcement ordinances, and paramilitary SWAT and antigang units. This underscores years of misplaced priorities and the development of systems of repression in Chicago aimed at managing the racialized poor and urban disorder stemming from employment stagnation and decline of social commitments. The human costs are stunning. In 2002, for instance, there were more black males in Illinois prisons than in college, while the total number of black males with a felony record (48% of whom were convicted on nonviolent drug offenses) was equivalent in number to 80 percent of the total adult black male workforce in Chicago (Street, 2002). Investments in policing have also been aimed increasingly at subverting and criminalizing dissent. For instance, in the wake of the Occupy Wall Street movement and a NATO summit in May of 2012, Chicago instituted emergency ordinances that enable police to suspend civil liberties and detain, search, and interrogate civilians outside established legal conventions.

Education Policy and Reform in Chicago

The Chicago Public Schools have been at the center of some of the most contentious political debates in the city's history. In the early twentieth century, Chicago was home to some of the most important thinkers in progressive education, such as John Dewey and Francis Parker, who stirred national debates about the centrality of public education in democratic life. Chicago has also historically been home to pitched battles over educational reform between a corporate class interested in making schools largely accountable to business interests, and progressive teachers' unions and community activist networks. Over the last two decades, public education has once again become a frontline political issue as Chicago has emerged as a leader of neoliberal school reform in the United States. Pauline Lipman (2003, 2011), who has written the definitive accounts of contemporary urban educational restructuring in Chicago, notes that the city "is more than a rich example. It is incubator, test case, and model for the neoliberal urban education agenda" (p.19). Today, the CPS serves approximately 400,000 students in 675 schools, making it the third largest school district in the United States. The CPS provides services to an overwhelmingly low-income population of mostly black and Latino youth. 85 percent of CPS students are visible minorities and 87 percent come from low-income families. Like other urban school districts across the United States, the CPS is plagued by inequitable access to resources, an appalling 55 percent dropout rate, and perennially low test scores.

Since the 1990s, Chicago's business and political elite have led the way in developing a variety of neoliberal educational reforms including high-stakes testing, top-down accountability policies, and privatization initiatives. For instance, Chicago's 1995 reforms served as the blueprint for what was to become the No Child Left Behind Act in 2001. These reforms largely rolled back efforts at increased decentralization and community governance that had been developed in the 1980s under the progressive administration of Harold Washington, the city's first and only African American mayor. As Dorothy Shipps (2006) documents, the 1995 reforms were largely the brainchild of business groups like the Commercial Club of Chicago, composed of the city's most powerful CEOs and financiers. The reforms granted Mayor Daley increased authority over education including the right to hire and fire the members of the Board of Education's Executive Committee and the power to select a chief executive officer for the CPS. The CEO became the primary authority over the district's principals, whose overriding mandate became implementing the directives of the Daley administration. This included the use of mandatory scripted lesson plans aimed at teaching basic skills for standardized tests. Further, the 1995 reforms also gave the mayor and his team the right to punish schools that failed to meet testing benchmarks with "probation," "remediation," and "reconstitution" if necessary. In 1995, Daley handpicked the state budget director Paul Vallas to be the new schools' CEO. Vallas, who was nicknamed "Chain Saw Paul," rapidly followed a neoliberal prescription by incorporating market competition, corporate management principles, and privatization into the CPS. This included, among other things, outsourcing numerous aspects of educational governance to the private sector while working to curb the power of the teachers' union. Shipps observes that in the late 1990s, under the market ideology of the Commercial Club and the authority of Daley and Vallas, the CPS essentially "became a deregulated agency of city hall" (p. 153). The 1995 policies with their emphasis on accountability and results were met with broad initial support by communities rightly fed up with decades of failure in the system. However, they have since become the object of extensive criticism and community opposition due to a lack of democracy and community input; a failure to improve systemic achievement; persistent charges of cronyism, fraud, and profiteering; and continued disinvestments in public schools and ongoing educational inequities.

Over the last decade, largely under the direction of former Chicago schools' CEO Arne Duncan (2001–2009), Chicago further consolidated and extended the 1995 reforms, mayoral control, and the influence of the Commercial Club in educational affairs. In 2002, the Commercial Club wrote *Left Behind*, a proposal that was to become the basis for the city's Renaissance 2010 school privatization initiative. The policy called for increased competition in education and the creation of an educational marketplace. This included closing up to 100 public schools and opening 60–70 charter and contract schools (publicly funded nonunionized schools run by contracted vendors) and a smaller number of performance schools (selective public schools subject to Renaissance 2010 guidelines). As of 2009, the city had closed or phased out 59 schools, opened 46 charters, 15 contract schools, and 31 selective performance schools. While touted as a bold and innovative initiative to dramatically improve public education through choice and market competition, Renaissance 2010 has not led to systemic improvement. Only 16 of the 92 new schools reached state testing averages in 2009. Among these, only 8 were charter schools. As it turns out, the successful schools benefited heavily from private foundation money, while the other 8 were selective magnet schools that choose their students based on ability and family connections (Catalyst, 2010). Critics have further argued that rather than promoting universal investments in order to improve struggling public schools, Renaissance 2010 has largely been geared to forwarding private control over public education in order to cheapen its long-term cost, dismantle the teachers' union, open up avenues for commercialism, and to remake neighborhoods in the interest of real estate speculation. Lipman's (2011) important analysis, for instance, points to how Renaissance 2010 has used school closings to lubricate gentrification by closing schools in conjunction with the demolition of public housing in African American neighborhoods in order to displace residents and use new schools of "choice" as real estate anchors.

While pioneering market-based educational policies, Chicago has also been at the forefront of redefining educational environments through new surveillance and crime control paradigms of security and discipline. In the wake of a fatal shooting at Tilden High School in 1992, Mayor Daley seized on school security issues and youth violence in the media in order to build support for mayoral control over public schools and to promote a range of "zero tolerance" and "exclusionary measures" that codified harsh mandatory punishments that soon "diffused across the country" (Hagen, Hirschfield, & Shedd, 2003). Daley also mandated metal detectors in all public high schools and created the School Patrol Unit (SPU) which greatly expanded police presence in CPS schools. In its first year alone, the SPU in conjunction with the "zero tolerance regime" made 9,822 arrests of students at schools in the CPS, most for low level and nonviolent offenses (Hirschfield, 2010, p. 42). Further, under Daley, the CPS incorporated a large number of security guards and surveillance cameras into schools, which were directly connected to law enforcement via the city's Homeland Security Grid. Currently, the CPS has over 2,000 security guards on its payroll at a cost of over $50 million a year, which incidentally, is roughly 15 times more than the district spends on college and career coaches (Voices of Youth in Chicago [VOYCE], 2011). This pays for an average of seven security guards at each school, with an additional "floating" reserve of guards that are dispatched to "hot spots"—schools that are identified through computerized risk assessment models as having immediate safety concerns. The research indicates that the law and order turn in the CPS has been responsible for dramatic escalation in suspensions, expulsions, and arrests in schools and the perpetuation of a school-to-prison pipeline (AP, 2005, 2010). It has also contributed to transforming educational spaces as the semiotics of the prison—guards, lockdowns, and containment—work to instantiate new punitive social relations and forms of social control in Chicago's schools.

Barriers to Inquiry:
Risk Culture and the Management of Social Research

In large urban districts like the CPS, one of the consequences of neoliberal governance is the enhanced difficulty of gaining access to research sites due to added bureaucratic obstacles and institutional forms of risk management. Access for the research conducted in the following chapters in Ellison Square involved a complex and protracted negotiation with the CPS. Beginning with my first trip to Romero High School (originally my proposed research site) that I describe in the opening paragraphs of this chapter, I began what turned out to be nine months of administrative gymnastics in order to gain access to the field. Before I was granted eligibility to apply for the CPS ethical review, I found myself having to acquire a variety of permissions beginning with the principal at Romero. As it turned out, the principal, while amenable to the project, would not provide her signed approval without a district supervisor's approval. However, the district supervisor, while also interested in supporting the research, would not grant his approval until the ethical review was completed. But the CPS ethical review board would not review my proposal without a principal's signature. While everyone I talked with expressed genuine interest in the research and agreed it was on an important topic, my impression was that both the principal and the district supervisor were both apprehensive (even fearful) to take responsibility for signing off on the project as the research dealt with the politically sensitive areas of security and inequality in Chicago and in the CPS.

My access negotiations dragged on for several months through the fall of 2009, until I finally acquired the permissions and signatures necessary to make my proposal eligible for review by the CPS. However, after approximately six weeks, the CPS ethical review committee rejected the proposal on the grounds that they would need the permission of the CPS director of the Office of Safety and Security, Mike Shields—a former police officer widely known in Chicago as Michelle Obama's cousin. Once his signature was obtained they would reconsider my application. After I was able to obtain his approval, the CPS had little choice but to accept my proposal but only after they restricted the amount of time I could spend in the field—cutting it down from two semesters to one—while also limiting the number of formal interviews with students and staff that I could conduct.[3] Moreover, it was at this point that the principal at Romero backed out of the project for reasons unknown to me. After networking through my contacts in Chicago I was able to find teachers interested in facilitating the research at Carter High School (CHS). The principal at CHS was also amenable, even enthusiastic, and I was able to receive approval for access nine months after beginning the process. To put this in perspective, my original proposal sailed through the International Ethical Review Committee at the University of Toronto on its first draft, certainly not unheard of, but notable because most submissions are returned for at least one round of revisions before acceptance.

My access negotiations reminded me of Franz Kafka's novel, *The Trial*. Like the character Josef K, no one would or could take responsibility for my case. There didn't appear to be a center, only an endless and impersonal bureaucratic authority as my case was passed from one official to another, all hoping, no doubt, that I would just simply admit defeat and go away. A former professor of mine who has done extensive research in the CPS remarked in an email that she was surprised that I was able to get as far as I did with this sensitive topic, and frankly, she was somewhat surprised that I was eventually granted approval at all. Apparently, these kinds of access problems have become routine. While school districts like the CPS are dealing with complex and difficult ethical issues and rightly want to protect young people and teachers from harmful or unnecessary intrusion, the difficulty of gaining access, particularly for qualitative projects that may take a critical perspective on current policy and practice, does raise important questions. For instance, under the current institutional climate, who has access to public spaces like public schools? What are the conditions of access? How does this institutional climate affect what questions can be asked and what methodologies can be employed to investigate them?

My access negotiation with the CPS speaks to the broader realities of conducting critical social research within neoliberal managerial culture. On one hand, qualitative researchers are contending with more intensive institutional efforts to govern risk through various technocratic procedures. This has meant increased bureaucratic obstacles in gaining access to educational sites and it has meant the enhanced surveillance of researchers once access has been granted. On the other hand, these obstacles to access have been concurrent with broader efforts to undermine and marginalize critical research. In the United States, this represents an attempt by the National Research Council, in collaboration with neoliberal and neoconservative think tanks and policy research centers, to legislate and discipline educational research under a narrow definition of "applied science" and a resurgent neopositivist "evidence-based" framework (Baez & Boyles, 2009; Lather, 2010). This has meant pushing for new guidelines and research standards rooted in a reductive notion of science that aligns with a corporate policy framework ideologically attuned to market oriented accountability mandates, basic skills curricula, data tracking, privatization, and standardized testing. Such efforts to domesticate educational research have created funding barriers and spurred attacks on qualitative research and researchers, particularly those who are critical of current educational reforms and practices. To be clear here, I am not arguing against the rigorous scientific study of educational processes and policy. Rather, my concern is how a narrow conception of science and scientific research functions to limit inquiry and screen out critical qualitative methods, projects, and perspectives.[4]

Certainly, such concerns are far from new as evidenced by various intellectual traditions which have called into question the contours of instrumental rationality and positivism in the social sciences. Here one might distinguish two broad lines of thought. First, there is the tradition in critical theory stemming from Max Weber that runs through the Frankfurt School and the constructivist approach to institutional sociology inspired by Michel Foucault (Weber, 1964; Horkheimer & Adorno, 2002; Foucault, 1977). This line of thought has sought to trouble assumptions regarding the inherently progressive character of modernist forms of reason and has made important contributions to the analysis of rationalization as an ideology and as a technology of discipline within various social contexts. Second, a variety of diverse theoretical perspectives have been developed over the last three decades in cultural studies, feminist and postcolonial criticism, and in the philosophy of science that have called into question representations of a pure objective image of science (Hacking, 1986; Harding, 1986 Latour, 1987 Said, 1989). This has included identifying the contingent and socially conditioned nature of all knowledge claims while uncovering how scientific methods are always already embedded within material and symbolic systems of value, power, and observer bias that work to shape research questions and outcomes historically in ways that have often justified relations of ecological and social domination. Contrary to advocating subjectivism, relativism, or irrationalism, the most astute of these philosophical perspectives have worked to deepen our understanding and ethical attunements to scientific inquiry as a value-laden activity. Far from rejecting science, they have sought to deepen its moral and empirical purpose.

In the contemporary moment where corporate power and the political right cynically appropriate the rhetoric of science (in the case of "evidence-based" educational policy and reform) or work to discredit it when it contradicts their interests and worldview (in the case of climate change), it appears that a critical and substantive debate over the democratic purpose of science remains of urgent public concern. Within this context it is imperative to understand how efforts to discipline social research in education within a resurgent positivism are grounded in neoliberal managerialism. Such an understanding is necessary for thinking through limitations and possibilities for what educational research and social science can and should mean within our current historical moment. Ultimately, these trends are leading to the marginalization of qualitative research projects: (1) lines of inquiry are limited and constrained; (2) social researchers increasingly have to justify the value of their projects within measurement-based logics; and, as a result, (3) the voices and experiences of teachers and students are devalued as sources of knowledge in both research contexts and within wider educational debates; (4) further, this marginalization of social experience and the reframing of research within a neopositivist frame inhibits broader analysis and discussion of the economic, social, and political valences of contemporary educational policies and practices; and, finally, (5) this contributes to undermining efforts to promote justice and equity within curriculum, schools, and communities and to critically evaluate and deepen the moral and ethical purpose of public education within a democratic society.

Taking the New Managerialism to School

Patti Lather (2010) notes that while many assumed in the late 1990s that the so-called "paradigm" or "science" wars were largely over and that qualitative research methodologies had found a secure footing in professional practice, a renewed neopositivism has emerged that tracks with the restructuring of institutional norms and practice under neoliberal governance and neoconservative politics. This is often described simply as the "new managerialism" or sometimes in slightly more Orwellian terms as Total Quality Management. It is characterized by a broad attempt to redefine institutional goals and values within a corporate framework of market calculation and a data-driven audit culture. As a dominant form of what Michel Foucault (2007) referred to as a "governmental rationality," the new managerialism links together systems of knowledge, technology, and practice at multiple scales from state formations and policy frameworks to institutional goals and forms of everyday culture and conduct.

The new managerialism works to legitimate itself largely through appeals to efficiency and through promises of less regulation, greater flexibility, and an end to the bureaucratic inefficiencies of the Keynesian welfare state. Within the context of school organization, including curriculum and research, measurement and outcomes-based practices such as standardized lessons, testing, teacher evaluation, and value-added assessments are held up as objective and supposedly progressive responses to long-standing educational failures. Numbers and measurable targets do not lie, nor do they have an agenda, so the popular wisdom goes. Additionally, holding teachers responsible for outcomes like meeting test-score benchmarks would appear on the surface to promote professional conduct, raise expectations, and ensure accountability. These logics have worked to lend moral justification and an air of "commonsense" legitimacy to the new managerial reforms. However, as Bronwyn Davies (2003) observes, the suturing of business-led data-driven policies and definitions of professional practice to the rhetoric of political neutrality and equity has worked to significantly suppress critical reflection and debate over the philosophical and ethical substance of the policies, particularly as they deprofessionalize teachers, limit research inquiry, and narrow the curriculum. Davies writes that it is not only the strong sense of inevitability of the new managerialism that limits critical reflection, but also pervasive insecurity and fear. She states that:

> Within the terms of the new system individuals will be presented with an (often overwhelming) range of pressing choices and administrative tasks for which they are responsible. But any questioning of the system itself is silenced or trivialized. The system itself is characterized as both natural and inevitable. Resistance to it by individuals…is constituted as ignorance of what the "real" (financial) "bottom-line" issues are, as sheer cussedness, or as a sign reminding management of individual workers' replaceability…the fact that much of the resource base that was previously available to support professional work has been redirected into surveillance and auditing somehow remains invisible…the individual's sense of agency and freedom through which professional energy, dedication and power were formerly generated are overlaid and in tension with an almost subliminal anxiety and fear of surveillance. (p. 93)

These observations can be extended to researchers and field work. The all-pervasive discourse of measurable outcomes collides with institutional cultures of risk management and surveillance to define what can and what cannot count as legitimate forms of methodology and inquiry leading directly to issues with access, funding, and restrictions on researchers in the field. In my field work for this research in Chicago, not only was the amount of time I could spend in the field narrowed from two semesters to one, along with the number of formal interviews I could conduct, but I also found that students, teachers, and administrators would initially demonstrate a high level of suspicion of my presence. I would often receive the question: "Are you from the board?" (meaning CPS headquarters downtown). What this meant was: "Are you here to spy and report on me?" As we will see in my analysis of life in Ellison Square and CHS in the following chapters, such a culture of fear and surveillance has become an utterly normalized aspect of daily school life for teachers, students, and researchers.

While the new managerialism purports to support democratic engagement and equity through appeals to liberal humanist values (i.e. "No Child Left Behind"), in practice, questions concerning the ethical substance of teaching, learning, and research are largely hollowed out. Within a fetishistic adherence to a market-based technical rationality, the system divests itself of discussion or debate over the actual substantive content and values that animate educational processes. Davies (2003) states that

> as long as institutional objectives have been specified and strategies for their management and surveillance put in place, the nature of the work itself is of little relevance to anyone. If the auditing tools say that the work has, on average, met the objectives, it is simply assumed that the work has been appropriately and satisfactorily tailored according to the requirements of the institution (and often the relevant funding body). (p. 92)

In the case of educational research this has meant that "the objectives will come first and the 'experimental research evidence' will be generated to justify them" (p. 100). Taking this argument further, Marc Fisher (2011) has suggested that the new managerialism must be read against a pervasive cynicism permeating neoliberal culture. He states:

> Neoliberalism reproduces itself through cynicism, through people doing things they "don't really believe"... people go along with auditing culture and what I call "business ontology" not necessarily because they agree with it, but because it's the ruling order, "that's just how things are now, and we can't do anything about it."

For instance, who actually believes that reducing learning to a test score actually serves "educational excellence"? Or that extending the criminal justice system into public schools through zero tolerance policies that send kids to jail for nonviolent school-related offenses is a positive way to handle discipline? Yet, these are the dominant policy frameworks in public schools today. In my own experience teaching graduate courses for educators in the Chicago area, I have yet to talk to a teacher, regardless of his/her political disposition, who believes that current fetishistic emphasis on testing is beneficial for student learning. This pervasive disillusionment, I would suggest, opens up important fissures within new managerial culture. It is worth quoting Fisher at length here:

> The idealized market was supposed to deliver "friction free" exchanges, in which the desires of consumers would be met directly, without the need for intervention or mediation by regulatory agencies. Yet the drive to assess the performance of workers and to measure forms of labor, which, by their very nature, are resistant to quantification [teaching for example], has inevitably required additional layers of management and bureaucracy. What we have is not a direct comparison of workers' performance or output, but a comparison between audited *representations* of that performance and output. Inevitably, a short circuiting occurs, and work becomes geared towards the generation and massaging of representations rather than the official goals of the work itself. Indeed, an anthropological study of local government in Britain argues that "more effort goes into ensuring that a local authority's services are represented correctly than actually going into actually improving those services." This reversal of priorities is one of the hallmarks of a system that can be characterized without hyperbole as "market Stalinism." What late capitalism repeats from Stalinism is just this valuing of symbols of achievement over actual achievement. (Fisher, 2009, p. 42)

Neoliberal managerial cultures in education largely fail on their own terms. They do not lessen regulatory authority and bureaucracy but vastly extend its scope while at the same time screening out deeper analysis of the ethical content of policies and practices within institutional contexts. As such, they are representative of what Fisher evocatively refers to here as "market Stalinism"—the subordination of all values to market imperatives while placing specific value on quantifiable representations without consideration of their underlying content or efficacy. For instance, the reduction of knowledge to measurable test scores appears as concrete "evidence" that something called "education" is being taken seriously and accounted for, with little in the way of critical analysis of the reductive assumptions embedded in excessive testing. Similarly, limiting what can be considered legitimate research to narrow questions and positivist methodologies prevents critical reflection on the meaning and purpose of research (beyond serving the status quo) as well as on the social, political, and economic forces that intersect with educational policy and practice in schools. Moreover, restricting researchers through either bureaucratic measures or through a narrow definition of science inhibits inquiry into how values and knowledge are struggled over in research contexts. It also inhibits inquiry into the perpetuation of issues that plague public education such as overcrowding, poverty, and/or lack of resources and equitable funding to public schools.

Conclusion:
Critical Ethnography as an Engaged Social Science

The narrative that unfolds in the following chapters grapples with the fragmentation of human security in relation to neoliberal schooling. Specifically, through the perspectives of young people and educators at Chicago's CHS, it brings to light human experiences of the systemic violence embedded within the decline of social democratic commitments to urban communities and schools. In contrast to the emphasis on technical market rationality implied by the new managerialism highlighted above, this narrative is informed by the principles of critical ethnography (Madison, 2012). As I wrote in the introduction, critical ethnography is foremost concerned with questions of meaning, power, and human agency as they become articulated and delimited within diverse social contexts and settings. Rather than attempting to isolate discreet parts of life in the interest of experimental testing and quantification, critical ethnography situates values and practices within the economic, cultural, and political forces that define and give them shape. This means that it is concerned with mapping wider social relationships and human experience from the local to the global and the universal to the particular. As a form of what Lather (2010) refers to as "engaged social science," critical ethnography enables us to gain access to how the broader forces of neoliberal schooling that I have described thus far are lived and experienced in everyday contexts such as in public schools like CHS and in the Ellison Square community in Chicago. Importantly, rather than attempting to serve the status quo, critical ethnography seeks to interrogate and challenge existing forms of knowledge and social relations in the interest of promoting human freedom, dignity, and greater democracy in public life. This firmly places critical ethnography in line with what the philosopher Immanuel Kant once referred to as "the public use of reason." In his commentary on Kant's essay, "What is Enlightenment?" Michel Foucault (1994) describes the public use of reason as a critical reflection on the present in the interest of determining what can be known, what can be done, and what can be hoped. For Foucault, the "critique of what we are is at the same time the historical analysis of the limits that are imposed upon us and an experiment with the possibility of going beyond them" (p. 56). It is in this spirit that part II proceeds.

Part II

Narratives of Enclosure and Possibility

3

Learning by Dispossession: Objective Violence and Educational Failure

Ellison Square and CHS are located several miles south of the landmark buildings and lakeshore attractions of Chicago's downtown. The neighborhood and school are marked by concentrated poverty and ethnoracial segregation. They also contend with persistent issues related to violence. Indeed, when I first arrived in Ellison Square during the first week of September 2010 to begin this research, I found a school and community under emergency conditions because of two recent shootings involving students from CHS. One of these shootings took place on school grounds in full view of students, police, teachers, and parents, the other in a vacant lot near the school. Neither incident was fatal, both were gang related.

> *Maya* (African American freshman): I was in my class. I was in my division. I was right there because we were looking through the window. It was hot so we had opened the windows and we were looking out the window and we just saw the boy had just got shot and he was just lying there and somebody was like, "Get help." And that's when the teacher told us to sit down. All I saw was a car pulled over and the boy was just walking and they shot him. And that's when the teacher was like, "Sit down, stop instigating" and stuff like that... I just felt hurt. Because it was like, it's probably because of the gangs and the bad decisions he chose and stuff like that.

While violence is not uncommon in Ellison Square or its surrounding neighborhoods, this was the first time in the 80-year history of CHS that such events had occurred during school hours and in such close proximity to the school. Statistically, public schools remain the safest places for youth even in tough urban neighborhoods like Ellison Square. However, these incidents foreground the persistent dangers and traumas confronting young people in our urban communities. Moreover, such instances of violence are profoundly affecting and understandably elicit strong responses to make neighborhoods and schools more safe and secure. The way we make sense of such violence, however, presents limits for how we formulate our efforts to promote greater human security for youth and more democratic and peaceful communities.

The philosopher Slavoj Žižek (2008) offers a useful diagram in this regard. He suggests that there are three interwoven types of violence. The first is the *subjective violence* carried out by "identifiable agents." The second is the *symbolic violence* embedded within language and aesthetic and cultural representations. The third is *systemic violence* which refers to the structural violence inhered within late modern societies. For Žižek, subjective violence is only the most visible of the three. This individualized form of violence appears to us as a disruption to the "normal" state of things, such as school shootings or spectacular acts of crime and terrorism. In contrast, as *objective* forms, systemic and symbolic violence refer to the violence inhered directly within this "normal" state of things—within the *"smooth functioning of our economic and political systems"* (p. 2). While objective violence may be less visible than subjective forms, it is no less visceral or real in its impact and effects. Žižek states that "systemic violence is thus like the 'dark matter' of physics, the counterpart to an all-too visible subjective violence. It may be invisible, but it has to be taken into account if one is to make sense of what otherwise seem to be 'irrational' explosions of subjective violence" (p. 2). Žižek's analysis suggests that rather than something exceptional, violence is, in fact, quite ordinary—a force embedded within our social systems and everyday realities.

This chapter explores neoliberal governance in relation to systemic violence and educational dislocation at CHS. I begin with a description of the historical, economic, and political dynamics underpinning school and community life. Next, I examine processes of privatization, social disinvestment, and curriculum management at CHS. I then extend this analysis by looking in detail at questions of security, conflict, and violence at CHS and in the lives of youth. These processes, I argue, are contributing to a climate of failure and alienation that is subverting the educative and human development function of public schooling.

Ellison Square and CHS

Ellison Square is a segregated, high-poverty community on Chicago's South Side. Since its founding in the late nineteenth century, the neighborhood has undergone significant, and at times deeply contentious socioeconomic and demographic transformations. In the 1920s, the neighborhood was inhabited mainly by Eastern European immigrants. CHS was built in 1929 on the cusp of the Great Depression and the New Deal. The single largest employer for the neighborhood during this time was the Union Stock Yards, best known perhaps for being the subject of *The Jungle*—Upton Sinclair's classic muckraking account of the dehumanizing aspects of Taylorist production and capitalist exploitation in the meatpacking districts of industrial era Chicago. The neighborhood and school remained solidly white and working-class until the civil rights era. During the 1960s, Ellison Square and CHS both became the targets of groups such as the Chicago Freedom Movement, co-chaired by Dr. Martin Luther King Jr., that organized and agitated for an end to restrictive employment and housing practices, as well as for an end to educational segregation and inequality throughout the city. In an iconic moment of the late civil rights era, King led a Freedom Movement march in 1966 not far from Ellison Square and CHS calling for economic as well as racial justice. The march was met by mobs of angry local whites hurling projectiles and racist insults. King himself was hit in the head by a brick. Many people in the area still vividly remember these events, providing living testament to the long legacy of struggles and conflicts over race and equity that continue to shape life in the community today.

CHS was officially integrated in 1972 despite significant opposition and even a boycott by white parents. The integration of the school, combined with the simmering racial tensions that defined the "urban crisis" of the late 1960s and early 1970s, signaled the beginning of decades of white flight, deindustrialization, and suburbanization, along with the ethnoracial recomposition of the neighborhood and school. In short, the whites began leaving for the suburbs and so did many of the jobs, thus leading to the effective desegregation of CHS. Currently, Ellison Square is a majority working-class Hispanic neighborhood. The student demographics at CHS are evenly split, however, between Latino/a and African Americans as the school draws its enrollment heavily from two adjacent historically black communities. The school itself straddles the borders of these three neighborhoods, linking them through their relationship to CHS. There are no Starbucks here or any of the other trappings of bourgeois living one finds in Chicago's gentrified professional class enclaves. The thoroughfares bordering Ellison Square and its surrounding neighborhoods feature a variety of businesses typical in such urban communities—fast-food outlets and used car dealerships with the occasional pawn shop, convenience/liquor store, church, and check cashing / payday lending outlet. The community is dotted with small brick houses interspersed with standalone two or three story "walkup" apartment buildings. On the afternoons that I spent walking around the community, people were open and friendly, if not seemingly a little perplexed by the young white man walking their streets.

According to research conducted by the College of Urban Planning and Public Affairs at the University of Illinois Chicago, Ellison Square is a neighborhood characterized by "serious economic decline." The neighborhood has been negatively impacted by the transformation and stratification of the new service-based "flexible" labor market and the attendant fracturing of living-wage employment opportunities traditionally available for the working-class. This has been aggravated by the twin fiscal crises of capital and the state stemming from the 2008 crisis and Great Recession. Unemployment in Ellison Square and the surrounding communities is estimated to run between 9 and 25 percent which does not include those who have given up looking for work altogether or those who are "underemployed"— attached to a part time or temporary job and unable to find full-time employment or meet their basic needs. The unemployment rate for youth is much higher, sitting at crisis levels of 37 percent for Latinos and 43 percent for African Americans between the ages of 16 and 25. Furthermore, foreclosure signs and boarded-up properties have become a common sight. Like other urban communities across the United States, Chicago's low-income racialized neighborhoods became a lucrative target for predatory subprime mortgage lending (Taibbi, 2010).[1] Indeed, the foreclosure rate in Ellison Square went from 5.3 percent in 2006 to 48 percent in 2008, while median home prices plummeted. The economic crisis has been accompanied by deepening economic dislocation in the community including a rise in homelessness and further cutbacks to social services and supports to CHS. People in the community frequently cite this pervasive insecurity, and the sense of hopelessness and demoralization that it breeds, as driving instabilities in home life, informal economic and gang activity, as well as conflict and violence in Ellison Square and CHS.

Ellison Square vividly represents the faltering promise of the civil rights era. Along with extensive economic insecurity, the neighborhood and surrounding communities are defined by race and class segregation and isolation. While the neighborhood is only a short distance from the landmark office towers, professional class jobs, tourist attractions, and trendy shops of downtown Chicago, it exists as a world set apart. The sociologist Loïc Wacquant (2008) has described Chicago's impoverished African American and Latino neighborhoods as "hyperghettos"—stigmatized zones of economic fragmentation and ethnoracial enclosure defined by the dual retrenchment in the labor market and social provision and the simultaneous extension of the surveillance and penal web of the neoliberal state. This is marked by limited access to stable employment opportunities, health care, transportation, and well-resourced schools. For many in Ellison Square, budget cuts have meant that a primary access to social services comes in the form of a Mobile Community Center operated by the Department of Child and Family Services. This is a bus that parks in the neighborhood once a month, offering limited access to job information, foreclosure assistance, health and immunization services, and a food pantry. On the other end of the spectrum, there is an intensive and extensive security and law enforcement presence in the neighborhood. It is impossible not to notice the dozens of police surveillance cameras that blanket the area, hanging like strange mechanical fruit from telephone and light poles, expanding the gaze of law enforcement to virtually every intersection and sidewalk in the community. It is routine to witness police officers interrogating local youth on street corners—or youth sprawled over the hoods or sitting handcuffed in the back of police cruisers. In these moments, the neighborhood has the feel of an occupied territory.

Institutional Snapshot of CHS

CHS and its grounds take up an entire city block. The 80-year-old school is a giant U-shaped red brick institution. There is an open space in the front of the building that features a handful of scattered trees and some patchy grass. My first visit to the school was on a mild and sunny fall morning and the neighborhood had a calm and almost idyllic feel to it. The area was alive with activity: groups of students slowly making their way to school, crossing guards watching traffic, parents dropping off students, teachers hurrying to get to their classrooms, and security officers and police keeping watch while clutching hot cups of coffee. Despite the prosaic character of this scene, one becomes quickly aware of the familiar markers of fortification that have come to define urban school contexts. CHS itself has the look and feel of a high-security containment center superimposed on the frame of a "traditional" public school: the majority of its steel doors are padlocked from the inside and/or are welded shut and there are countless surveillance cameras surrounding the building—hung over doors, mounted at the corners, and placed seemingly at random on the building's flanks. At the back of the school is a parking lot with a 20 ft high fence rimmed with barbed wire that borders a sparse athletic field. Signs dotting the perimeter capture in language the palpable sense of fear embedded within the architecture—*Warning, Safe School Zone!*

On entering the school, one is greeted by uniformed security guards, armed police in bullet proof vests, airport style x-ray screeners, scanning wands, and metal detectors. Inside the school, metal cages on the windows, steel cages over doors, cages that can be expanded across hallways during "lockdowns," ubiquitous surveillance cameras, and dim fluorescent lit hallways—all conjure prison aesthetics. Upon entering the school, students and visitors are required to go through a screening process that involves feeding your possessions through an x-ray scanner and being led through a metal detector and given pat downs by uniformed security personnel. After passing through security, one realizes that this new security infrastructure is layered on top of a historical foundation marked by all too visible signs of disinvestment and neglect. The clocks are mechanical artifacts from the 1960s and many do not work. Many of the wooden doors in the school are worn out and some have been reinforced with steel. Classrooms have aging but generally well-kept interiors with desks in various stages of disrepair. Several classrooms are missing ceiling tiles that expose rusty plumbing along with the soft cotton-candy-like tufts of fiberglass insulation. There are two gymnasiums, an auditorium, and a library that serves as a quiet meeting place and de facto computer lab. The school has a fenced-in courtyard that features several red box-like "mobile classroom units"—essentially wood/fiberglass trailers that serve to alleviate overcrowding within the main building.

Throughout the day, the hallways intermittently fill with students as they walk, laugh, jostle, and talk on their way to and from their classes, breathing intermittent bursts of life into an otherwise drab institutional space. Teachers and administrators can be seen talking together or walking to and from their classrooms and offices. The school is also populated by a sizable contingent of uniformed and nonuniformed security officers and police who patrol and monitor the hallways. As part of what educational sociologists have referred to as the "hidden curriculum," intensive security and law enforcement presence combined with deteriorated physical environs send powerful messages to youth that inscribe norms and mediate identities, aspirations, and ways of being and understanding (Brown, 2010; Wotherspoon, 2004). As I will return to in more detail in the following chapters, the intertwined governmental and aesthetic dynamics of securitization and social neglect work to shape the students' sense of self-worth and agency as well as their perceptions toward schooling, community, and the future in complex ways while normalizing particular relations of subjectivity, power, and authority at CHS.

Carter's enrollment during the 2009–2010 academic year was just under 2,000 students, roughly evenly split between Latino/a and African American youth. This mid-size public school serves primarily high-needs and high-poverty students. Better than 90 percent of the students at CHS qualify for free or reduced lunch, 97 percent qualify as low income, 18 percent are special education, and 8 percent are English language learners. The school has 200 staff members that include teachers, administrators, paraprofessionals, and other support staff. The majority of the teachers are "highly qualified" as stipulated by the No Child Left Behind Act and many have advanced degrees. The official curriculum, however, often limits the professional autonomy of this teaching force. Despite the efforts of teachers to provide meaningful and engaging lessons, there is a strong feeling among faculty that they are limited by an inflexible "direct instructional" and "scripted" curricular approach that emphasizes basic skills and standardized testing. This curriculum, much of it developed and contracted out to large educational corporations, is often of questionable relevance to students' lives and experiences. According to its District Report Card, CHS has a 55 percent dropout rate and only about 10 percent of its students make or exceed state standards on standardized tests. The school is thus on probation for "low academic standing." This means that it consistently has not met Average Yearly Progress on high-stakes tests mandated by No Child Left Behind. This can lead to disciplinary sanctions including the loss of crucial funding, and eventually can lead to being targeted for closure or turnaround, which typically means that the entire staff will be fired and the school will likely be converted into a privately operated charter or contract school. Many believe that in time this will happen to CHS.

CHS struggles to cope with persistent gang problems, conflicts, and student emergencies of all kinds, while trying to provide educational services under difficult conditions. Not surprisingly, the people who inhabit its corridors, classrooms, and offices have complex and, at times, conflicted feelings about the institution. For instance, teachers speak often of their devotion to the students, who they describe almost universally as "good" kids, many of whom are struggling under extraordinarily difficult circumstances. While most teachers speak passionately about their commitment to teaching and to the students, they also express a deep sense of collective frustration with the conditions and policies that they work within. Many feel overwhelmed and unsupported. Conversely, many students feel alienated and disengaged from the standardized official curriculum and frustrated by the conflicts that plague social relations among many of their peers, as well as with the security and disciplinary apparatus of the school. However, many students also expressed affection and a sense of loyalty to the institution and to their peers and teachers as well as a strong desire to commit to their education and go to college despite the significant barriers standing in their way. Furthermore, in their conversations with me, teachers, students, and other staff would often seek to disrupt the palpable sense of stigmatization and failure that haunts the school by highlighting the many positive aspects of life at CHS. Indeed, despite the many challenges, positive and inspiring things occur on a daily basis at CHS. Amid the difficulties there are incalculable moments of inspired teaching and authentic student engagement, while countless healthy and supportive interactions and relationships take root and flourish. These moments offer a glimpse of the latent, and too often subverted, promise of public schools as potential centers of community building and democratic opportunity.

Privatization and the Production of Failure

It is common to hear urban public schools like CHS described in the media and elsewhere as "dumping grounds," "schools of last resort," and as "drop-out factories." These terms, of course, are pejorative and speak to the broad stigmatization of urban public schools as they are consistently linked in the media, along with their teachers and students, to "failure" and "crisis." Behind this rhetoric, however, lies a constellation of policies designed to integrate market forces into education through privatization, testing, and accountability arrangements that have placed significant strain on public schools like CHS. As I outlined in chapters 1 and 2, this has corresponded to disinvestment in public schools and youth, the extension of various centralized layers of administrative control, and the creation of an increasingly unequal school system in Chicago. While schools like CHS have been labeled "failures" and stigmatized in the media, they have been simultaneously subjected to resource scarcity, overcrowding, and painful sanctions.

Like other neighborhood public schools in Chicago and elsewhere, CHS has become increasingly socioeconomically and racially segregated as families with the material resources and cultural capital have pulled their kids out of public schools throughout the city. This has been accelerated by privatization initiatives, particularly under Renaissance 2010. As I detailed in chapter 2, Renaissance 2010 is a policy platform designed by the Commercial Club of Chicago and implemented under former mayor Richard M. Daley and former Chicago schools' CEO Arne Duncan. Drawing on neoliberal theory, the policy calls for the transformation of the city's schools by injecting market competition and business management into the system through privatization and the creation of an educational market (Lipman, 2011). The policy has worked to close or "turnaround" dozens of public schools in high-poverty neighborhoods and replace them with privately run and nonunionized charter and selective enrollment schools.

Research has shown that selective enrollment and charter schools have skimmed off students, funds, and social supports from public schools like CHS (Catalyst, 2010). As these schools are often free to select their students, and as school funding and contract renewals are increasingly linked to test scores under high-stakes accountability measures, "high performing" students become "valued commodities" while "low performing" students, students with learning disabilities, and English language learners are made into "undesirables" and "outcasts." In the wake of school closures and turnarounds, the vast majority of students—who are typically the most academically and socially in need—are sent packing. According to the Consortium on School Research at the University of Chicago, only 6 percent of displaced students from school closures end up enrolling in academically "strong" schools. The majority of displaced students, some 82 percent, reenter other "low performing" public schools such as CHS (Gwynne & de la Torre, 2009). The research also indicates that while privatization has proven a lucrative enterprise for corporations in the education market, and despite the fact that many charter and contract schools are beneficiaries of millions of dollars in supplementary funding from corporate philanthropies such as the Broad, Walton Family, and Gates foundations, privatization, closures, turnarounds, and charters have failed to produce significant systemic or school-based improvement (CREDO, 2009).

Privatization has placed significant strain on CHS, generating obstacles to providing high quality education and social opportunity for its youth. Teachers I spoke with referred to how school closures and the city's privatization agenda have impacted the school. Mr. Gates, a teacher at CHS, explains:

> *Mr. Gates*: When they made Jones, we got all the kids that they didn't want. Same thing happened when they did the one on Davidson as a selective enrollment school. So they get to pick and choose their kids and we got all the ones they didn't want.
>
> *Alex*: So they get to pick and choose which students they want and the rest came here?
>
> *Mr. Gates*: Yeah, and Harvey. We got the kids that they didn't want. Then Thomas had some problems a year or two ago and they redid their school and we got all those kids. And kids apply to these schools and they don't get accepted so we get those kids. I don't know. I don't call it [CHS] a dumping ground but kind of. It's not really just a neighborhood school.
>
> *Alex*: I hear people refer to it as a school of last resort.
>
> *Mr. Gates*: Kind of. And there is a lot of kids who are like, "I've been accepted at Lawrence" and I'm like, "No you didn't. I know who they're accepting and you're not that kid."

Under the rationality of consumer choice, school privatization and the creation of educational markets and "urban portfolio districts" have been positioned as a means to "empower" parents to "shop" around for the best school. These notions of choice have been understandably appealing for many families justly frustrated by conditions at their neighborhood public schools that have suffered decades of dysfunction and neglect by the state (Pedroni, 2007). Yet, as Mr. Gates points out, his students at Carter—whether because of their cultural capital, ability, and/or test scores—are not afforded the choice to attend the new selective schools. Rather than improving public schools for all youth within public norms of universalism, equity, and cooperation, privatization contributes to sorting the most disadvantaged into a bottom rung of disinvested public schools like CHS through the individualized market norms of competition and consumer choice.

These processes have created the general feeling at CHS that privatization is contributing to a climate that is setting the school up for failure. This is an excerpt from an exchange I had with Ms. Douglas, a veteran language arts teacher:

Alex: How do you understand and make sense of barriers to success here at CHS?

Ms. Douglas: The school has been set up by the system for failure. Basically, we have magnet schools that skim the more academically aggressive kids and the kids whose parents can find a better option so we're kind of known as a school of last resort. There is a set-up right there. Number two, we must take every-body who comes, so we get the kids that are kicked out of charter schools, we get the kids that are getting let out of jail and coming back from alternative schools and we take everyone. At the same time, when you have selective enrollment schools skimming your most academic students and then you get the reputa-tion of being a school of last resort then there is some issues with the attitude people have toward the school and sadly a mindset on the part of the kids. So we're set up for failure in that way. The other way the system treats us is like a number. Every four hundred kids, one security guard. Eighteen-hundred kid school and we are entitled to four security guards which is preposterous so the school has to dip into its own discretionary funds and buy security guards with it. So instead of lowering class sizes, adding more teachers or resources, or any of those choices that would help the kids, our school has to buy security guards in order to have a greater adult presence... it would be great to have resources put into more social workers or psychologists that really could help the kids with some of the incredible issues that they bring to school, including anger over everything that they are dealing with. But instead those meager resources go into security personnel. So instead we get all the kids that are kicked out and a disproportionate amount of kids that are lower academically than the selective enrollment schools. We have a disproportionate share of Special Ed students and yet we are compared to these schools with different circumstances and labeled as a failing or struggling school.

Ms. Douglas here reiterates how privatization has led to the concentration of the most disadvantaged students at CHS. Combined with extensive resource scar-city, this generates numerous problems. In particular, like others I encountered at CHS, Ms. Douglas discussed how privatization and disinvestment create a cul-tural stigma at CHS and a profound sense of failure.

Alex: This goes back to what you were talking about earlier in terms of reputation and that students feel that attached-stigma as a place of failure and the argu-ment on one side is that what needs to be done is the school should be closed down and we should totally revamp the whole thing so we can get rid of that sense of failure and start over, maybe make a charter school. What would you say to someone who would make that argument?

Ms. Douglas: That argument is being made as we speak. UNO—the United Neighborhood Organization is a political organization wired to the Daley administration. They get Hispanic votes for the mayor. They have eight charter schools right now and they want eight more and they are going to the next board of education meeting to get a charter for an Ellison Square High School. With all of their connections, they have capital development money from Springfield.

They bought a plot of land [near CHS] and they are going to grab the best of the kids that we have here, primarily Hispanics. The UNO charter schools are 97 percent Hispanics. The board is turning over eight schools with the wishes of UNO to get eight more. They have basically a school district within a school district right now. They have four thousand kids in their existing eight schools. So they are gonna come into the community with a brand new building and new computers and the latest of everything and come to our school and obviously parents will say, "brand new school that doesn't have the stigma of CHS, we're going there." So CHS loses personnel, kids, resources because every kid that walks out of here and to the UNO school, the per-pupil expenditure of eight thousand and change goes with them. So all these years we've been under-resourced and under-funded with one social worker for eighteen hundred kids and four security guards provided by downtown and at constant threat because our test scores are low. We're then blamed for the failure of the kids who remain.

Alex: How would you respond to criticisms that ultimately place the blame for failure on teachers as they are the ones foremost responsible for the quality of education in a school like CHS?

Ms. Douglas: Is it extremely unfortunate that 50 percent of the kids graduate from CHS who start here? Absolutely. Is it the fault of the teachers and all the teacher bashing that goes on in the media? Absolutely not. I've taught for a very long time and I have never seen such an educated, committed faculty as we have here. Like any school, there are people who could be improved but on the whole, Chicago Public Schools have the most educated teaching force that they've ever had. Is it a lack of care with the teachers? Absolutely not. I can say that with the utmost conviction that the overwhelming majority of my colleagues care about these kids, buy them prom dresses, buy them graduation jackets, and help them in any way possible. And deeply care about these kids, take them on college tours by themselves because the parents are unable to or are unwilling. So is it the teachers? Absolutely not. Does poverty play a role? Absolutely yes. It's just more expensive to educate a poor child who shows up in kindergarten with half of the word knowledge of a more advantaged kid. As the years go by, those two sets of kids improve, improve, improve but the gap doesn't close because they start from so much further back. So we were under threat this year because of budget cuts and they were gonna have thirty-five or more kids in the high school classroom. The fact is that the system has set up schools like ours as targets and then wonder why, when they close surrounding schools and those low performers come to the school that is open, that the scores remain low. It's just a vicious cycle and I just can't get the logic of turning over schools to private organizations when in fact the leadership of the city is supposed to be in charge of them. It makes no sense. They neglect these schools, under resource them and then blame them and say, the answer is to turn them over to outside groups. It makes no sense.

Ms. Douglas points to how poverty and the external funding and political connections of charter networks like UNO contribute to deteriorating conditions at public schools like CHS. Moreover, Ms. Douglas challenges directly the dominant narrative that teachers are largely to blame for the failures of public schools.

As she describes in the above passage, teachers in the CPS are overwhelmingly dedicated professionals who consciously make the decision to work at schools like CHS in order to make a positive impact in the lives of young people. Ms. Douglas was far from a unique case in terms of my interviews. I found that despite the often trenchant criticisms and palpable frustrations, teachers by and large were deeply invested, both professionally and emotionally, in CHS as an institution and in the lives of their students. Here, I ask Ms. Douglas how she interprets and understands the politics of the privatization agenda and the marginalization of CHS within the system.

> *Alex*: To me, what you are describing points to a marginalization not only of public schools, but of commitments to the public in general. How do you understand that?
>
> *Ms. Douglas*: Well, the public sees a new gleaming charter school with state of the art technology and they see a hundred year old school with a bad reputation. At the same time, the leadership of the city under the control of Mayor Daley has promoted this as the renaissance of the public schools, turning them over to outside groups to run. At this point there are seventy existing charter schools and recent legislation to allow forty more. So the public has bought the notion that Chicago Public Schools are failing our students. Obviously you can see that the statistics are dismal, so this is being presented by an unquestioning media as the way of improving school reform when, in fact, in the last fifteen years under Mayor Daley the graduation rates have remained stubbornly the same. From Paul Vallas to Arne Duncan and now Ron Huberman, one draconian approach after another has not produced. Turning the schools over to charters has not produced. I'm sure you've seen the Stanford study that shows traditional neighborhood schools do better than 83 percent of charters. So we are destroying a public school system on the basis of a policy with a 17 percent success rate. So it makes no sense, but maybe now there's an opportunity, but maybe not. It's gonna be a continuation of the privatization of everything that moves in Chicago. I think that's why. It's systemic. And I think that we represent kids that nobody cares about. Their parents are perhaps unwilling, unable, or too overwhelmed to be active in the political arena. The people with more resources send their kids to private and catholic schools and move to the suburbs. These are the kids that don't have the advocates in the public arena beyond their teachers and when their teachers are vilified and undermined and our schools are presented as failing schools and so it must be the teachers. Their only allies are being scapegoated as well.

Ms. Douglas' comments undermine assumptions regarding the relative engagement or disengagement of teachers. She is an articulate voice and is invested in her school and its students. This is not to say that all teachers at CHS are perfect. There are moments where even the most dedicated educators become overwhelmed, frustrated, and/or cynical about their work. A small handful of teachers "burnout," a few "checkout." However, this remains the exception, not the rule. In the course of my research, I found that while many teachers feel disempowered, they remain dedicated to their work and to students. Moreover, like Ms. Douglas, many harbor a well-developed understanding of the policies they work within. As Ms. Douglas intimates, these policies erode the capacity of teachers to meaningfully address the educative and social development of their students.

In terms of content, Ms. Douglas raises a host of important issues that corroborate what I found in my research at CHS, and the broader research as well, where privatization has been found to have significant local impact on public schools (Burch, 2009; Lipman, 2007, 2011). These findings which corroborate and extend Lipman's findings can be summarized as follows:

(1) Privatization has meant that public schools like CHS receiving students from turnarounds and school closures find their resources strained as they attempt to handle the influx of new students who typically have the greatest needs.

(2) Privatization produces a climate of anxiety and fear as public school teachers, students, and families confront the possible closure of their public school.

(3) Privatization negatively effects teaching and learning as class sizes swell and public schools are denied adequate funding and resources.

(4) Privatization has contributed to conflict and violence due to students having to cross gang lines in the wake of school closures and due to the increased stresses that accompany overcrowding and enhanced competition over educational services within schools.

(5) Privatization has made public schools and communities feel like they are being "set up for failure" as they are starved of resources and forced to incorporate new influxes of students.

(6) As privatization places strains on public schools, the difficulties that arise become more fuel to discredit public schools and their teachers while legitimating further privatization agendas in the city.

(7) Privatization is also producing resentment over lack of transparency and the disregard of community voice in matters of school governance.

(Lipman, 2007).

In contrast to promoting a high quality, universal, and equitable school system in the best tradition of democratic education that stresses integration and inclusion, privatization and free market incursions into educational policy have contributed to sorting the most disadvantaged and academically challenged students into a bottom rung of disinvested and segregated public schools. Simultaneously, neoliberal culture and policy is eroding the resources and sense of collective social responsibility necessary for realizing academic development and securing social advancement in these schools. This sorting process bears a significant responsibility for promoting failure at CHS while eroding its capacity as an institution to effectively promote the social and educative well-being and human security of its students. Finally, the deliberate underfunding and warehousing of the most disadvantaged students in public schools like CHS and the resulting educational failures become a potent ideological justification for the further privatization of every aspect of public education under neoliberal governance.

Social Disinvestment and Abandonment of Youth

Alongside privatization, patterns of austerity and scarcity are having a profound influence in shaping life at CHS. Many students at CHS have never been to Chicago's downtown, to one of its cultural institutions, or to its famous lakefront. Many struggle on a daily basis to secure their basic needs such as food and shelter. Largely invisible in a world of receding economic opportunity, soaring inequality, and hardening attitudes toward the poor, they face a precarious and volatile present/future. This has intensified since 2008 and the turn to austerity by state and city governments. Students and teachers frequently spoke of how economic insecurity and the Great Recession have impacted food security, homelessness, mental health, and the stability of home life in the community. Mr. Bradley, a teacher, describes some of these difficulties:

> Lots of kids have lost their place and have had parents who have lost their jobs and have been foreclosed on. There are students who are just simply homeless. This one girl in my AP class, her family is intact and they seem like a great family, but the father lost his job and then they lost the house and so now they have been living out of a car for a while. So homework becomes out of the question and her focus has shifted from school to finding a job in order to help her family. And she is not the only one. And you know, you hear on like Oprah that inspiring story about the girl who overcomes that and goes to Harvard and that's awesome, but that girl is not like the rest of us. She is to be admired, but such things are not done even by the best of people, it's just too much to overcome.

This type of instability can be understood in terms of what Slavoj Žižek refers to as the "objective systemic violence" inherent within the routine operation of our economic and political systems. Combined with the lack of access to basic services such as adequate health care and employment opportunities, this insecurity (homelessness in this case) can only be understood as a central factor driving instability in the school and community as well as in creating significant barriers to educational engagement and achievement. It is extraordinarily difficult if not impossible to think about things like meeting state standards on high-stakes tests and/or filling out college applications when you and your family live in a car or when you do not have enough food to eat. Malia, a thoughtful African American sophomore, explained that problems at CHS often begin from such places of basic deprivation: "some kids come in and make trouble, well maybe they didn't sleep that night or they haven't eaten in three days and they are stressed out."

When considering urban schooling, inevitably questions arise concerning parenting and home life. Many students at CHS come from broken homes, have absent parents, parents in jail, parents struggling with unemployment, and parents with mental health and addiction issues. While it is common to hear youth and teachers speak to the central importance of parental involvement in students' lives and be critical of those parents shirking their responsibilities, there is a general recognition that instabilities in home life are intimately connected to poverty and the dire economic situation facing many families in the broader community. The following comments by Mr. Bradley are paradigmatic:

> Poverty is a central aspect of what goes on around here. If more parents had decent paying jobs and/or didn't have to work three jobs just to make ends meet then maybe the situation would be radically different. If they didn't have this crushing weight over their heads, I think then a lot of the kids would certainly have more stable home environments and would be more likely to succeed at school. I don't think it's the only factor the leads to that instability, but I think that it is a major one.

Social science research overwhelmingly corroborates Mr. Bradley's intuitions that economic condition and social class are the most significant factors in predicting educational engagement and achievement (Wotherspoon, 2004). While race, ethnicity, and gender remain salient features defining relations of power and inequality in education, impoverished students at the bottom of the class structure regardless of race, ethnicity, or gender, are far more likely to fall behind in school, drop out at higher rates, and fare more poorly on standardized tests. The reasons for this are complex, involving the intersection of economic, environmental, and cultural factors that impact child development and school learning and interactions (Lareau, 2003; Rothstein, 2004). Jean Anyon (2005) cites extensive research indicating that despite neoliberal and neoconservative assertions regarding the "disincentivizing" and "dependency" breeding effects of welfare, it has been consistently demonstrated that even meager economic supports to families in poverty correlates directly to marked improvements in student academic engagement (pp. 64–67). Similarly, Darling-Hammond (2010) documents that social investments in instruction, well rounded curricula, and smaller class sizes play a significant role in school success. Further, Rutgers school-finance expert, Bruce Baker, has concluded after analyses of data from across the United States "that increased funding levels have been associated with improved outcomes, and that more equitable distributions of resources have been associated with more equitable distributions of outcomes" (Bryant, 2011). In short, social investments in the amelioration of poverty and inequality combined with ensuring economic security and social provision are central factors in promoting the success and/or failure of individual students and in creating safe and effective schools.

Despite the preponderance of evidence, educational and social policies inflected by neoliberal and neoconservative rationalities have come to reject structural explanations of poverty and its impact on schools. In this milieu, teachers, students, and localities are made solely responsible for the problems of school failure, while public schools, especially those serving the most disadvantaged, are consistently asked to do more with less. Simultaneously, as health and social services are reduced or exposed to privatization, public schools become one of the last institutions providing any kind of a safety net, while at the same time they are denied the resources necessary to adequately perform all of the numerous responsibilities charged to them. As science teacher Ms. Lorrie explains, CHS is governed largely by a reactive logic driven by scarcity:

> I feel like the schools are looked at as this net that is placed below the community, but not just a net because we obviously have the primary focus of educating the kids which will hopefully help get them out of poverty, but I feel like anything else that might impact our primary focus, we are expected to catch the community. Like, "Oh well, your kids can't focus because they are hungry so we'll have reduced breakfast and lunch and summer meal programs" and things like that. Like, "Your kids can't get access to health care so we'll have the immunization bus come out once a year because they have to have that to get into school." Like, "There was a shooting last night, so we bring in crisis counselors." But I feel like it's not even a safety net. I feel like it's just reactionary. I feel like the school is just scrambling trying to figure out how to provide the bare minimum so that kids can potentially have a half of a prayer of getting out the door with an education.

In my observations as well as in my conversations with students and teachers at CHS it became clear that the lack of adequate resources and supports in the school and community contribute to various problems. In particular, teachers and students often spoke of connections between poverty, emotional trauma, and violence at CHS and there is a broad feeling and recognition that the services available for students in the school and community are totally inadequate for addressing these concerns. For instance, CHS has only one social worker and students are allotted a maximum of 15 minutes per month with her. This underscores a more general absence of social-emotional support services for students. Again Ms. Lorrie:

> Our kids deal with more issues than kids in other schools that would cause them to benefit from social work services. Even some of my kids that have some problems and want to go down to see the social worker have to go down and wait. In terms of what they're allotted—they get fifteen minutes a month. They do have counselors for kids, but again there's only one or two of them in the building and psychologists are here only once or twice a week for a couple hours a day. I haven't even seen her here yet this year. We share one nurse with several other schools and they are never here, which is another issue and if they are having an issue and they need to talk to someone they've got nobody to talk to about it. But again, it's money. We don't have the money to do that here. And I think we could make an impact if we just had more resources and staff.

Teachers like Ms. Lorrie feel a deep sense of frustration over the absence of resources that might enable the school to effectively address the emotional, physical, and social insecurity of youth at CHS. The lack of support services for youth only underscores more general conditions of austerity and disinvestment at the school. Many classrooms do not have enough desks for students as budget cuts have swelled class sizes. It is common to see packed classrooms with students sprawled about haphazardly, sitting on the edges of the class and on the window sills, even some standing without desks. Teachers often complained that they had 40 or more students in their classes despite the fact that this violates district and union rules, not to mention any nominal standard of pedagogical efficacy. This places limitations on the provision of educational services as well as on the capacity of teachers to develop supportive relationships with students. Mr. Parks, a veteran teacher at CHS, expresses his frustration over the class size issue:

> I had to go to the programming office and say, "Are you people not looking at the numbers?" I don't have desks. There's just a steady stream, every five kids that comes in changes the chemistry of the class again. That's not rocket science. That's anybody who can look at such a scenario and see that's a recipe for disaster. But they just shrugged and said this is the new normal and I better get used to it.

The class size issue underscores a more general absence of books and other essential resources. Teachers routinely reach into their own pockets in order cover the costs of basic supplies, such as photocopies of class textbooks, due to their insufficient number. Further, the school has not only a shortage of supplies but a shortage of teachers as well. Over the summer of 2010, the school had to lay-off 15 percent of its faculty due to budget cuts in the aftermath of the economic crisis and recession. In the wake of the layoffs the school is using what they call "place-holders," transient substitutes that are something like the educational equivalent of the service sector "perma-temp." There is significant resentment among faculty and students regarding the layoffs and the use of permanent substitutes. According to Mr. Parks:

> When teachers are laid off it affects morale and the culture. And now we have all these sort of transient substitutes. Kids are going to classes where there might be a different teacher everyday and I think that creates some tensions because students don't feel like they are being treated respectfully or that they should even care. Students need to have regular adults in their classes that they can feel comfortable with where they feel like they can bring up issues that are affecting them and where they might have some chance of getting some help.

Marcus, an African American junior, commented on the teacher cuts, "It was a big deal to a lot of kids. A lot of kids were mad about that. Me and a bunch of other kids considered leaving because they had taken a lot of our favorite teachers. But we don't have anywhere else to go." I asked him how he thought the teacher layoffs have affected the school. He put it bluntly, "Now you tell me, how you supposed to run a school without teachers?" When I asked him how the layoffs had affected his education he responded, "My second period math class has had like 15 different teachers this year. No one cares. Everybody just laughing and talking. It's like whatever, this is a joke." Indeed, it wasn't difficult to recognize what Marcus was talking about. Walking the halls of CHS one often gets the sense of an institution barely holding itself together. There is an undercurrent of frustration and fatigue that marks the atmosphere and culture. While many feel disaffected and disempowered, teachers make legitimate attempts to provide educational and social guidance under difficult conditions. However, many students appear to just slip through the cracks with little in the way of the individual attention, guidance, and care they all need and deserve.

Along with Marcus, various teachers, students, and administrators linked disinvestments in the school and the teacher layoffs to straining teacher-student relations and to general conditions of disorder in the school and alienation among students. Students rightly perceive that their education and needs are not being taken seriously and that their interests, moral development, and input are not highly valued. As a result, relationships fracture and an often corrosive tone of disaffection and disengagement is set in place throughout the entire institution. Many students thus engage in resistant acts such as disrupting class or withdrawing, arguing with security in the halls, and generally disregarding the school authority that many do not view as being legitimate. As Marcus points out, a lot of kids care deeply about their teachers, but they regard the policies that remove them from their lives and the school as nothing more than a cruel joke. This sense of betrayal extends beyond the loss of teachers to the broader institutional and social structure. In the interview I conducted with Mr. Parks, whom I quoted above, he stated that he believes the current round of layoffs and austerity measures are "systematically dismantling the education of our youth" and that "one could not have created a better breeding ground for violence and a culture of fear."

Curriculum Management and the Perpetuation of Redundancy

There is good teachers here but it's hard to because a lot of what they're teaching…like a lot of students just don't care. I mean we all have to strive to get an education and do our work but a lot of times it's just like, there's a lot of stuff that goes on around here. I would say that classes need to be more toward the students, what we care about, like projects and stuff. Most of time around here it's just like do this, do that, here's this assignment. It doesn't work for a lot of kids.

—*Rose, CHS Student*

Ninety percent of the incidents that occur are because no one is listening to these young people, they are bored, they're not engaged, and they don't see how the stuff that you're teaching is indicative of their real world day to day.

—*Mr. Charles, Youth Worker at CHS*

It's like, every time you turn around, this vendor or that vendor—just looking at the monthly board meetings and the vendors that get approved for professional development services, for testing services, technology programs, for curriculum, for textbooks, notebooks, everywhere you look there is the corporatization of curriculum and education. And again, if the teachers in the school were presented with these options and looked to decide which ones might best meet our needs, that would be one thing, but that's not how it goes. It's all top-down mandatory. And they'll be able to see in the computer whether you've done it or not.

—*Ms. Douglas, CHS Teacher*

Over the last three decades, urban educational systems have become increasingly subject to market management and centralized forms of accountability that seek to regulate and discipline processes of teaching and learning. These policies are commercializing and narrowing the curriculum while limiting the professional autonomy of teachers to meet the needs of students, particularly in low-income schools. In the semester I spent at CHS, I observed scores of classes across subjects from English, Math, Social Studies, JROTC, and Computer Science, conducted in-depth interviews, and had many informal conversations with teachers. I observed a range of engagement at CHS from focused concentration and enthusiastic discussion to repetitive scenes of standardized nullity and the disaffected boredom that comes from classes dominated by scripted lessons and test preparation. Unsurprisingly, both students and teachers reported dissatisfaction with the curriculum. Many feel that the pressure to gear lessons toward district mandates and testing is failing to engage youth and to address their diverse interests and needs.

Like schools throughout the CPS, CHS has largely dispensed with vocational training. The rationale has been that in the global knowledge economy all students need to go on to college in order to be ready for the jobs of the twenty-first century. Just what these jobs are exactly or how CHS students will fit into them is unclear. However, sorting processes at CHS no longer function in terms of strict divisions between "academic" and "vocational" tracks but instead work via the division of instruction along academic lines with an honors track and a lower general curriculum that includes both in-stream and pull-out special education instruction for kids with learning disabilities and special needs. CHS is one of many schools in the CPS that now utilize a program called AVID (Advancement Via Individual Determination) that is designed to prepare students for college, particularly kids in the "middle" of the academic register. The school also has two supplementary programs that give students additional options, CTE (Career and Technical Education) and ETI (Equipment Technology Institute) that are geared toward college enrollment and career training. While these programs emphasize college readiness and are popular with students, the bitter reality at CHS is that relatively few of the youth who start their high school career at the school make it on to college and fewer still attain college degrees. Over 50 percent of students at CHS end up not graduating at all. Out of those who graduated in 2009, 40.3 percent did enroll in some type of college program. Of those who graduated in 2009 but did not enroll in college, 60 percent were unemployed in 2010. Employment statistics for dropouts are not available for former CHS students, but the broader evidence would suggest that their labor force participation is much lower, signaling a profound crisis.

While CHS has made efforts to utilize supplemental programs like AVID, CTE, and ETI explicitly for college prep, much of the instructional focus is geared toward teaching to meet state standards and boosting student performance on state tests like the Prairie State Achievement Examination (PSAE), Illinois Alternative Assessment (IAA) and the American College Test (ACT). These tests are used to measure Adequate Yearly Progress for the requirements of the NCLB, Carter's own state and district ranking and report card, and for determining college eligibility for its students. During the semester I spent at CHS, the school was rated a "low achieving school" and was "on probation" (a term taken, it can be noted, from the corrections lexicon) for poor performance on the tests, a distinction that the school has held for several years. While the pressure to perform and prepare youth for standardized testing has become a central part of schooling, teachers were often critical of these educational practices. In particular, teachers repeatedly sought to highlight how a top-down emphasis on scripted curricular mandates was infringing upon their capacity to meet the needs of their students. The majority of the curricular mandates represent commercial programs that have been contracted out to educational corporations and then pushed on teachers under threat of disciplinary sanction. Teachers often express their sense of frustration at the arbitrary nature of these programs and the climate of fear that accompanies them. The corporate curricular and accountability mandates have contributed to undermining their professional knowledge and voice while creating a bewildering set of protocols and reductive requirements that are replacing more progressive teacher and student centered forms of pedagogy and curriculum. Teachers also report that the mandates have been accompanied by new forms of surveillance and sanctions for those who fail to comply.

> *Ms. Douglas*: So now this school is under some program called IDS, a scripted curriculum mandate that the school is forced to have because we're on probation so we must spend hundreds of thousands of dollars of our own discretionary money into programs like this that are scripted, rigid, that downtown can see how your scores are. Just even the online grade book programs where anybody downtown can just peek right into your classroom and see how your kids are doing. There is a balancing act because we're criticized if we have too high of a failure rate but at the same time we have to be showing progress on all these indicators. But the insanity is that they just spin around like crazy where a new guy comes in and that program is out and this program is in and they are trying to teacher-proof the entire curriculum. It is a basic lack of faith, instead of saying, "Let's hire good people and then give them the professional discretion to do their thing." So for instance, before the IDS stuff got mandated our English department was just cooking with a fabulous curriculum with freshmen and it trickled into the sophomore and junior years as well. But that just got dumped when the next thing came in and this was mandated and we were a probation school so we have to do this. So after putting out so many years of working on this curriculum and then having it all just tossed out of the way, it's very frustrating.

Mr. Wilson, a math teacher, extends these observations by describing just a few of the scripted curricular mandates that he is supposed to fulfill:

> Last Friday we had a professional development meeting with our district leader about classroom management and testing practice. It follows this CHAMPS model. Conversation Level, Help, Activity, Movement, Participation, Success. And it's like this is the fifth week of school and now we are supposed to trash our management style that we have developed that works for us and our students and we are supposed to do CHAMPS for everything. We were told that within two weeks they were going to come to our school and do a walk through and come into our

classrooms to see if we have CHAMPS posters for independent testing practice and procedures and warm-ups and that all the students should know the program. We were then told that principals are going to come in and pull out students from class and ask them questions like, "What does conversation level 1 look like." And if that isn't explained within your classroom then you will have a debriefing and you are no longer a good teacher. And so that is one that came out on Friday. Another one is RTI (Response Through Intervention) which is a literacy program we are supposed to do every Tuesday and Thursday. On this one we weren't given any information accept the name of a website we were supposed to go to and download the forms to teach ourselves what RTI is which no one has any experience with. We are supposed to do these strategies and every student is supposed to achieve 80 percent mastery on them and the ones who don't are supposed to go to some sort of pull-out program. So there are all these things like High Quality Instructional Task vs. Powerful Practice that we have to include and be labeled and have an agenda and I could go on and on about these. So there are all these sort of mandates that we are required to do and if an administrator walks into your classroom it better be posted, done, explained to the students along with all this other stuff like remediation plans and so it leaves very little room for creative teaching and we are told that if we don't do these things then we are not effective teachers. And it's like that's not what an effective teacher is to me but that's how they define it and in this whole culture of fear people feel a lot of pressure to do this stuff and not stand up and say, "Hey this is dumb, today I am doing something else." I feel like this is really stifling teacher creativity which then leads to killing the creativity of the students. And it's just crammed down our throats and we are reminded every week to do these things and if I write up a lesson plan and submit it to my department head and it doesn't have these things on it then it will be sent back and I have to redo it so it conforms to these prescriptive mandates.

Each of the curricular and accountability mandates is attached to a different district contract with educational corporations and foundations. These programs often work at cross purposes, and as Mr. Wilson's comments indicate, they place a heavy emphasis on teaching standardized "skills" as opposed to promoting more creative and exploratory forms of learning. Mr. Parks further discusses these phenomena:

There are four sets of clipboards that come through my classroom. Number one is IDS. But IDS is not aligned with RTI. RTI is not aligned with Area 23. And Area 23 which wants the skills and standards to be the Illinois State are not aligned with the College Readiness. So unless I know who you are coming into my classroom, I don't know how to sequence the skills that my kids need to be learning in order to meet the expectations placed on me to teach these ridiculous things. As their teacher I've got a pretty good idea of which skills I need to start sequencing to get them to the level in which to function in today's society, but those four competing clipboards have no relevance. They're each connected to different money and different programs that each have a competing and conflicting interest in what happens in my classroom. The curriculum is not just the curriculum, it's a loaded political football from the Gates Foundation to IDS and Kaplan that's making an awful lot of money on what I'm teaching. And in this day and age content is just not all that important. It's about the skills being taught and that's really not all that content-based.

Market governance is presented as a progressive force that can break down rigid bureaucratic structures and empower individuals to realize their potential in more open and decentralized institutions and systems of organization. However, as the current efforts to control the curriculum through top-down commercialized accountability mandates makes clear, rather than reduce cumbersome and autocratic bureaucracy, market governance and the proliferation of corporate contracting and influence of corporations in the planning and delivery of curriculum has vastly expanded it. The education market has changed dramatically in the last two decades. It is now a global multinational business that includes textbook publishers, software and online learning companies, for-profit school management and charter corporations, consulting and curriculum businesses, and for-profit testing, tutoring, and test-prep corporations, each vying for a piece of the growing educational market estimated at $600 billion a year in the United States alone (Ball, 2012). Each year, the CPS issues millions of dollars in contracts to educational corporations such as Kaplan, Princeton Review, EdisonLearning, Literacy for All, ILearned Online, Sylvan, Non-Public Educational Services, among many others. The influence of educational companies can be seen as having less to do with seeking to support teachers as professionals and more with how to profit from and control what they teach. The imposition of scripted commercial programs and the disciplinary systems put in place to enforce them represents a key formal characteristic of neoliberal governance in schools today. It relies on centralized forms of authority that click with neoconservative emphasis on "getting tough" on schools and on teachers, while at the same time it forwards market-oriented solutions and policies designed to integrate commercial interests and profit-making into the institutional fabric. As this analysis suggests, market-based forms of governance and external forms of centralized control are far from contradictory logics. Rather, they require and inform one another in the daily operations of public schooling.

There are a number of observations that can be made regarding the management of curriculum at CHS and the intersection of market logics and centralized control. Foremost, it is eroding teacher autonomy. Teachers simply no longer have the same degree of professional freedom to make connections between their students' experiences and unique needs and the planning and delivery of curriculum. Much of the curriculum is being planned by educational companies and their internal "experts," many of whom may know little if anything about the culture and needs of students in schools like CHS. The curriculum is primarily created in order to align with state standards and tests and then sold to the CPS. Not only does this remove control over curriculum from the professional discretion of educators and the voice and input of communities, but it also elevates the role of the private sector in determining what knowledge is taught and how it is taught. Further, and related, through a network of administrative strategies derived from the central office and carried out by district and school administrators, teachers are placed under intensive surveillance and can be severely penalized for failing to comply with the mandates. Such a disregard for the voice of teachers has a demoralizing effect that I found common among educators at CHS who do not feel like they are treated as valued partners in curricular decision-making.

Further, and as a result, teachers have few options but to become active agents of neoliberal policy (Davies, 2003).

Beyond the erosion of teacher autonomy and the institution of new forms of teacher surveillance and discipline, efforts to manage curriculum at CHS are revealing of differential and inequitable approaches to education.

> *Mr. Parks*: At the present time, every week we get something else added to our instructional clock, to our curriculum, and administrators have stopped even trying to justify their way. They've just been mandated, that's why we do it. And that's where children of poverty and children of such institutions continue to be raped by the educational system. It's because if you try to get away with mandating this at a middle class suburban school like Walter Paten or North Side high school in the city of Chicago you would be burned at the stake. Who in the hell gives you the right to do it to our school?

Mr. Parks here uses strong language to describe the inequality embedded within scripted test-based forms of curriculum. As researchers like Jonathan Kozol (2005) have noted, the technocratic management of curriculum has been enforced most intensively in low-income schools serving high proportions of impoverished black and Latino/a students. This differentiation and emphasis on scripted curricula and testing in low achieving and socially disinvested public schools leads to the further stratification of educational and social opportunities for youth. This can be explained, in part, by how scripted test-based curricula constructs knowledge. Reduced to a set of procedural skills, knowledge becomes an inert and lifeless object—a thing to be consumed and mastered as opposed to something that is open, contestable, and dynamic. Scripted pedagogy socializes students to accept knowledge as something detached from power and everyday life. As opposed to teaching students about a complex and increasingly interdependent and inequitable world to which their histories and experiences are intimately connected, the emphasis on teaching skills for tests socializes students to believe that learning and thinking involves finding one correct answer out of a small handful of decontextualized and static choices. Moreover, the imposition of scripted "teacher proof" curriculum limits the capacity of teachers to make meaningful connections to the cultural location and experiences of their students and their unique geographies, needs, and interests.

Such an approach to knowledge does not impart the kinds of creative thinking and high-end analytical skills that are said to be required for the new global information economy. Instead, it teaches conformity of thought and the ability to follow basic directions in order to perform repetitive tasks. Mr. Wilson refers to this as a process of "institutionalization" which he describes as follows:

> It's like being treated like a number. Like you're a number almost in a factory worker sense like you come in to the school as a number, you come into class and I give you something to fill out, I record it and you get a grade and that is the extent of our education. The students are just treated as little pieces and I think a lot of students feel that way. And that comes from everything from security to curriculum to the way the rooms are designed.

Realities at CHS present distinct contradictions to claims that market reforms in public education are preparing youth with the skills they need to find stable work in the global economy. The impact of social disinvestment combined with the reductive organization of curriculum appears to do little to support and prepare these youth for knowledge work and professional class opportunities. Instead, it reproduces broader conditions of economic and social inequality. Their labor largely no longer needed in the new economy, these youth become cast-off populations fit primarily for low-wage and no-wage futures and/or the burgeoning for-profit prison system. Shahrzad Mojab and Sara Carpenter (2011) describe such pedagogical relations as a form of "learning by dispossession," whereby young people are disconnected from the modes of learning and knowledge necessary to understand, overcome, and transform the social conditions that confront them. The impersonal systems of curriculum management tend to objectify relationships between students and teachers, and students and knowledge, producing an environment of disaffection, insecurity, and alienation. Such forms of learning disarticulate those relationships and forms of knowledge necessary for youth to critically map the social, economic, and political forces which impact their lives and, in the process, leave pressing forms of objective and symbolic violence unexamined and unchallenged. It thus disconnects students from the support and social relations needed to imagine alternative and more just and democratic frameworks of educational and social life.

Circulations of Violence

When you have a boring curriculum you create an opportunity for other things to be of interest that should not be in the building because you are simply not keeping people's attention with the curriculum. You're not pulling out the potential of the youth for the most part without taking away that there are good programs and teachers that care. But for the most part the culture of that place turns into one that is—education is fleeting and you're walking on your tippy toes not to fall into the cracks. But there's a whole other school culture of cliques, of violence, of he said she said, of respect and disrespect and upholding that. That becomes so much more important than everything else.

—*Mr. Charles, Youth Worker at CHS*

I really like it here but the violence that is going on is too much and I was thinking about transferring for my sophomore year because I feel like—I like it here. I like the teachers, I like the students but I feel, I just don't feel comfortable here.

—*Maya, CHS student*

If I could change one thing about this school, it would be all the drama.

—*Sasha, CHS student*

In the previous sections, I have pointed to how privatization, social disinvestment, and the organization and management of curriculum contribute to a climate of insecurity, teacher and student alienation, and educational failure that limits the capacity of public schools like CHS to provide substantive forms of social support and meaningful educational services and experiences to students. In short, they contribute to perpetuating what Žižek describes as *objective* and *symbolic* violence and insecurity in the lives of youth and in the everyday structure of school life at CHS. In this section, I discuss how this climate has also fed into and contributed to conditions of *interpersonal conflict and subjective violence* at CHS. While it is important to be cautious about ascribing direct causality between subjective conflict and violence and the political economic and governmental trends I have outlined thus far, it is clear that privatization, disinvestment, and the neoliberal management of the school's curriculum are part of a broader context of insecurity and dispossession in which such phenomena emerge and flourish.

Expressed in the intensive fortification of the school and throughout daily interactions, conflict, or "drama" as the students refer to it, appears as a taken-for-granted part of everyday life at CHS. One source of conflict is derived from neoliberal policy and race and class contestations over space and social resources in the city.

> *Mr. Wilson*: Since Chicago is so divided, everything east of Markham Avenue is primarily African American and everything west is Hispanic. Our school is situated on this border essentially. So while Ellison Square is mostly Hispanic this doesn't really represent our school which is 50 percent African American. I think that causes some tension, people coming over and crossing these boundaries. So the community is very segregated and the school boundaries do not really match up with the community boundaries and I think that causes some tensions.

As in all large urban centers, there have been historical frictions between various communities in Chicago. These tensions have primarily revolved around the uneven distribution of access to affordable housing, employment, and high quality education (Street, 2007). Moreover, class and racial divisions have been repeatedly exploited by the political elite in the city in order to divide loyalties, acquire allegiances, and to maintain power (d'Eramo, 2002). In recent decades, race and class tensions have been further aggravated by extensive gentrification, real estate speculation, the demolition of public housing, and the privatization of schools in the city (Koval et al., 2006; Lipman, 2011). These processes have contributed to the displacement and the intensified concentration of low-income African American and Latino residents in hypersegregated residential zones while sending students displaced by public housing and school closures outside their neighborhoods and across often hostile gang territories. This has led to conflict. Connections between the privatization of schools and social conflict have been repeatedly raised in local communities across the city by parents, teachers, students, and activists and have been consistently ignored by the political class in the city. Mr. Charles, a young African American youth worker at CHS states:

> Organizations five years ago reached out to the mayor before some of these school closings were about to happen and they said, do not close these schools for safety reasons because of where students were gonna have to go. And that didn't happen, schools were closed, people went places, overcrowding. Now we've got problems. What you've seen as a result of not listening to the community is a rise in school violence.

Mr. Charles' comments point toward the empirical linkages between the exclusion of community voice, privatization, and the elevation of security related concerns at public schools. According to research conducted by journalist Sarah Karp (2009), amid a broader decade-long decline in overall youth crime and violence, at the height of school closures in the late 2000s there was a system-wide increase in school security and discipline issues in the CPS. For instance, violations of the CPS discipline code at the most serious levels of 4, 5, and 6 code violations have risen steadily, from 5,762 in 2006–2007, to 12,058 in 2007–2008, to 15,094 in 2008–2009. Reports of students bringing dangerous objects to school rose 43 percent and reports of fighting, gang activity and bullying rose 18 percent during the same period. These concerns over physical security and violence are no doubt connected to multiple factors including economic pressures stemming from the Great Recession. CPS officials, for instance, cite enhanced accuracy in the reporting of school incidents. However, the evidence strongly suggests that the effect of disinvestment in public schools and the arbitrary shuffling of kids through market experiments has likely played a significant role. As public schools become collection centers for the most socioeconomically distressed and academically challenged, coupled with the neglect of these same institutions, conflict and insecurity inevitably emerge.

At CHS, this manifests in three general areas of concern over physical and personal security: (1) weapons; (2) student conflicts; and (3) gang violence. The concern over weapons is certainly justified considering the reality of gang-related shootings in the community; however, despite troubling periodic warnings of the presence of guns, teachers and students that I spoke with indicated that they did not believe there had ever been a documented incidence of a firearm in the school. With this being said, students have been found in possession of knives and other weapons. While weapons are rare, student conflicts are common. These conflicts have many sources. They start as the result of different factors including gang disputes, petty gossip, bullying, sexual harassment, and frustrations brought to school from conditions at home. Sasha, a freshman student of Mexican and African American descent, describes some of these issues.

Alex: What's it like to be a student at CHS?

Sasha: For me it's decent. I mean, I haven't gotten into any fights yet. I've gotten into arguments which is the problem with me because I don't like when people—I don't have good people skills.

Alex: Really? That's surprising. You seem like you have pretty good people skills.

Sasha: No, nice people I do but people who have conflict with me for no reason, I don't like that. For me it's okay right now.

Alex: So sometimes you get into arguments?

Sasha: Yeah. But never fistfights.

Alex: So it sounds like what you're saying is that school is pretty good except for these conflicts. Tell me, why do these conflicts happen?

Sasha: I don't know. Like, yesterday I was in my next class that I have after this one and there was a girl—what was I doing? I was playing music because we were in the gym and she was like, "turn that shit off" and I was like, "what?" I wasn't doing anything to her, she just started a big argument with me and was like, "I'm not a talker, I'm a fighter" and I was like, "Okay." So I don't know. Little stuff like that just gets into people's head and just messes with me.

Alex: Where does it come from?

Sasha: I don't know! It's really stupid stuff. Most of it is over boys, some of it is over "he said" "she said" stuff. It's basically what every fight is about in CHS.

Sasha here describes the everyday conflicts that are a common feature of life at CHS. As she describes in this passage, these conflicts often spring out of ordinary everyday situations and most are over seemingly inconsequential or "stupid stuff" as she puts it—rumors, everyday frustrations and acting out, bullying, romantic relationships. It is vital that strategies are developed that constructively address such conflicts, particularly as the current security and disciplinary climate fails to. Sexual harassment, bullying, homophobia, and other forms of everyday conflict contribute to a culture of fear that can lead to pushing students out of school. These concerns need to be addressed through the development of holistic and restorative approaches to school organization, a point I take up in greater detail in the conclusion.

While most conflicts at CHS manifest as personal and verbal disagreements as outlined above, physical altercations between students do occur. During the semester I spent at CHS, there were several such incidents. For instance, one afternoon as I was leaving the building I suddenly heard all of the security radios going crazy. I could hear the word "fight" and "police" being repeated amid a barrage of radio squawks and static from the security guards' two-way radios. Security immediately began scrambling into their "lock down" mode. The guards began closing doors and blocking off hallways with steel gates. I ran upstairs to where the incident was unfolding. Just adjacent to the cafeteria in air thick with adrenaline and the unmistakable tang of processed school lunch there were about 25 students excitedly milling about. In the middle, several security guards were breaking things up and calling for students to exit the area. Up the stairs behind me came four plain clothes police officers clad in body armor and semi-automatic pistols. The officers entered the scene but remained passive observers, allowing the security staff to control the situation. I saw a school security guard lead away a skinny freshman girl who could not have weighed more than about 80 pounds and who was apparently one of three students involved in the fight. Slowly the crowd of students dispersed. The police stood back and watched things unfold. They gave me looks like, "Why aren't you doing anything?" They obviously thought that I was a teacher and had no way of knowing that it would ironically be a legal liability for me to get involved.

Paradoxically, despite the threat of serious punishment, physical altercations like this one often take place in the school precisely because students believe it offers a sense of safety. Students will choose to have a brief "face saving" altercation in a school hallway where they know it will be broken up by security rather than take their chances in the streets where the feeling is "anything can happen." However, while the school's security and disciplinary apparatus was successful in diffusing this unfortunate incident, it is not organized to take these kinds of nuances into consideration. Such incidents immediately elicit a militarized threat posture defined by the symbolic codes of "lock down," body armor, and weapons. This does indeed serve to break up fights when they occur, but does little to prevent them and often works at cross purposes to counseling those engaged in the actions. This is aggravated by conditions of overcrowding, scarcity, and neoliberal accountability as educators and administrators are not afforded the time, resources, and support needed to attend adequately and substantively to the many needs and problems of their students. In the incident described above, the three female students were subject to automatic suspensions while one was detained on a potential criminal misdemeanor. As I describe in the next chapter, such a reflexive turn to the criminal justice system does little to teach, uplift, or to address the underlying problems, while furthering a culture of suspicion, fear, and punishment that erodes the educative and social foundation of public education as a space of democratic human development.

While the majority of conflicts between students at CHS do not represent a serious threat to student safety, violence remains a serious and legitimate concern, particularly the threat of gang violence. One teacher described CHS as the "Middle East" of gang activity because the school sits on the boundary of as many as six rival gang territories. Problematic metaphors aside, this crossing of gang boundaries poses serious problems as these rivalries can and do lead to violence and conflicts in the school. However, with this being said, the question of gangs at CHS is far from straightforward as the question of what actually constitutes a gang is itself highly contested. The general consensus seems to be that a relatively small percentage of CHS students, perhaps as low as 7–12 percent, have an actual affiliation with a known street gang such as the Latin Kings, Satan's Disciples, and the Black Stone Rangers, three of the active gangs in the area. With this said, there remains a pattern among students to form "cliques" or "crews" which resemble gangs. These cliques and crews are typically groups of youth from the same neighborhood block. They may or may not have anything to do with illegal or violent activity. Many simply exist as a support network that offers friendship, belonging, and a sense of security and protection. A Latino sophomore named Raul explains:

Alex: What can you tell me about gangs here at CHS?

Raul: Gangs are what cause most of the problems around here. Everyone has to protect themselves because things that go on in the streets might come into school. So everybody has to have a crew to protect themselves.

Alex: So then some students are in gangs just to protect themselves from other gangs?

Raul: See it's not like everyone is in a gang. But sort of. You need someone watching your back...It don't mean like you are like selling drugs or causing mayhem or whatever. It's just like you have to have a crew, if you don't, no one is gonna have your back if someone tries to mess with you. So a lot of students have their own crews but that don't mean they are doing the gangbang.

Rose, an African American freshman, adds:

> *Alex*: Why do students join gangs?
> *Rose*: For safety. Mostly because they think if they're in a gang with this person that it can protect them. It's like, "If I stay with these people they'll help me out and I'll help them out" and stuff like that but it's not really like that because if you get caught up in something they're not going to jail with you.

My research suggests that the forces driving youth gangs and cliques at CHS are very much in line with the broader social science research. As John Hagedorn (2008) demonstrates, gangs are deeply connected to and shaped by multiple overlapping forces such as broken families, racial oppression, and entrenched poverty and social inequality.

> *Mr. Wilson*: Right now gang violence is exploding all over the place and it's because no one has money or jobs and so they are selling drugs and fighting over territory. This school year has been the most violent by far and it's because of the economic depression. Two kids shot on school property already this year. Like that has never happened before. So I see a definite connection between the economy being worse and the recent violence.

Contrary to dominant narratives that depict gangs as simply a manifestation of social pathology, gangs persist today because they provide youth who have been abandoned in a world of crumbling public institutions and savage inequalities a means to form local solidarities and to exert some sense of power and agency within struggles over urban space, economic opportunity, and social status and recognition. After all, despite the fact that most gang affiliations do not translate into much more than a subsistence income for the majority of those involved, the urban "drug dealing" gang member can be understood as representing nothing less than the inverted image of the rugged entrepreneurial subject mythologized by neoliberal ideology—a street corner CEO hustling in a competitive market to maximize his/her flow of capital and to outcompete their rivals by any means.

Pointing out the underlying forces driving gangs and gang violence is certainly not the same thing as romanticizing them. At CHS and in Ellison Square, gang rivalries take a tragic and destructive toll on the social fabric. While gangs do function as an informal sphere of social organization and a means for youth to exert some sense of power and to exercise a form of entrepreneurial initiative, they too often prevent larger and far more important solidarities from developing while contributing to nihilistic violence and social fragmentation. The two gang related shootings involving CHS students that I discussed in the introduction to this chapter certainly speak to this stark reality. Moreover, while youth violence has declined overall since the mid-1990s, each year scores of young people are shot and killed in Chicago, many related to gang disputes of one form or another. Importantly, however, an understanding of violence cannot be limited to gangs. To do so limits not only our ability to understand the persistence of gangs, but also our understanding of violence itself as a *systemic* and *objective* force implicated in broader patterns of oppression and social insecurity in schools and communities. As scholars have pointed out, the violent historical and institutional realities of racial oppression, stigmatization, and the inability to enter into stable employment contribute to a landscape of broken families, demoralization, trauma, and cycles of violence (Alexander, 2010; Wacquant, 2008, 2009; Wilson, 1996). Based on my observations and conversations with those in the community, I conclude this chapter with perspectives for thinking through the circulation of violence in Ellison Square and at CHS. These perspectives, I would argue, are necessary to consider if we are to rethink security in schools and communities from the standpoint of equity, human development, and democracy as opposed to punishment, containment, and exclusion.

First, *violence is embedded within economic insecurity and inequality*. The inability to find employment, to provide for one's basic needs, and the physical and emotional wreckage that poverty and unemployment exerts in the lives of individuals and families is itself a form of objective violence as well as a source of subjective violence.

> *Alex*: What do you think are the primary factors driving the violence in the community?
>
> *Ms. Douglas*: Poverty. We've got ninety percent kids that qualify for free lunches and breakfasts. Poverty drives a lot of the crime, especially the theft. Certainly family issues and family breakdown. I have a lot of kids where I don't know how they get themselves here every day. They don't have anybody at home getting them up for school or somebody there getting them out for school. In some cases, like a student that never comes I called her father and he said, "Well I don't know if she goes to school or not. I'm up and out to work at six a.m." That's one case where there is a parent in the home and they're working but they're not aware whether their daughter is going to school. In other cases it might be that there is no parent there or no parent that is up in the morning to get them up and out. So some of it is the attendant issues of poverty, unemployment, family breakdown.

In their book, *The Spirit Level*, epidemiologists Richard Wilkinson and Kate Pickett (2009) present a transnational comparative study of sociological data that unequivocally concludes "the association between inequality and violence is strong and consistent; it's been demonstrated in many different time periods and settings. Recent evidence of the close correlation between ups and downs in inequality and violence show that if inequality is lessened, levels of violence also decline" (p. 144). Wilkinson and Pickett indicate that the linkage between inequality and violence is multidimensional, involving struggles over access to economic and social resources as well as over cultural capital and social status. However, in their trenchant analysis of the transnational data they find that the social factors that contribute to high levels of subjective violence such as low educational attainment, family breakdown, high levels of stress and depression, drug and alcohol abuse, and social mistrust all correlate to the relative distribution of income, power and wealth in a society. In short, what matters is not how affluent a society is but how unequal it is—the more unequal the society, the more socially atomized and objectively and subjectively violent it becomes. As I have described in this chapter, the hard realities of homelessness, food insecurity, and rampant poverty and joblessness among families in Ellison Square serves to erode the conditions in which young people can secure their daily life and future. This means, for instance, that when families lose their homes through foreclosure and are forced to live in the streets, it not only erodes the necessary conditions for youth to "perform" in school but also contributes to the splintering of the social fabric and to the proliferation of subjective conflicts in the school and community. In Malia's words, "some kids come in and make trouble, well maybe they didn't sleep that night or they haven't eaten in three days and they are stressed out."

Second, *violence not only stems from economic dislocation and inequality, but also emerges out of various interlocking forms of trauma and oppression.* The historical legacies of slavery and Jim Crow along with contemporary institutional realities of racial inequality, stigmatization, and the inability to enter into the formal sector of work and employment produce a landscape of broken lives and loss of hope. Mr. Charles here powerfully links the lure of gangs and violence to demoralization and stigma of failure.

> I think it's deeper than hopelessness. It's deeper than despair. We're talking about all-out failure and disbelief. How do you live without belief? What does the classroom represent to people who are not doing well in school? Failure. What does school represent as a building? Failure. So when I get suspended, that's cool because I don't have to go to that space where I am a failure. So how are you gonna convince someone who is trying sometimes but they are failing for whatever reason. So when the building and the space and the curriculum and the assignments represent failure, how do you increase one's belief that this is actually important to them? As a survival mechanism I have to tell myself that this is no longer important to me and I can survive without this because I can't do it and I've been told I can't do it and that I'm horrible. Well okay, I can make this money. I can organize this or plan this. That makes sense.

Orlando Patterson (1982) has suggested that histories of racial oppression and contemporary racial inequality and despair perpetuate a form of "social death," which he defines as the combined socioeconomic and political processes that deny the fundamental dignity of human beings. As Mr. Charles describes above, poverty, societal racism, and intergenerational trauma contribute to the normalization of conflict and violence. He suggests that CHS, as it is currently organized, is failing to make up for the deficit of hope and belief that emerges within this milieu. Rather than a source of inspiration and uplift, for many youth CHS represents more failure and a seemingly unrealistic option for a better future. This lack or absence of belief feeds into the lure of gangs and the streets. While the picture painted here is terribly bleak, I would suggest that while hopelessness and despair are no strangers to young people and adults at CHS, this only tells one part of the story. As I will suggest in chapter 5, there is also a tremendous amount of resilience and hopeful engagement among educators, youth workers, and youth at CHS. While the situation is indeed dire, there nonetheless exists powerful, yet all too often subverted, forms of critical knowledge, desire, and cooperation for promoting more peaceful, just, and ethical social relations at CHS and in the community.

Third, *violence is connected to struggles over social status and respect*. Adults and youth at CHS frequently link subjective acts of violence to conflicts over status or what they refer to typically as "respect." Links between violence and status relations are well documented in the social science literature. For instance, Harvard psychiatrist James Gilligan (2003) has argued that almost all acts of violence stem from feelings of shame and humiliation. Based upon long-term research with violent offenders in the Massachusetts prison system, he states that "the basic psychological motive, or cause, of violent behavior is the wish to ward off or eliminate the feeling of shame and humiliation—a feeling that is painful and can even be intolerable and overwhelming and replace it with its opposite, the feeling of pride" (p. 1151). Drawing on the work of Gilligan, Wilkinson and Pickett (2009) further argue that poverty and inequality drive feelings of power-lessness and in turn, conflicts over status. In this framework, "respect" becomes of heightened importance to youth who, in a context of poverty and powerless-ness, possess little of the material or symbolic capital valued within the broader culture. The desire to maintain dignity and to demonstrate self-respect and pride then becomes not only a source of potential conflict as when someone feels dis-respected by another, but also an important survival mechanism. Raul defines respect as such:

> *Alex*: So what does respect mean to you?
> *Raul*: Respect means that you have pride in yourself and that you aren't going to let anybody mess with you. It means you stand up for yourself and your people.
> *Alex*: Why is respect so important?
> *Raul*: Well it's kind of about who you are and having pride in yourself. Like you respect yourself and you won't let anyone take that away or disrespect you in any way. And like also if someone thinks they can get over on you then you are in trouble. If you get checked and you like, back down, they're gonna think that you're a punk. Then you got trouble.

Respect is one of the single most important issues for youth and informs the way young people perceive themselves and others in relation to their world and future. As Raul explains, "respect" has a dual significance. It refers to a person's sense of self-worth and dignity. It is also something one must have in order to protect oneself against subjective violence. Each of us understands how impor-tant it is to feel valued and respected by others. The powerlessness and loveless-ness that young people too often experience in their daily lives, and that we all bear a responsibility for perpetuating, can translate into feelings of shame and ultimately feed cultures of conflict and violence.

Fourth, *violence is articulated via raced and gendered social relations*. As a vari-ety of researchers on urban schools and young people have observed (Thomson,

2002; Fine & Weis, 2005), questions of violence are experienced differently for young people across the lines of social difference including class, race, sexuality, and gender. At CHS, for instance, male students report that they are more likely to be pressured to join gangs and are more often confronted or "checked" on the streets by gang members than female students. Male students also articulate that they are more likely to experience harassment by the police when in school and out in the community. This exchange I had with Darien, an African American junior, describes these phenomena:

> *Alex*: What's the relationship like between the police and students in the neighborhood?
>
> *Darien*: I think the relationship is that the police, when they see people outside sometimes—it depends on who it is but sometimes the cops, they're around and trying to figure things out and catch what's going on but sometimes the police officer there will let you go if you give them information. Sometimes they come up to you for no reason and try to get information out of you.
>
> *Alex*: What kind of information?
>
> *Darien*: Information like, "Do you know this person?" or "Where this person be?" or "What did they do at this person's house?" and things like that. Sometimes the police officers—there are racist police officers around here. Like, a couple of months ago a detective car, they grabbed this one guy like they were gonna arrest him and put him in the back of the car and took him somewhere and they beat him up and then they put him back in the car and dropped him back off and things like that just for no reason.
>
> *Alex*: Has this kind of thing happened to you?
>
> *Darien*: It happens to me all the time. I'll be outside and they'll stop me and pat me down and ask me questions. Like, one time they stopped us we were just walking down the street and this was before curfew, so we were just walking down the street and this cop pulled over and pulled their guns on us and pushed us against the car. That was unnecessary, we wouldn't have resisted. When they pulled up next to us we stopped, we didn't keep going we stopped and I just think all of that is unnecessary.

While Darien shows remarkable restraint in his comments regarding such hostile violations of his and others' bodily integrity and civil rights, he highlights what has long been a reality for young men of color in urban America, which is to be always under a constant state of siege either from forces of violence on their streets or under suspicion and threat of racist violence from police. As Paul Street (2007), Loïc Wacquant (2008, 2009), and others have noted, the rise of a neoliberal economic and social milieu of declining economic opportunity and the turn to mass incarceration as a central mode of governance of the poor has meant that black and Latino men, in particular, have become increasingly subject to enhanced police scrutiny and victimization via law enforcement profiling and brutality. In Chicago, for instance, between 2002 and 2004 alone there were more than 10,000 complaints of police brutality with only 18 of these resulting in meaningful disciplinary action of police.[2] It is little wonder that issues of respect and status assume such heightened importance to young people who often witness such blatant acts of disrespect and violence by authorities.

While also exposed to these same forces, female students cite sexualized violence and harassment as primary concerns. As Sasha describes:

> As a female I've been checked by a lot of grown men and that's what I've gotta worry about. For example, me and my cousin we used to go to the store outside and people would stop their cars and try to talk to me and stuff like that. And I try to avoid that because my dad is really overprotective of me because I'm an only child and my mother passed away so he's really protective of me. And if he ever sees something like that he's gonna go crazy. That's why I try to prevent everything from happening.

Confirming Sasha's concerns over sexual harassment, McCormick (2003) found in her study of youth in an urban school in New York that female students experience the "twin abuses" of both racism and sexism in their everyday lives at school and in their communities. McCormick observed that female students often have to develop strategies, as Sasha intimates above, to "shield" themselves from unwanted sexual attention, harassment, and intimidation on the streets and in their schools from young men as well as from adults. I will come back in more detail in the following chapter to how this sexualized violence is articulated amid the militarized security culture of CHS.

Fifth, *heavy-handed suppression efforts do not work to prevent violence.* Over the last three decades, the United States has poured billions of dollars into expanding state power in the realm of policing while concurrently it has slashed investment in communities, families, and schools. What has emerged is a penal net that functions as both a growing sector of the new economy and a source of violence unto itself. As Barry Weisberg (2010) has argued in a special report for Chicago Public Radio:

> In the United States the twins of crime and crime control are big business. The wars on crime, drugs, gangs or terrorism perpetrate violence in the name of public safety. In the attempt to control the toxic consequences of inequality and racism, some local police have become armies of occupation and oppression. Cops, courts and corrections account for half of the budget in some cities. This will never lead to functional families, successful schools or healthy communities. (p. 1)

A 2007 report by the Justice Policy Institute suggests that despite unprecedented investments in heavy-handed suppression efforts, a general strategy of surveillance and mass incarceration has failed miserably to reduce gang membership, crime, and violence in inner-city neighborhoods. The report goes on to state that in Chicago "a cycle of police suppression and incarceration, and a legacy of segregation, have actually helped to sustain unacceptably high levels of gang violence" (p. 6). Rather than continuing the failed trends of state repression, Weisburg (2010) argues that "the values, behaviors and institutions of violence must be replaced with the values, behaviors and institutions of peace-building in families, schools, businesses, communities and cities." This remains a fundamental necessity and challenge.

Public schools have often been referred to as a "social leveler" enabling youth at the bottom of the socioeconomic pyramid to have a chance at opportunity and a decent life. As a result of changes in global capital and labor coupled with the rise of a neoliberal culture of market values and social fragmentation, social mobility in the United States has all but evaporated over the last 35 years (Stiglitz, 2012). Many youth, like those at CHS, now form a surplus population outside the needs and demands of the current system. In relation to the realities I have thus far described at CHS, it is not difficult to understand how educational policies and public schools have played a role in contributing to this insecurity, stagnation, and downward mobility. As my analysis thus far suggests, neoliberal reforms have generated educational failure in public schools like CHS while contributing to the exacerbation of deepening systemic educational dysfunctions and inequities. In this climate of disinvestment and narrowing of educative goals and substance, the promise of public schooling to provide human security and hope to struggling youth and communities is subverted. In place of broad-based social and democratic commitments to investing in young people and their future are sown the seeds of conflict, violence, and alienation. In the next chapter, I extend these perspectives through a discussion of the how these systemic conditions of violence and inequality are increasingly managed through a prism of crime control and surveillance at CHS.

4

Criminality or Sociality: A Zero Sum Game?

The sole effect of extemporary police actions is to render the need of further police actions yet more pressing: police actions, so to speak, excel in reproducing their own necessity.

—*Zygmunt Bauman*, "Interview—On the U.K. Riots"

The School Safety Office, home to officers Duggan and Jones, is tucked away on the first floor and down a back hallway. After finding the office one morning, I proceeded to knock on the plain wooden door. After some audible shuffling around inside, a burly white cop with cropped brown hair opened the door. "Yeah, can I help you," he said, in the flat unmistakable cadence of a working-class Chicago accent. This was Officer Duggan. He told me to come in. As I entered the small office I noticed two desks against the opposite wall. At one of the desks sat Officer Jones, a middle aged white female officer in a blue bullet proof vest. Against the other wall I noticed a skinny African American student in a gray T-shirt and jeans. I guessed that he was probably a sophomore or junior. After a quick double-take I realized that the student was handcuffed to a steel ring protruding from the wall. The kid gave me a wry smirk as I introduced myself to both Duggan and Jones. Duggan motioned toward the student and said, "We can't really talk right now cause we have this problem over here." "Problem?" I asked. "Yeah, we gotta wait for the paddy wagon to come pickup this goofball." "Come back in a couple hours and we can talk," he said. On my way out I wondered if the "goofball" was going to be handcuffed to the wall for the next "couple of hours?"

Since the 1980s, a punitive neoliberal culture has emerged that has supplanted social democratic visions of collective security in favor of market governance, privatized visions of security, and the extension of state surveillance and retributive policing. David Garland (2001) has argued that this has engendered a "culture of control" that is more "exclusionary than solidaristic, more committed to social control than to social provision, and more attuned to the private freedoms of the market than the public freedoms of universal citizenship" (p. 193). Within cities this has translated into new systems of repression. Amid the realities of insecure work and soaring inequality, systems of militarized surveillance and crime control have become central organizing strategies of governance, producing new experiences of space, subjectivity, and inclusion and abjection through the institutional and everyday circulations of urban life (Graham, 2010; Simon, 2007) As the above image of a student handcuffed to the wall of the School Safety Office at CHS suggests, a punitive climate of security and criminological discipline has been imported into urban public schools. These new security environments have inaugurated a set of practices rooted in a culture of mistrust that has tended to reframe all forms of student rule-breaking in criminal as opposed to social terms. In the name of safety and order, the new security culture tends to overwhelm educational and social alternatives as well as sustained consideration of the economic and political conditions that drive human insecurity and violence in public schools and communities. Here security becomes imagined almost exclusively in terms of surveillance and crime control as opposed to the social and human development of young people. In what follows, I examine these processes of surveillance and criminological discipline at CHS and their impact on school culture and the human and social security of youth.

Surveillance and the Culture of Control

When visiting CHS in the morning, one will find two lines on opposite ends of the building, one of female students and the other of male students. CPS policy encourages "where possible" for female security guards to scan and search female students and male guards to scan and search male students during security checks. At the front of the female line, one security guard monitors the contents of book bags via an x-ray machine and a closed circuit television monitor. The other guard beckons each student through a metal detector, then proceeds to give each student a once over with a metal detecting scanning wand. Both the security officers bark directions: "Hurry up now!" "Take of those belts!" "Bags on the left!" "Let's go!" "Move it!" "Off with the jewelry!" "Move along!"

The students are visibly annoyed. Eye rolling and talking back are standard operating procedure. As the students proceed through the metal detector, one security guard, a middle-aged African American woman in a dark blue SECURITY jacket, sweeps each student with the electronic wand. The other guard sits on a stool watching the CCTV monitor viewing an x-ray image of the contents of each book bag as it passes through the device. "How does this thing work, and what are you looking for?" I ask. The guard replies, "Drugs, weapons, anything that they aren't supposed to have. They come through and we check them. They have to remove anything that might set off the alarm. We use the wand to make sure they aren't hiding anything." A guard asks a student to remove her belt, the student responds: "Damn, why do you have to waste my time every morning?"

A similar scene unfolds at the male entrance where I stand with a talkative security guard named Alberto. As the male students line up for their screening, I notice that Alberto is dressed in the same dark blue SECURITY jacket as his female counterparts and I can see that he has handcuffs on his belt. There is no electronic wand on the male side and the scene is remarkably more tranquil. The students line up calmly and without protest. Many of them look tired as if they just rolled out of bed and they all seem more or less resigned to the security process. An African American youth in a black jacket sporting a neatly trimmed low-rise afro sets off the metal detector (BEEP!). At this he is promptly frisked head to toe by Alberto. Out from the kid's pocket emerges a red cigarette lighter. Neither Alberto nor the other nonuniformed security guard appear concerned by the lighter. "You know you can't bring this in here…what are you thinking," Alberto says as he sets the lighter in a little yellow container next to the screener. As he lets the kid pass through security and into the school, Alberto remarks: "When the metal detector goes off we pat the students down. Mostly it's nothing but sometimes we get lucky and find things they aren't supposed to have like drugs and weapons."

Alberto tells me that he has been working security in the CPS for 11 years. I ask him his opinion of the security situation at CHS. He says that "the teacher layoffs are making things more difficult" and "without the teachers things have been more hectic." He is also frustrated that some of the other security guards do not always act professionally. Some apparently do not always wear their uniforms, do not show up to work regularly, or come to work on time. "Some of them just don't care," he says. As I talk to Alberto, a stocky white male teacher with a ponytail walks past us carrying a small green plant. I notice he is wearing a T-shirt that says "I Love Standardized Testing." He offers us a cheery "Good morning!" A skinny boy in a red sweatshirt and jeans, who looks like he might be a freshman or a sophomore sets off the alarm again (BEEP!). Alberto's partner, a nonuniformed male security guard, tells the kid in a less-than-sympathetic tone, "Take out those earrings. Next time I see those I am going to suspend your ass."

As conveyed in this description, the scanning line is a complex site of social interaction. It can be a stressful place as well as a place of monotonous repetition and routine. Every day the security guards and the students engage in a variety of power struggles, most of which are trivial and tangential to any serious security concerns—guards checking IDs and dress code while students shift about in line fretting over being late for class. However, despite the seemingly benign nature of the scanning process, the failure to comply is backed up with the threat of exclusion and physical eviction from the school: "Take out those earrings. Next time I see those I am going to suspend your ass!"

Maryann Dickar (2008) has used the notion "cleansing ritual" to describe this scanning process. In her research in New York City, she observes that intensive scanning systems in schools institute "safety" by "making student bodies fit for the institution by removing the element of the street" (p. 65). She argues that "such practices work to identify certain items and cultural markers as 'unclean'" (p. 65). In particular, the scanning ritual, in conjunction with the school's dress code policy, tends to target styles that are associated with black and Latino/a youth culture and specifically anything that might be perceived as "gang" related. Dickar states that "one of the symbolic roles of scanning is to clearly differentiate school space from street space by coercing students to remove such styles, at least at the entry point" (p. 65). Such processes discursively produce meanings of "safe," "compliant," and "acceptable," along with "dangerous," "unruly," and "criminal" that are inscribed onto students as they pass through the scanning system. Surveillance thus produces and inscribes distinct meanings and understandings of both virtuousness and deviancy within the process of schooling. The scanning process is designed to produce a safe and protected space whereby the ordered and functional business of education can proceed beyond the supposed threats posed by the unruly and dangerous norms of the street. However, such meanings produce powerful overt and tacit understandings of power, place, and identity, signaling who belongs and who doesn't in this space (Gallagher & Fusco, 2006). These understandings impact how students perceive themselves and their relation to authority as they are immediately confronted upon entry to the school by a mesh of security procedures that are both concretely and symbolically designed to make their bodies and appearance "suitable" to the institution—in a sense decontaminated of those elements that are deemed potentially threatening. Olivia, a junior who self-identifies as "mixed-race" remarks:

> It's so ugly. Because there's a line of girls that lead off of the stairs. And it's all these people in this tight little spot and they tend to get loud and kind of uncontrollable. So of course security has to respond to that and a lot of times it's them yelling at us, us yelling at them. It makes you later than you have to be and now these girls are angry because they're late and you know they're getting checked and a lot of times you'll walk through the metal detector and it will beep and now you have an attitude because now you have to take off whatever may have made the metal detector go off, whether its your earrings or your belt or whatever, hold up the line and go back through. It's an irritating and not a fun way to start your day. It's not good energy. And that's one bad thing. And everyone else is dealing with that bad energy too. And who knows whatever other bad issues are going on throughout the school. So it's like bad energy just carries itself through. I don't know how you would address that. How could you tell someone to not feel a certain way in the morning? Honestly it's frustrating. But there isn't anything you can do but just take it.

Kristina, a Latina freshman adds:

> I have learned from experience that if you go through a metal detector you feel like you're in a prison like, "Check here. Check there. Take off your coat." They are like, "Good morning kids, get in there. Take off your coat and make sure you're ready," and blah blah blah. It isn't a warm welcome, it's more like a, "Here we go again, more daily routine." It's more like that.

Christian Parenti (2003) has documented that technological developments in surveillance have historically been linked to the desire to know and control the movement and behavior of racially suspect and criminalized populations. He documents how the earliest forms of surveillance technologies in North America were information systems such as identification systems designed to restrict the movement of runaway slaves, immigrants, and political dissidents. Today, surveillance practices such as CCTV cameras and digital data tracking systems

sort people according to various threat assessment and risk management criteria which single out particular individuals, behaviors, and groups for scrutiny
within sites as diverse as hospitals, airports, schools, streets, and shopping malls.
This contributes to differentiated forms of mobility (Bauman, 1998; Salter, 2004),
various racialized and gendered effects (Haggerty & Ericson, 2006), as well as
discourses that work to justify and expand a culture of control and punishment
(Garland, 2001).

Public schools currently utilize a variety of surveillance technologies for a
range of purposes: human, electronic/digital, data analysis, record keeping,
profiling, and spatial manipulation. In the name of security, these practices
target and affect teachers, administrators, students, and researchers in diverse
ways throughout the school. Like the scanning process at CHS described above
where students are scrutinized upon entry to the school, they operate to sort and
regulate bodies and behaviors based upon criteria that work to define notions
of the virtuous and deviant and the included and excluded. They also function
to socialize students to accept a penal web of surveillance as natural and inevitable while learning to identify as either potential victims, suspects, or criminals within a neoliberal landscape of generalized social precariousness and mass
incarceration (Kupchik & Monahan, 2006). In what follows, I am interested in
outlining a few examples of how surveillance redefines security from a concern
over social security and human development to relations of mistrust and criminological control.

Data Tracking and the ID System:
Monitoring the Criminogenic Environment

At CHS, students are under the gaze of surveillance from the time they leave
their homes to when they return at the end of the day. To be a student is to be
watched, tracked, monitored, and under suspicion by authorities at all times.
Cameras on the street corners record their movements for real-time inspection
by law enforcement. Once they arrive at school they are met immediately by a
thick mesh of security and scanning procedures: security guards, cameras, scanning wands, and x-ray screeners. As students pass through and beyond the scanning system at CHS, and have entered the gated and securitized school, they are
promptly confronted by additional layers of surveillance and control. One of the
most prominent is an intricate web of data tracking.

Data tracking is a central form of surveillance at CHS aimed at the regulation
and monitoring of students as well as teachers and other staff. The modes of data
tracking vary from the attendance system; accountability policies and computer
software that monitor test scores and student achievement data; lesson plans and
the record keeping of teachers; to the district wide software system "Verify Net"
that tracks student disciplinary infractions. Perhaps the most significant form of
tracking surveillance is the school's ID system. All students and visitors, including researchers, are required to have and display an ID at all times. On the front
side, the IDs have a photo, name, grade level, and a bar code. On the back side,

they have a school timetable and the individual class schedule of each student. Each ID can be scanned into a computer system, where, depending on the level of clearance, one can access student records and input new information on students including grades, schedule changes, and disciplinary infractions.

Administrators, teachers, and security are constantly checking IDs throughout the day in efforts to monitor the flow and traffic of students in the building. Combined with the extensive security infrastructure, the ID system contributes a broader control network whereby students become a tracked and "knowable" population whose mobility is always subject to scrutiny, enacting what Foucault called a "grid of visibility" (Foucault, 1977). This serves to enforce to students their place within the hierarchical and authoritative structure of the school environment. Kristina comments on the apparent dehumanizing aspects of surveillance: "It makes me feel like it's a jail, like Cook County or something, with the IDs, like I'm number 4025. You might as well just tattoo it on my forearm."

The ID system is used not only to monitor the movements of students throughout the building but also to keep track of who has been suspended or expelled in order to control access to the securitized school itself. Each day a list of students who have been suspended or expelled is compiled and this information is then converted into dossiers with large color photos, student names, and other identifying information. These dossiers are generated and distributed to security guards throughout the school who then use them as tools to control and deny access to the building. Some schools in the CPS apparently keep bulletin boards by their front entrances with the photos of those students who have been suspended or expelled displayed prominently for all to see—enacting a spectacle of punishment and public shaming. At CHS, the guards keep the dossiers on clipboards and/or have them available for review at the security desk near each entrance.

The ID system is also implicated in processes that move beyond the monitoring of school space and symbolic criminalization. The ID dossiers, or "most wanted" lists or "mug shots" as I came to think of them, are also used by the disciplinary staff to build cases against students in coordination with law enforcement. For instance, the ID dossiers are often used as identification tools in the wake of violations of school rules and/or laws. If an incident occurs, police and school staff can use the photo dossiers to verify the identity of potential perpetrators in a way similar to a police lineup. After lunch one day, I found myself standing in the hallway outside the central office talking to the freshman dean, Mr. Meyer. Ms. Jacobs, a vice principal, approached us and handed Mr. Meyer several student dossiers. She informed him that these students had been accused by another student of assault in an incident that took place outside the school the previous afternoon. Ms. Jacobs gave Mr. Meyer instructions to go and show the dossiers to the accuser in order to make a "positive ID" before involving law enforcement and before pursuing a potential "mob action" criminal charge against the accused youth. I went with Mr. Meyer as he took the dossiers to find the accuser. After pulling the young man out of class, Mr. Meyer proceeded to acquire a positive ID based on the dossiers. Next, Mr. Meyer informed CHS' two police officers, Duggan and Jones, that an identification had been made in the case and that charges may need to be filed. The police then proceeded to make arrangements to bring in the accused for questioning and to potentially pursue arresting the youth.

Such incidents are a regular occurrence, demonstrating how forms of data-driven surveillance become implicated within a larger web of crime control at CHS as information is freely shared and integrated through technological tracking systems between school and police officials. The incident is revealing of how surveillance works to link the administration of the school and law enforcement in a direct and unmediated way as administrators and deans frequently work together to build cases that funnel students into the criminal justice system. One of the most troublesome aspects of this is that because the accused are being directly connected to police in the confines of the school, their First Amendment rights to due process are subject to violation, as interrogations routinely occur without the presence of parents or legal representation (Robbins, 2009; Ruddick, 2006). While unfortunate incidents of this type are sometimes handled in-house through administrative intervention and counseling, students are often simply sent directly to the police for questioning, which can lead to arrest and criminal charges. Such examples highlight how surveillance is implicated in processes that link the movements and behavior of students to law enforcement while in some cases divesting them of rights to due process. They become a targeted population excluded from the rights and protections supposedly afforded to all citizens within the very institution responsible for developing their moral and civic potential.

The Camera Network and the Institutionalized Mistrust of Youth

Beyond data tracking and the ID system, CHS relies on a sophisticated network of CCTV cameras in order to keep watch over all aspects of life in and around the school. In 2003, the city of Chicago was awarded a $48 million dollar grant by the Department of Homeland Security and has spent tens of millions more of its own funds including $50 million in 2007, in order to link emergency communications systems and CCTV cameras into an integrated Homeland Security Grid. According to an article in the Associated Press, Chicago now has "the most extensive and sophisticated video surveillance system in the United States, and one that is transforming what it means to be in public...in less than a decade and with little opposition, the city has linked thousands of cameras—on street poles and skyscrapers, aboard buses and in train tunnels—in a network covering most of the city" (AP, 2010). This network includes over 10,000 cameras, 6,500 of which are located in public schools making educational institutions the most watched spaces in the city. This includes CCTV cameras that now have the capacity to zoom, scan, and pivot along with a new generation that are "covert," meaning that they can be as small as a thimble and are designed to be hidden and thus go undetected. The CCTV cameras are accessible in real time via an internet network where city officials and police officers can log in and literally "surf" surveillance cameras throughout the city, representing a vast expansion of state surveillance into schools and communities.

The camera network at CHS is integrated directly into the broader Homeland Security Grid. The security grid has been presented to the public as a security net designed to prevent terrorism and crack down on crime. However, the integration of school cameras into the Homeland Security system blurs the material and symbolic lines between militaristic, post-9/11 antiterrorism discourses, and school governance. The grid is used to neutralize external enemies and monitor internal populations who might pose a threat to public order and national security. In the case of educational surveillance, it is targeted at monitoring youth who are deemed unruly and criminally suspect. As part of the broader antiterror security grid, images from the cameras at CHS can be accessed and monitored anywhere with an internet connection by city officials and police.

One morning while in the School Safety Office with police officers Duggan and Jones, I was shown firsthand the extent and power of the CCTV cameras. During our discussion we somehow moved onto the topic of the cameras and Duggan said, "I'll show you how they work." He then proceeded to log in on his computer to the city's surveillance network. He asked: "What do you want to look at?" "You want to see a train?" "How about the Red Line Stop at 95th and Western?" Within seconds, he had multiple surveillance cameras pulled up on his computer screen. It looked like the interface featured in some post-9/11 Hollywood film. I could see three different real-time images from around the 95th EL stop not far from where my sister lives and teaches. In the far right-hand corner of the screen, I could see people on the train platform and others waiting for the bus outside the station. "How about one a little closer to us," he said. He then demonstrated how he could pull up cameras from other schools, cameras downtown, and indeed from the hallway outside their office at CHS. We saw students and security guards walking the corridor of a nearby public school and people walking the sidewalks in the Ellison Square neighborhood. They demonstrated how they could pull up a camera from the neighborhood and use a zoom function to read the license plates of cars and even peer into the windows of houses. "I didn't realize you guys could remote view all these cameras," I said. "Oh yeah, we have the entire city covered."

The camera network at CHS operates on multiple levels. Its official function is to act as a deterrent to crime and as a system for identifying suspects in the event of an illicit incident. Indeed, administrators have used the network in conjunction with police to identify students who have committed legal violations inside and outside the building. Unofficially, the cameras are also integrated into the broader cultural fabric and "hidden curriculum" of the school. Here they stand as a symbolic warning to students and others that they are always under the watchful and criminological gaze of authority. Peter Kelly (2003) has referred to this as representing the "institutionalized mistrust of youth" where surveillance cameras are symptomatic of what has become an often excessive effort to police student behavior for any sign of criminality, either real or imagined. For instance, one afternoon I was sitting in the hallway outside the Dean's Office with two female African American students. They said that they had been caught ditching class. The freshman dean, Mr. Meyer, had dropped them off to talk to the acting dean of students, Mr. Morris. The three of us began talking about what kind of music we like. I told them that I like the hip-hop artist NAS, which immediately made them laugh hysterically at me. Next, one of the girls made a joke about the artist T-Pain and the girls started giggling and performing a knowing handshake. At this gesture, I heard a security officer approaching us from down the hall yell, "Hey where do you think you are…I'll write you up on a gang violation…look up at that camera right there [the guard points to the surveillance camera above us]…you are on camera gang banging right here." The girls responded, "No we ain't, we just playing around!" The guard pointed at the camera and said, "Don't you see that camera? We got you on film. We'll have you written-up and arrested for a gang violation right now." Overhearing the commotion in the hallway, Dean Morris called the two girls into his office where he proceeded to give them a suspension warning for skipping class. He also proceeded to warn them again against any future handshakes in the school hallway on threat of being charged with a gang violation.

In this example, CCTV cameras become integrated into a culture of security, suspicion, and criminalization at CHS. I do not know if these two young women were in fact engaging in a "gang" related handshake. It is entirely possible that they were, but it is also just as likely they were not. As my comments regarding the reality of gangs at CHS in chapter 3 suggests, there is an often ambiguous line between "innocent" affiliations between students and supposed "criminal" gang activity. In either case, the girls' behavior did not in any way pose an immediate threat to student safety as we were the only people in the hallway. Cameras are thus not simply performing a security or safety function by warding off potential gang activity, which is a serious and legitimate concern, but are also serving to expand and legitimate a gaze of punishment that criminalizes even those interpersonal expressions among students that are deemed illicit and/or potentially dangerous according to rationalities and definitions held by authorities. Here, surveillance becomes directed as much at the possibility or potential of illicit conduct as actually "catching" or neutralizing violations or threats to safety. While these two students were not arrested for this particular incident, it became clear throughout my observations of daily life at CHS that the behavior of students is always under a kind of criminological scrutiny subject to the potential involvement of police. This modifies the distribution, composition, and authority of school governance and generates a culture of suspicion and social control rooted in the norms of criminal deviance. In this case, two students who had skipped class found themselves potentially drawn up on criminal charges via evidence from the CCTV cameras. I found that the cameras and the security culture in general had this kind of multiplying effect or what Foucault (1977) once referred to as "a state of conscious and permanent visibility" (p. 201), proliferating the possibilities within given times and spaces where students could be monitored and potentially punished, or as I will describe in upcoming sections below, formally charged with crimes. The cameras thus occupy part of a broader culture of suspicion permeating daily life at CHS that presents a challenge to our understanding of the educative purposes of public schooling in the contemporary moment as the security of young people becomes framed largely in criminal as opposed to social or democratic terms.

Environmental Design and Internal Confinement

Another prominent form of security and surveillance at CHS concerns the built environment itself and the management of space. As Foucault noted in his historical studies of modern institutions, architectural arrangements in places like schools, factories, and clinics represent rationalized processes and forms of knowledge that are designed to maximize visibility, regulation, and order (Foucault, 1977). In schools, this has historically meant dividing, tracking, and ranking student populations by age and ability; creating hallways, stairwells, and open spaces that enhance the regulatory gaze of adults; and organizing classrooms with straight mathematical rows of desks and chairs that place the instructor prominently at the front of the room ready to administer examinations, keep order, and maintain individualized student records.

In schools like CHS, this industrial-era model of factory discipline has been overlaid not only with the extensive systems of digital networking technologies outlined above, but also with new strategies of spatial repression. These strategies click with the current realities and concerns over violence, crime, and student disorder. Taking cues from Oscar Newman's (1972) notion of "defensible space" and from "Crime Prevention through Environmental Design" (CPTED), schools like CHS have experimented with new mechanisms for managing space so as to maximize control and minimize disorder and threats to safety. At CHS, this has meant sealing off doorways and limiting access points to two secured entrances, keeping certain bathrooms under lock and key, posting security guards at strategic locations to monitor hallways and flow of students, mobilizing CCTV cameras and wireless communications, and periodically performing "hall sweeps" and instituting "lockdowns," where steel gates are used to block hallways and students are confined in their classrooms for intermittent periods of time.

One of the most extreme environmental/spatial arrangements that CHS has experimented with involved the internal containment of a specific population of students. Teachers and students alike often shared their frustration in describing the most disruptive students at the school. I found that it was common for teachers and students to indicate that 10–12 percent of the students were responsible for the vast majority of the school's discipline problems including classroom disruptions, fights, and disorder in the hallways. These concerns are quite real. CHS and schools like it do indeed deal with persistent issues concerning disruption and conflict. However, in a neoliberal economic and sociopolitical environment where grinding poverty and loss of hope meet the realities of the neglect and the criminalization of institutions like CHS, they are not entirely surprising or unpredictable. During the 2009–2010 school year, the school attempted to directly identify and isolate the most disruptive youth by separating them from the "general population." Lists of students were drawn-up and these students were mandated to be confined to the "mobile" classroom units in the school's inner courtyard. In these windowless fiberglass and wood trailers, the identified youth were assigned their own internal security force of guards to monitor them. Teachers brought the curriculum to the students as they were not allowed to circulate among the broader population of the school. Administrators, and even many teachers, argued that the "solitary confinement" of these students was a way of improving the learning environment for the majority. However, the project broke down as the detained students began openly rebelling and parents and district officials became aware of what was happening and forced an end to the program.

I do not think it is hyperbolic here to suggest that this experiment in the spatial isolation and exclusion of this "problem" population represents the extent to which the prison has become the model and imaginative horizon of the disciplinary authority of the urban public school. As with each of the surveillance practices I have described in this section, this example also signifies how schools like CHS are increasingly becoming less invested in counseling and rehabilitation and more oriented toward warehousing and containing threats posed by certain populations of youth. Such processes of warehousing and containment need to be understood in relation to the broader transformation of security under neoliberalism, which has eroded social democratic referents and promoted criminalizing practices within an urban context of social fragmentation, poverty, and limited economic and social opportunity. As Henry Giroux (2009) notes, in an age of neoliberal disposability and austerity, "students are being miseducated, criminalized, and arrested through a form of penal pedagogy in lock-down schools that resemble prisons" (p. 102). According to Giroux, this represents a "cruel reminder of the degree to which mainstream politicians and the American public have turned their backs on youth in general and poor minority youth in particular" (p. 102). The temptation to isolate and exclude may perhaps be somewhat understandable for teachers and staff overwhelmed by real problems of disorder and conflict in schools. However, such measures do nothing to address the root causes of these problems, or the problems youth bring with them to school, nor does it function as an effective strategy for constructively and ethically addressing them. Instead, it contributes to a climate of punishment and exclusion as opposed to uplift and healing.

Criminological Discipline and Authority

Thus far I have profiled the use of surveillance technologies at CHS and how these technologies frame questions of security through the lens of criminological control. In this section, I examine criminalizing processes of discipline and authority. This includes analysis of an authoritarian zero tolerance culture of suspensions, expulsions, and arrests instituted by security guards, disciplinarians, and police.

Due to consistent community opposition, the CPS officially ended "zero tolerance" as a district policy in 2007. However, thus far this has proven to be largely a rhetorical measure. The uniform discipline code still assigns mandatory "Interventions and Consequences" for each of its six levels of infractions that proceed from the least serious, Level 1, that includes such violations as "persistent tardiness" or "making noise in hallway," to the most serious, Level 6, that includes "robbery," "murder," and "arson."

Between 2002 and 2008, under Arne Duncan's tenure as the Chicago schools' CEO, suspensions nearly quadrupled in the CPS from 23,942 to 93,312 per year. In the 2009–2010 school year, there were more than 89,336 suspensions, equivalent to 1 suspension for every 8 CPS students (Dignity in Schools, 2010). Most of these suspensions were for low-level and nonviolent incidents and African American males, constituting only 25 percent of CPS students, represented 45 percent of all suspensions and 60 percent of all expulsions (Catalyst, 2009). Students at CHS are routinely suspended for lower level violations and are sometimes even referred to the police for potential criminal charges for such subjective and undefined infractions as "disorderly conduct," a Level 4 violation that might include persistent "insubordination," among other things. During the 2007–2008 school year, there were 750 suspensions and 23 expulsions at CHS while in 2008–2009 there were 1,126 suspensions and 39 expulsions. This is equivalent to having 7 out of every 10 students suspended at some point during 2008–2009.

> *Chris* (an African American senior): If you are involved in anything you immediately get suspended. And these range from things as small as loss of ID to things as big as fighting. You are immediately suspended for X amount of days without trying to understand why something happened. Like when students get suspended for fighting, you never knew why the fight started, it's automatic suspension. Just like ID, you don't know why the person lost their ID or don't have their ID but after a few questions they are immediately suspended.

The research is clear that reliance on suspensions and expulsions is associated with various negative consequences. Extensive research compiled by the High Hopes Campaign (2012) in Chicago indicates that:

- Suspensions and expulsions do not make schools safer and do not improve students' behavior.
- Suspensions and expulsions have long and damaging effects on student behavior and learning.
- The higher a school's rate of suspension and expulsion, the lower the academic achievement of its students even when taking socioeconomic status out of the equation.
- High levels of suspension do not make students and teachers feel safer— instead, they can negatively affect the school environment by creating distrust.
- School districts which have focused on decreasing suspensions have seen an increase in graduation rates. For example, Baltimore City Public Schools lowered suspensions from 26,000 to 10,000 and experienced an increase in their graduation rate by 20 percent.

Beyond suspensions and expulsions, scores of students are arrested every year at CHS. Data on these arrests is difficult to obtain. After filing a Freedom of Information Request with the Chicago Police Department, I was told that they keep track of student arrests by police districts in the city and do not delineate arrests by school. During my observations, however, I witnessed that arrest was a routine phenomenon at CHS with multiple students leaving school in handcuffs each week. This lack of transparency in the availability of arrest data has become a common concern of scholars and civic groups increasingly blocked from obtaining reliable information on juvenile arrests in schools. What we do know is that arrests of students in the Chicago schools are a matter of routine. In 2003, for instance, there were 8,539 arrests in the CPS, the majority of which did not involve injuries, weapons, or serious crimes (AP, 2005). In the 2008–2009 and 2009–2010 there were 9,683 arrests at Chicago schools (Project NIA, 2010).

In the name of safety, order, and violence prevention, school security and discipline has come to operate on the presupposition that criminality is an ever present feature of school life—thus naturalizing the presence in schools of external forms of power and authority such as security companies, security guards, and law enforcement. This generates numerous effects that are often at odds with the democratic aims of schooling. For instance, research has shown that these security environments and excessive reliance on suspensions, expulsions, and arrests correlate to student disaffection and insecurity in schools, higher dropout rates, poorer academic performance of schools, and racial profiling (AP, 2005, 2010). Students suspended, expelled, and/or arrested in their schools has also been shown to correlate to a greater likelihood that they will spend time in jail even as adults thus creating a "school-to-prison pipeline" (AP. 2005, 2010). These processes represent a distinct challenge to the human development mission of public schools and the capacity of young people to secure their lives and future.

Security Guards:
Professional Misconduct and the Mind/Body Division

Alex: When you think about security at CHS, what do you think about?
Chris: Security Guards. It reminds me of an overseer at a plantation. It's very strict and authoritative, the security guard relationship with the students at CHS. Almost like police and inmates. The security guards in the hallways have more power than the teachers when you are in class.

Security guards are the most visible and controversial layer of disciplinary authority at CHS. The guards are charged with performing most routine surveillance functions in the school as well as serving as the front line of discipline and behavior management. CHS has seven full-time district appointed security guards. However, this number periodically goes up to 12 or more during those times when the school's threat level is raised making it a "hot spot." At these times, typically in the wake of heightened gang activity or violence in the community, the CPS sends over additional security guards. The security guards play a key role in controlling access to the building and they actively patrol the hallways and monitor the flow and behavior of students. Throughout the day, guards are posted in strategic locations in the school—at the entrances, the ends of hallways, outside the cafeteria, and so on. During class sessions they make sure that students are not lingering in the hallways and/or avoiding their classes. They also are periodically called into classrooms by teachers in order to address disruptive students. Sometimes security guards engage these students in dialogue and give verbal warnings before sending them back to class and at other times they end up referring students to the dean for disciplinary action. During passing periods, the guards hasten the students to class and attempt to enforce the ID and uniform requirements. When problems arise during passing periods, including potential student conflicts, security guards are there to address them.

Students have hundreds of interactions with security guards throughout their days, weeks, and months in school. Some of these interactions are positive and even educative while others are harmful, inappropriate, and have a poisonous effect on school culture and the learning environment. Through my observations and conversations with security guards, I discovered that some guards strived to be a positive presence in students' lives, while others were far less committed to such ethical aspirations. Among students and staff, certain security guards have better reputations than others. The guards with good reputations are known to take their jobs seriously and many attempt to provide guidance to students and help them solve various problems ranging from replacing a lost ID to lending out bus fare to students in need. However, there is also a widely acknowledged dark side to the presence of security guards at CHS. Security guards throughout the CPS have minimal training and are not required to have any background in adolescent development, counseling, and/or conflict mediation and resolution. As a result, norms of professional conduct are close to nonexistent. Students and teachers both voiced a litany of concerns over the professional conduct of the guards. I was told that certain guards over the years have been involved in various unprofessional and unethical behaviors including suspected drug trafficking, gang activity, and sexual harassment. I also encountered credible stories from both youth and from other adults that some guards have even attempted to frame certain students for crimes. One of the most often repeated accusations was that male security guards have engaged in sexually harassing female students.

Such outrageous and shameful conduct contributes to a hostile environment for all students that can be understood to perpetuate cynicism among youth and disorder in the school. Mr. Burke, a teacher, here gives voice to some of these concerns:

> *Alex*: So you have said that security guards act in unprofessional ways, do you have any examples that you've seen of this?
>
> *Mr. Burke*: I have heard about male security guards giving notes to female students with their phone numbers on them or inappropriately touching or speaking to female students. Those are just the ones I've heard about but if they're getting to me then I'm sure there's a lot more like that that we don't even know about at all and have been for years. Some curse at kids and the automatic lack of any type of care or respect for the kids. This causes the school to be a little bit—it takes away from the atmosphere of the school. If kids don't trust the security guards who are they gonna trust besides their friends? It's their friends and them.

Such behaviors work to produce a culture of fear that contributes to gendered violence and the insecurity and alienation of all students. As intimated by Mr. Burke, amid such conduct, the only thing binding students to the authority of the school are authoritarian norms of force and threat of punishment. As a result, the relations of trust between students and the school break down, eroding the social contract underwriting the democratic and educative purposes of schooling and undermining the capacity of students to secure their own sense of personhood and well-being. Such a climate, where present, has to be understood as connected to the persistence of high dropout/pushout rates among students across the CPS while feeding the escalation of various forms of oppositional behavior among students. As the female student exclaimed in the scanning line, "Damn, why you have to waste my time every morning!" These resistances are born out of frustrations and routine violations of students' sense of humanity. However, they often serve to block students' capacity for agency and voice. Rather than being understood as a predictable reaction to physically and spiritually adverse conditions, oppositional behaviors are criminalized and translated into exclusionary suspensions or worse.

These tensions between the unethical conduct of security guards and student resistance is revealing of deeper transformations in the socializing mission of public schools. For instance, in his study in New York City, John Devine (1996) observed that the presence of security guards creates a division in schools. On one hand, the classroom becomes a separate, enclosed universe where "learning" is conducted under the authority of teachers responsible for the "minds" of students. On the other hand, the school corridor becomes a space governed by security guards and police who operate less as an extension of the school's educative and democratic mission than as an apparatus of containment directed toward disciplining the student "body" that is thought less in terms of an investment in the future and more as a potential threat to order. As a result, public schools like CHS that rely heavily on the disciplinary authority of security guards who are untrained in the professional care and guidance of youth, abdicate much of their role as key sites for the holistic and democratic development of youth. Instead, by relying heavily on the normative parameters of criminal discipline, these prison-like environments contribute to pushing students out of school and into a school-to-prison pipeline (AP, 2005, 2010).

The Deans:
Prescriptive Punishment, Counseling, and the Criminological Limit

Beyond the security guards, the next line of disciplinary authority at CHS resides with the two deans. During the time I spent at CHS, the head dean of students was off on medical leave and Mr. Morris, normally the head of the security guards, was standing in for her. Mr. Morris grew up near CHS and many feel his roots in the community give him credibility with students. Mr. Morris views his role largely as enforcing the rules as they are articulated in the CPS uniform disciplinary codebook. As a result, Mr. Morris relies heavily on suspensions and the threat of arrest and expulsion in his disciplinary oversight. In my interactions with Mr. Morris it became clear that this attitude derived from a belief that without potentially severe consequences, order would further break down. Despite his comportment toward following the prescriptions laid out in the code-book, Mr. Morris was constantly making judgments based upon his own discre-tion, his knowledge of the students, and what he thought was appropriate given the context of an incident. However, despite using his discretion, Mr. Morris relied heavily on the use of suspension and expulsion as a primary means of dis-cipline. He stated to me that, "If you do the crime, you have to do the time."

In contrast to Mr. Morris, the perception among many students and teach-ers is that the school's discipline system and its heavy reliance on suspensions, expulsions, and law enforcement is largely ineffective. In fact, I didn't speak to any students or teachers who thought that the current system of discipline is broadly effective in deterring misbehavior or for promoting safety.

> *Alex*: As far as suspensions and expulsions, do you think they're effective for cor-recting student misbehavior?
> *Malia* (African American sophomore): No, I do not think they are effective.
> *Alex*: Why not?
> *Malia*: Because most of the students who get suspended, they don't take it as a, "Well, I need to get back on track and not get suspended anymore." They will come back and get suspended right the next day. There's more to it than getting suspended. You have to actually communicate.
> *Alex*: So how could the school do better as far as discipline? What do you think would be more effective than suspensions and expulsions?
> *Malia*: Detention, but not the regular detention that you usually have just sitting there being quiet. They should have a circle where everybody explains why they are in there and what happened and then maybe the students around them could be like, "It could have been handled differently." It should be something like that instead of automatically suspending someone for ten days because it's not gonna get you nowhere but missing your classes and falling behind.

Malia's comments reflect a much broader critique against the overuse of suspen-sions and expulsions at the school as well as a real hunger for a more commu-nicative and educative approach to discipline. Students I talked with seemed to universally believe that the disciplinary system fails to serve the needs of students and that the school should make greater efforts to counsel students and to work through problems in more constructive and communicative ways rather than to simply banish students from the school via suspensions, or, in the case of expul-sion, to push them out for good.

While the school does rely heavily on prescriptive zero tolerance forms of pun-ishment, there are significant attempts made to talk things through with students when they break the rules. The freshman dean, Mr. Meyer, in particular values such an approach. Mr. Meyer is a young Afghan War veteran with a penchant for striped ties and for casually addressing students as "pal," buddy," and sometimes "dumbo." He has been at the school for four years, at first in the capacity as a World Studies and an AVID teacher, but took his current job as freshman dean as he faced the prospect of being forced out of his job due to the teacher layoffs. Mr. Meyer is a key point person at the school for security and discipline and he is quick to recognize the limits of the school's security and surveillance system and the need to work more proactively with students in a counseling and restorative capacity.

> *Mr. Meyer*: We can flood this place with security guards and all that stuff and at the same time there is gonna be fights and all that stuff because these kids bring problems off the streets and they have this idea that even the slightest look of disrespect equals a fight. It's the culture. I don't know how to do it, but we gotta get out there and get these young kids to realize that you don't always have to go to blows. There's things that can just be talked out.
>
> *Alex*: How do you personally approach disciplinary issues?
>
> *Mr. Meyer*: You have to ask yourself, what's the situation, have you dealt with the kids before? If so, how have you dealt with them? What kind of situations have you dealt with them? And also for me, can you get the situation under control without taking it to the next level. A lot of these kids out here just don't have the skills of confrontation and knowing how to confront a teacher and knowing how to effectively deal with the situation so they explode. So my biggest goal is to teach them how to deal with those situations. I don't just take them, not listen to them, suspend them and be done with it. I take them, I listen to the teacher's side, I listen to their side and I try to get them to understand how they are dealing with the situation, bring them back to the teacher and have them deal with the confrontation a better way and the teacher is almost always like, "Okay great, no problem. Come back to class." Now it's different obviously with a violent situation or something like that but as far as most situations you have to go off of your discretion—how well do you know the kid, what's the situation, what did they do, how are they reacting to you in the office, how are they explaining things to you, are they freaking out, are they threatening. It depends on the situation.

Mr. Meyer's approach to discipline is broadly respected by teachers and students throughout the building. Mr. Parks states that "Mr. Meyer represents a personality type, a disciplinarian that is personable and personal and kids like him although they may be frustrated by him sometimes. I think that represents a more realistic approach—we tend to have the police commander type in which the kids are adjudicated as opposed to a parental style that listens and teaches." Cynthia, a female African American sophomore, agrees with Mr. Parks saying that, "Mr. Meyer is good because he will actually listen to what you have to say and try and help you, he doesn't just suspend you for no reason."

While he is technically in charge of freshman, Mr. Meyer's presence is felt throughout the building. During the day, he is roaming the halls, counseling students and encouraging them to get to class—a major headache for staff as students love to linger and avoid their classrooms (the security guards and the deans wage daily pitched battles against tardiness). Periodically, he receives calls that he is needed for any number of reasons: to help break up a fight, to meet with a parent, or to diffuse a conflict. One morning I was with Mr. Meyer as he was sent to pick up two female students from their classes who were seen having some sort of verbal conflict during the previous passing period. Both young women were African American, one a junior with short curly hair and a bright smile and the other a skinny freshman with grey jeans, a black jacket, and medium length braids in her hair. At first the two students denied even knowing one another. "I don't know this girl," the junior girl said, "She's just some freshman." At this, the freshman rolled her eyes. After some prodding by Mr. Meyer they admitted that "words were going around"—that is, rumors were being spread. After some discussion in the hallway. Mr. Meyer then took the students to his office. After we sat down he asked, "Tell me, what do you two believe is worth fighting over?" The junior said, "My people." Similarly, the freshman responded with, "My family." Meyer responded, "If these are the things that you think are worth fighting for then why on earth are you fighting with each other over some rumors that you don't even know are true?" "You know that rumors are spread by people who just want to see a fight." The students agreed that their differences were "petty" but they couldn't seem to move past the problem they had with each other.

After a particularly passive aggressive exchange, Mr. Meyer lost his patience. He exclaimed, "I have had enough, apparently you don't understand who you are talking to. You may not know me but I am not here just to pass my time. I know a few things about protecting and losing friends. I was in Afghanistan, and I lost friends over there. When I was over there I realized that the things we fight over here are just incredibly stupid. Just because some girl gives you a look in the hallway that is no reason for fighting! That is just STUUUPID! You two need to figure out a way to let this go. If I hear that you two end up going at it, you are going to be arrested. Is that what you want? To mess up your life over some look or some rumor?" The two girls both responded with almost simultaneous recitations of the word "no." Meyer continued, "This is your warning, if you two decide to settle this through a fight then you are going to be arrested. You both need to go about your day and ignore one another." He proceeded to send the girls back to their respective classes. To my knowledge, the problem between them was resolved.

This incident is telling because it represents a genuine attempt to resolve student conflicts through dialogue without automatically resorting to immediate arbitrary punishment—a style that Mr. Meyer has sincerely tried to cultivate. However, here Mr. Meyer relies ultimately on the threat of arrest as a way of deterring these students. While a sincere effort is made to counsel students and to promote dialogue and healthy problem solving, it appears that law enforcement and arrest represent the final authority through which student conflicts are to be ultimately mediated. It thus functions as a kind of criminological limit and final arbiter of student misconduct to which even those like Mr. Meyer, who believe in counseling and dialogue, submit. This exchange represents a broader pattern at CHS, as the threat of arrest was one of the most common deterrents I witnessed adults use to correct student behavior. Over and over, I saw students threatened by security staff and administrators with criminal charges for things ranging from everyday conflicts similar to the one described above, to more mundane things like uniform violations and/or signs of "disrespect" toward adults. While Mr. Meyer places more emphasis on trying to cultivate a more humane and democratic approach to discipline, ultimately even he submits to law enforcement and the criminal justice system as the overriding and final authority on matters of corrective punishment.

The Cops:
Policing and Arresting Youth

This brings us to our final layer of disciplinary authority at CHS—the police. CHS has a significant police presence. Probation officers often meet with students at the school; detectives and plain clothes officers also meet with the deans and other administrators to investigate incidents; and additional officers enter the school during "lockdowns" as a show of force and to keep order. Duggan and Jones, however, are the primary police presence at CHS. They monitor the outdoor spaces before and after school and they walk the hallways, adding yet another layer of surveillance and discipline at CHS. But their most significant responsibility is to investigate incidents and make decisions over charging students with crimes such as in cases of theft, conflicts and physical altercations, and the possession of drugs or other illegal contraband.

Duggan and Jones state that they use arrest only in the most exceptional circumstances and that they prefer to "talk things out rather than lock kids up." This might involve having a meeting with students, issuing a warning, or organizing student and parent meetings in order to try and resolve a problem. This is not always successful. In one such parent meeting that I observed, a father was adamant that two students who had assaulted his son outside the school be criminally charged, despite efforts to resolve the incident in another way. Despite apparent efforts by Duggan and Jones to minimize criminal charges at CHS, arrest is used throughout the building by security and the administrative staff as a threat and is often supported by mandatory punishments in the CPS uniform discipline code that provides a pretext and mandate to arrest youth for specific types of violations. As I mentioned above, students are often warned by security guards that they will be arrested if they break this or that rule or if they show disrespectful behavior toward adults. Duggan and Jones claim that they do not arrest students under such circumstances even though security guards routinely request it. This does not mean that arrest and criminal convictions do not occur. On a weekly basis, multiple students are led away from CHS in handcuffs and sent to the police station to be booked on criminal charges for a range of offenses. Duggan and Jones stated to me that they are present at CHS only to handle the most serious or exceptional incidents. The problem here is that the nature of an event is always subjective. For instance, how does one distinguish a relatively harmless altercation from a criminal assault? Or a young person testing the boundaries of authority from disorderly conduct?

Stories relayed to me from students indicate, for instance, that students live in almost constant fear of being arrested for even minor and trivial kinds of rule breaking. Here a Latino junior named Javier describes his run-in with police during a water fight outside school during a heat wave the previous June.

> *Javier*: You know how last year the school didn't let us go to water fountains when it was really hot. So what we did is we got a couple of water bottles and water balloons and just started playing around. And I had a couple of water balloons…
>
> *Alex*: Was this outside?

Javier: Yeah, it was outside. And then I had two water bottles that I was hanging on because my friend had gone inside school and he had just opened up a water bottle on my bag so I was waiting outside and I had two water bottles and I was hiding them just in case I saw him so I could get him wet—and then one of the cops came up and he told me—I don't know why but my first instinct was to run but then I took four or five steps and I thought, "Why am I even running. I don't have anything." So I turned back and they handcuffed me and searched me. The thing is when you're running from the cops there are certain alley ways you can take and they started searching me and they said that if they find a gun that they were gonna arrest me for it. I was like, "Why? You can finger print me it's not mine." All I had were these two water bottles but they had me on the floor. They had me on my knees, they had me handcuffed and they kept asking me what I am and I kept telling them, "Nothing, nothing, I'm not a gang member. I only have these two water bottles." And they asked, "Why did you run?" And I was like, "Because I don't want to get arrested!"

Students I talked with referred to the water fights as the "Great Water Balloon Controversy." This would sound almost comical if it weren't for the brutal treatment exercised by the police as relayed by Javier and for the fact that students were branded and treated as criminals simply for participating in what was perhaps a disruptive but ultimately harmless water fight on a hot day. Here, Javier's first instinct was to run from the police out of fear of being arrested for little more than carrying a water bottle. The police proceeded to threaten and pin Javier to the ground. Such negative encounters with law enforcement and authority not only do violence in the lives of young people but also add to a climate of insecurity and social distrust between youth and authorities. While Javier was here only aggressively threatened with arrest, another female student was apparently arrested on a disorderly conduct charge for participating in the water fights.

CHS has uniform discipline policies in place for serious infractions such as weapons and drug violations. However, decisions on most behavioral incidents—as to whether the police should become involved—are left to the discretion of administrative staff and security officials. Such discretion is crucial. School officials need to be the first line in terms of understanding the context of an incident and the background of the students involved so that they can mediate incidents in a restorative manner without involving the police. While the school does attempt to handle problems in this manner, too often students are just simply dumped on the police because the police happen to be there. This allows security and administrators to avoid responsibility and liability for security and discipline.

Discretion is thus only as ethical as the norms of professional conduct that guide it. Moreover, if we take Duggan and Jones at their word, there would be far more arrests at CHS if they did not try to avoid them. This consideration does not always extend to their peers. For instance, there are law enforcement officers stationed at other schools in the CPS that indiscriminately arrest first and ask questions later. Duggan and Jones claimed, for instance, that a particular officer at a nearby high school openly brags about personally arresting 180 students during the 2009–2010 academic year. This suggests that zero tolerance and uniform punishments are applied in highly uneven ways. I found that when it comes to student criminalization, professional norms of ethical conduct, or the lack thereof, play a fundamental role in the number of students funneled directly into the criminal justice system. These arrests have far reaching consequences for young people and have been shown to significantly increase the likelihood that youth will fall behind, drop out of school, and spend time in jail or prison as adults (AP, 2005, 2010).

Police presence at CHS is contested. For instance, students often report feeling more safe because of the police. Further, Duggan and Jones do make attempts to constructively work with students rather than just simply applying reactionary punishments. However, I also witnessed many incidents of police and administrators working together to build cases against students accused of violating school rules in ways that erode the line between the criminal justice system and the school and extend the gaze of police into the community, while socializing youth into the norms of criminological authority. Similarly, Aaron Kupchik (2010) found in his study of four public high schools that police in schools "help school administrators run the school and the police department regulate communities, enhancing the school's control over students and the police department's surveillance of communities" (p. 133). According to Kupchik:

> Officers affect the overall school climate. Having an officer can escalate disciplinary situations; increase the likelihood that students are arrested at school; redefine situations as criminal justice problems rather than as social, psychological, or academic problems; introduce a criminal justice orientation to how administrators prevent and respond to problems; and socialize students to expect a police presence in their lives. (p. 115)

Despite the fact that Duggan and Jones did voice criticisms of the tendency of the school to rely on arrest as a central mode of discipline, their presence and actions nonetheless contribute to the general criminalization of youth, the naturalization of penal systems of authority, and an invasive web of crime control in the life of students. Ultimately, public schools need to reclaim their mission in the social and human development of youth. This would necessarily mean reducing the disciplinary role and the presence of police in schools, and the creation of restorative systems of investment and school authority rooted in social norms as opposed to the authoritarian logics of containment and criminalization. I will return to these themes in the next chapter and the conclusion.

Beyond Criminological Security and Control?
The "Culture of Calm" and Neoliberal Decomposition

In recent years, the security, surveillance, and disciplinary culture that I have described in this chapter have come under increasing criticism from scholars, communities, and activists as evidence suggests that these practices are not only harmful to youth but are also ineffective at preventing violence and at promoting healthy and democratic school environments. Public concern over these issues became particularly intense in Chicago during the fall of 2009 in the wake of the death of Derrion Albert. Albert, an honors student at Fenger High School on the South Side, received a fatal blow to the head as he was caught in the middle of a fight involving two groups of students on his way home from school. The incident was captured on another student's cell phone camera and the footage turned up on YouTube. It then went viral before becoming an international news story culminating in several CNN specials on youth violence in Chicago.

Critics began to point out how the demolition of public housing projects combined with gentrification and school closures under the Renaissance 2010 policy had led to escalating youth violence on Chicago's streets. Before 2006, there were on average 12–15 deadly shooting of CPS youth in Chicago each year. At the height of school closures in 2006–2007, there were 24 deadly shootings involving CPS youth. 2007–2008 brought 23 deaths and 211 shootings and 2008–2009 saw 34 deaths and 290 shootings (none of which took place at a CPS school, it should be noted) (NBC, 2009).[1] In the case of Albert's tragic death, the fight involved youth from the Altgeld Gardens housing projects, who had been arbitrarily transferred to Fenger as their former school was converted into a selective military academy despite significant community opposition. This created overcrowding and tensions at Fenger which ultimately led to the fight that took Albert's life. Amid the bad publicity and political circus that involved, among other things, an Illinois state representative calling for the military occupation of Chicago's poor neighborhoods by the national guard, the secretary of Education, Arne Duncan (one of the principal architects of the Renaissance 2010 plan), was dispatched by Barack Obama along with Attorney General Eric Holder to meet with CPS officials and Mayor Daley.

What came out of these meetings was an antiviolence and school safety plan called the "Culture of Calm." On the surface, the plan appeared to recognize not only the failures of the past but also the need for a more robust social response to the issue of neighborhood and school security. The $60 million dollar plan was made possible largely from stimulus grants from the federal government. It was intended to be a two-year pilot project that focused intensively on 6 schools but also provided services to 32 other "high risk" schools, including CHS. The Culture of Calm was largely the brainchild of then CEO of the Chicago schools, Ron Huberman. A former police officer with an MBA, Huberman is a proponent of data-driven statistical models of governance. As such, the plan was designed to focus resources on the schools and students deemed at highest risk for violence as identified through computer and statistical models. Those schools and youth would then supposedly have resources directed to them, including opportunities for one-on-one mentoring, social work services, and help finding part-time employment. The program also planned to initiate programs to promote alternative and restorative disciplinary practices in schools and to create healthier school climates. It also provided funds to hire community members as part of the Safe Passage initiative that helped walk students to and from their schools. These aspects of the Culture of Calm represent a step in the right direction. Based on the realization that the status quo at schools like CHS is fundamentally intolerable, the program was presented as a way to redirect policy toward providing services to students and to transform punitive security environments.

Between the fall of 2009 and spring of 2011, the CPS claimed the program had significantly reduced suspensions, incidents of misconduct, and violence in the schools and communities receiving services. However, the plan provided services to only a small number of schools and students. Further, it did not seriously attempt to alter or address many of the systemic problems that create insecurity and violence in schools. It transferred significant resources to provide services to selected schools and students but according to reports there were various problems with the implementation of these services (Karp, 2010, 2011). CHS was one of the targeted schools under the Culture of Calm. However, there was very little implementation of the program at the school while I was there. In fact, I was surprised to find that many students and even some teachers and administrators appeared to know very little about it except for one program that proved to be somewhat controversial. As part of the Culture of Calm, the CPS awarded a large contract to Luster Learning Services, an educational consultancy firm headed by Jai Luster, the executive director of Mesirow Financial, one of the largest hedge funds in the United States. At the beginning of the 2010–2011 academic year, teachers at CHS participated in a professional development session led by Luster in order to learn the secrets of his patented "Calm Classroom" method. Within the Calm Classroom every teacher is assigned a "Zynergy Chime" to intermittently ring as they lead their students through a series of deep breathing exercises. Based on a mystical "new age" sensibility, the exercise is designed to "control and concentrate the mind, enhance alertness, improve physical stamina, decrease stress, and find greater personal satisfaction" and thus ultimately to create a "culture of calm" in the school (Calm Classroom, 2012).

In the fall of 2010, CHS teachers were mandated to integrate Luster's Calm Classroom method into their homeroom routines. There isn't anything necessarily wrong with such a practice. Having a built-in period of quiet meditation during the day could very well have positive benefits. However, for many in the community, in light of serious concerns over violence, resource scarcity, and other cutbacks to services including teacher layoffs, the program appeared as an absurdity. Mr. Bradley and Malia both weigh in on the Culture of Calm:

> *Malia*: They're doing a thing called Culture of Calm where I think during second period they take ten minutes out of your day and they've got this little chime and they hit it and it's like "ding" and you're supposed to meditate but a lot of kids are not okay with that at all even though it's supposed to like make you want to chill out and relax. Sometimes it makes kids pretty angry. And a lot of teachers don't like it either because it wastes class time.
>
> *Mr. Bradley*: The CPS is spending all this money on this and we all get a glossy meditation book and a Zynergy Chime and another teacher and I looked those up and they are $14 dollars on Amazon. I mean the people who pay taxes in Chicago are paying for Zynergy Chimes when there are still some kids who don't have textbooks here; or houses! Copies are a problem, and when you don't have textbooks you need more copies. I would trade all the Zynergy Chimes in the world for just a second copy machine that always had paper in it and worked.

The implicit message of Luster's meditation program is that youth violence has little to do with matters of economic fragmentation, structural inequality, and/or misguided policies that disinvest in communities and the human development of young people. Instead, these issues are imagined as something that can be overcome through a retreat into the individual psyche. Here the effects of poverty, racial oppression, and disinvestment are thought to simply melt away through the pursuit of "greater personal satisfaction" and "a heightened sense of calm." While CHS was one of the schools targeted by the Culture of Calm which was widely touted in the media as a bold plan to address youth violence, they received little more than a corporate new-age meditation program and a few boxes of Zynergy Chimes that psychologized systemic problems and the insecurities of youth while doing nothing to address the roots of violence. Currently, the future of the Culture of Calm initiative hangs in doubt as the grant money has expired and the city embraces austerity measures to control its budgetary deficits.

The story of the Culture of Calm at CHS finds commonality with a broader narrative concerning the limits of security in the neoliberal city. Surprisingly, at least to me, one of the most critical perspectives on governance at CHS and larger security politics in the city that I encountered in my research came from officers Duggan and Jones. Over the course of several informal meetings that ranged from 1 to 2 hours in length, these police officers shared various trenchant critiques concerning connections between public school governance and the governance of the Chicago Police Department. These perspectives shed light on the more general hollowing-out of institutional and public life in the city.

For Duggan and Jones, the Culture of Calm, and indeed the broader surveillance and disciplinary structure at CHS, share a common foundation, one of the core elements of which is an increased emphasis and reliance on data-driven surveillance technologies and systems of risk measurement. This reliance on data-driven technology and auditing can be seen in how both teachers and police are increasingly governed through intensive accountability and productivity targets. For teachers, this is based on test score benchmarks, and for police it is based on tickets written, dispersals made (where police break up groups of loitering young men typically on street corners), and bodies locked away. These numbers are then used by those in positions of power in order to make a case to the public that something like education and something like public safety is taking place, when in fact both of these social services are being hollowed-out and redefined in ways detrimental to the public interest. In the case of the Culture of Calm, the program did not seek to fundamentally alter existing institutional, economic, or social relationships but to target resources at a small handful of schools and students identified through data mapping as "hot spots" and "at-risk." This may have played well in the media and even accomplished some positive things in some schools, but it has done little to address the broader problems and underlying conditions of violence and insecurity in neighborhoods like Ellison Square or in the lives of youth at schools like CHS.

Duggan and Jones were highly critical of the so-called high-tech revolution in law enforcement, dismissing data driven technocratic governance as nothing but "smoke and mirrors" justifying extensive cut backs to schools and communities.

They feel that the reliance on numerical targets and computer models of policing are largely projects that funnel money away from supporting police on the streets into the coffers of security companies while redefining police work from community work to mass incarceration.

> *Duggan*: It's just so some higher up can point to the cameras and say, "Look we are utilizing technology to protect you." While at the same time all this money is going out the door to these security companies. Its money plain and simple... politicians out there saying, "Look what I got for you." Meanwhile there aren't any cops on the streets doing their jobs for the community. It's all bullshit. Boiling everything down to numbers, to productivity targets, dispersals... it's not about police work. We are judged by the numbers, bodies locked up, dispersals made, tickets written.

They offered several interrelated examples of what they view as systemic corruption in security and policing. First, they cited the surveillance camera network as a massive corporate giveaway (some cameras costing as much as $60 each) with little merit in terms of crime prevention or prosecution. They pointed out that it is impossible for police, who are already stretched thin, to be watching the 10,000 plus cameras in order to prevent crime and they do not believe they deter or catch criminals. Jones stated, "They don't deter anybody... people know where they are and if they are going to do something they just pull a hood over their head." Because they do not have the capacity to watch all the cameras, one solution that was floated was to have available officers spend a certain amount of time watching a camera each week—just sitting at a desk in front of a monitor hoping to randomly spot a crime. According to Duggan and Jones, the Chicago Police Department even proposed pulling patrol units off the street one day a week in order to watch cameras which they described as, "an utterly absurd waste of time and resources." Second, and related, the officers cite how the economic crisis led the city to cut back in the number of officers on patrol in the community. They feel that this prevents police from building meaningful relationships in communities, which they claim translates into more arrests and more antagonism between residents and police. The political class has justified the cutbacks by stating that new technologies will offset the reductions of police, but Duggan and Jones insist that no amount of data mapping can replace community policing and the process of relationship building. Third, the officers claim that the so-called high-tech revolution in law enforcement has been ineffective in crime prevention because it focuses its effort on prediction and reaction as opposed to community policing, prevention, and rehabilitation for those convicted of crimes. Duggan and Jones point to the two shootings at CHS as evidence that these processes fail to prevent crime. For example, they point out that what is jokingly referred to as the Chicago Police Department's "Crystal Ball Unit," which is a computer modeling and data tracking program used to identify potential hot spots for crime, failed to identify CHS in either incident as a place where a shooting might occur.

Within this framework, Duggan stated that all we are left with is a "law enforcement system that only knows how to lock people up... that's all we do in Chicago, we just lock people away." For some, it might be difficult to take at face value the critical perspectives of CPD officers who represent a police force that has been embroiled in countless scandals involving all manner of charges of racist brutality and abuses of power—charges that were made real to me in discussions with youth in Ellison Square who relayed countless stories of police harassment. Regardless, what I think one can take away from the implementation of the Culture of Calm at CHS and the corruption that Duggan and Jones describe, is that they are both indications of the deep systemic rot at the core of the neoliberal project. Here, the web of state surveillance, policing, and control can be seen as representative of the loss of public ethics and endemic exploitation and profiteering that speaks to the dysfunction and corruption spawned by free market governance (Bauman, 2001; Brown, 2005; Giroux, 2009). In the context of CHS, it represents the social and moral disinvestment in the future of young people.

Coda:
Limits to Control and the Occupied Imagination

In this chapter, I have described some of the ways in which security is imagined and operates at CHS. I have suggested that in the name of security, surveillance and disciplinary practices contribute to a punitive culture of suspicion and mistrust that blurs the lines between schooling and the criminal justice system. As one would imagine, attitudes toward these practices at CHS are complex and often conflicted. For instance, there is no shortage of critiques of these practices and there is a broad recognition and concern at CHS that security technologies and disciplinary procedures are contributing to a harmful climate of fear and criminalization. Mr. Wilson elaborates:

> They [students] are immediately under suspicion almost like they are being considered guilty before being proved innocent. It is just assumed that since you come from this community that you have to walk through a metal detector because you might be carrying a gun. And that's just an assumption that is made around here, and there are certain things that are just put on the students that are not always fair. Like you are an urban youth in an impoverished area so therefore you must be a criminal. And that's not true for the majority of our students. It takes away a little bit of their youth when adults assume they are guilty before even knowing them.

I also found that there is a sense at CHS that the heightened security atmosphere and emphasis on monitoring, IDs, uniforms, and other surveillance practices are representative of misplaced energies and priorities that often overshadow or subvert educative and pedagogical concerns.

> *Mr. Wilson:* When it comes to instruction. Learning is not the primary focus. So like I can be in the middle of a lecture and a key point is about to come up and it just comes blaring over the loudspeaker that all students without IDs need to come

down to the auditorium and you are like, "Can that wait?" And it's like, "Is that really that important right now when we are trying to learn something." And so all this energy is being spent on what are largely trivial things.

Furthermore, there is also a strong sense that the surveillance and security apparatus of the school is plagued by questionable efficacy.

> *Mr. Parks*: I'd like to brainstorm the removal of the metal detectors. The notion that we have metal detectors is so fucking stupid...It takes a 14-year-old freshman 30 minutes to figure out nine ways to get a gun and if they wanted to get one into the building they would. And I've been here 12 years and we've never found one. Think of the hundreds of thousands of repetitions through a metal detector which we play this silly game that we're protecting anybody. So deconstruct it. If you want a safe place, then have greeters. Welcome students into the school, actually try and create a culture of calm as opposed to promoting fear.

While many individuals shared concerns over the effects and the efficacy of the surveillance and security process, for many adults and youth at CHS these practices appear nonetheless as inevitable. Despite the problems that these practices generate, many people expressed that at the very least, they provide a modicum of safety amid real concerns over violence. Olivia comments:

> The metal detectors only detect so much. And I can't even tell you how the metal detectors work because a lot of times they don't really do what they were made to do. Metal gets past the metal detectors very often. Sometimes the metal detectors are pointless but they provide a sense of security. And even if they don't work they make people feel safer and that's just because they're there and they make you go through this long process. And that's a bad way to start your morning anyway.

Similarly, Mr. Burke here expresses his view that despite the questionable efficacy of the metal detectors and surveillance cameras they are not only inevitable but necessary in order to promote safety and security.

> The cameras are on the corners, they are everywhere now and there's only gonna be more in the future. I think we need that stuff. Especially the metal detectors and the cameras too. There's been multiple times when we've been able to go back to the camera, pick out a kid who did something and actually prove it. They don't work all the time because some are in bad condition. We just got new ones and it's still really hard to see anything when you're watching the cameras, but I feel like a lot of our kids without that wouldn't feel safe.

What the comments by Mr. Parks, Olivia, and Mr. Burke capture is a sense that the surveillance and security practices function largely on an emotional or psychological register, what might be described in Raymond Williams's (1977) terminology as a "structure of feeling." For Mr. Parks, the metal detectors are of such questionable efficacy that he views their negative impact on the culture to outweigh whatever safety they may or may not provide. He also feels that there may be more holistic ways to create a culture of security. However, Olivia and

Mr. Burke seem to suggest that despite their obvious limitations they at least make people feel safe, even if this sense of safety is largely illusory. Further, Mr. Burke's comment that "there will only be more cameras in the future" gels with a broader sense of inevitability that I found at CHS among youth and adults who express their belief that there isn't really anything that can be done to change security policies at the school. Many recognize the negative consequences of intensive surveillance measures, but aside from Mr. Park's wish to remove the systems altogether, many appeared to lack a language to describe alternatives. Kathleen Gallagher (2007) has referred to the sense of inevitability of intensive security and crime control practices in schools as representative of an "occupied imagination." Here neoliberal ideologies, forms of governance, and insecurities stemming from extensive economic fragmentation and social disinvestment have become so entrenched that even while there may be broad recognition of the harmful consequences of intensive surveillance and security cultures, there is often a limited sense of alternatives. While surveillance technologies and punitive disciplinary policies may not be proven to effectively prevent violence and make the school a truly more safe and socially uplifting place for youth, they appear to many as the only option. This ultimately collapses into a socially degraded vision of security.

> *Chris*: Instead of being so harsh and pursuing the zero tolerance policy we could talk and get a better understanding of what's going on in the school outside of harsh discipline that is already happening. Even though we have this harsh discipline at CHS it doesn't work because the crime still builds inside the school. Crime gives verse to crime in this school. I wouldn't necessarily say that security encourages it but they don't do anything to prevent it or stop it from happening the next time.

Rather than investing in public education and other social measures that could work to reduce conflict and gang violence and promote the human development and security of young people, neoliberal policies have contributed to pouring resources into technological security and law enforcement measures that while they may provide a veneer of safety within the very real threat of violence in and around poverty stricken urban schools, do little to address the root causes and insecurities driving conflict and violence. In other words, these practices do little to provide youth with the material or emotional support or sense of purpose, belonging, and hope necessary to break the cycle of gangs, oppression, and social fragmentation permeating their lives. This means that the school suspends, expels, and arrests youth for what are often nonthreatening and minor forms of conflict and misbehavior as opposed to instituting restorative justice, remediation programs, and social services. Not only does this fail to create a culture of healthy conflict resolution and pedagogies of peace, but it also fails to promote collective responsibility as it denies students a voice and ownership in school-based issues, contributing to student disengagement and alienation. As a result, the roots of conflict and violence go unattended, while the monitoring, containment, and punishment of students become a central overriding objective of school governance. This tends to overshadow the sincere efforts of educators and others at CHS to teach, to heal, and to promote social development. With this being said, despite the near-penal atmosphere at the school, there remains an intensive desire for change and transformation among students and faculty. The next chapter grapples with how educators and young people struggle with tensions between oppressive forms of authority and possibilities for reform.

Searching for Human Security and Citizenship

Hope is not just a question of grit or courage. It's an ontological dimension of our human condition.

—*Paulo Freire*, Pedagogy of Freedom[1]

This chapter explores tensions between various forms of social enclosure and how students, educators, and youth workers at CHS imagine their own sense of responsibility in relation to possibilities for democratic change. To begin with, I examine the experiences and perspectives of students, their criticisms of schooling, and their anxieties and hopes regarding their lives and future. Next, I discuss how teachers understand and negotiate their professional responsibility and ethical obligations to students in relation to neoliberal accountability and management. In the second half of the chapter, I profile two different models of nontraditional education at CHS. I critique the structural and pedagogical relations articulated through the Junior Reserve Officers Training Corps (JROTC) program at CHS, highlighting in particular its position as an "exceptional" form of social and civic development at the school. Lastly, I discuss how youth workers and organizations are utilizing the principles of social justice education to engage youth at CHS and throughout Chicago in order to pressure political changes within Chicago schools and broader society. Throughout, I highlight how these different social actors (students, teachers, soldiers, and activists) struggle with understandings of individual responsibility and the need for collective action in order to develop more ethical and restorative approaches to schooling and to promote more substantive and transformative forms of security and hope in the lives of youth.

Students:
Resisting Resignation and Imagining Change

Young people in the neoliberal city face a growing set of challenges in their communities, schools, and daily lives. This includes staggering economic insecurity and loss of social opportunity, an unresponsive state wedded to corporate inter-ests and far-reaching public and social disinvestment, and the rise of a puni-tive culture of criminalization and social control. These factors present distinct barriers to promoting human security, equity, and democracy in the lives of young people. Further, youth who inhabit spaces at the margins of contemporary urban geography along with their struggles, hopes, perspectives, and dreams are largely absent if not rendered completely invisible in broader public consider-ation. When they do appear in the media, youth who live in poverty, especially in racially segregated urban communities like Ellison Square and its surrounding neighborhoods, are too often painted in one dimensional terms as either danger-ous objects of fear and derision or as helpless victims in need of pity and salva-tion. In my research, I have found that youth at CHS broadly defy and reject these stereotypes. They do not see themselves as victims and they do not view themselves in need of saving. Like all young people, what they want above all is to be treated with respect and to have an opportunity to find dignity, peace, and a fulfilling life.

The young people I talked with at CHS are diverse in background and per-sonality. And, like all young people, they had complex and often contradic-tory feelings about their lives and future. Young people in Ellison Square and CHS often demonstrated significant awareness of the social conditions that confronted them. However, due to a variety of factors, many felt incapable of impacting or meaningfully transforming these conditions. This is inextricably tied to how youth relate to CHS as an institution and to how they perceive the broader role of education in their lives. In what follows, I mark out contra-dictions and tensions in how young people view life at CHS between, on the one hand, critical understandings of the forces impacting their lives, and on the other hand, the difficulty of finding openings for social advancement and change under present conditions. I focus here largely on the perspectives of two students named Olivia and Javier. By focusing mainly on Olivia and Javier I hope to offer a more personalized narrative and analysis of how youth frame their experiences at Carter.

Young people at CHS have a strong intuitive sense of how the neighborhood and the school are positioned in relation to broader socioeconomic realities. For instance, students often describe Ellison Square and CHS as a "ghetto" neighborhood and school. On the one hand, "ghetto" is used among youth as a pejorative to describe behavior among their peers that is deemed unruly, uncouth, violent, or embarrassing: *"Oh, that girl, she's so ghetto!"* "Ghetto" here has connotations of internalized negative social status. This negative social sta-tus clicks with feelings of stigma, indignity, and shame about living in Ellison Square and attending CHS. On the other hand, the term is used to materially locate the neighborhood and school as spaces of poverty, neglect, and racial segregation. In this manner, students often describe CHS as a "ghetto" school out of a sense of frustration and awareness of the conditions in which they live and learn: *"I swear, this school is so ghetto!"* This usage has a critical edge to it. It is an act of naming certain interlocking realities, injustices, and assumptions that have concrete effects on the social and cultural fabric and life and identity in the community. Olivia comments:

> When you go to this neighborhood you might see the signs in the yards that say "Bank of America failed this home and I lost it to foreclosure." Things like that affect people's mentalities. Again maybe if we were in a suburb where everything was nice and clean and it was low gang violence outside of school then maybe the inside of school would be a less violent place. But because of the fact that this place is ghetto or whatever, it's just the mentality that we bring in. I hear people say all the time, "Well, it doesn't matter. It's just Ellison Square." Well, that's just the culture of this school.

Olivia points out how larger social, political, and economic forces such as the foreclosure crisis impact the perceptions and attitudes of families and youth in the community. As intimated in Olivia's comments, there is a strong sense among young people of the inequalities and injustices that permeate the spaces they inhabit, their own identities, and their life chances and opportunities. Importantly, there is an understanding that the material and symbolic forms of violence and deprivation that they face occur in relation to other spaces of affluence such as the "suburbs" that Olivia describes here in idealistic terms as "nice and clean" spaces relatively free of gangs and violence. Such observations concerning the construction of space, inequality, and identity contain intrinsic judgments on the operation of race and the distribution of relative opportunity.

> *Alex*: When you talk about the "culture of the school" and "student mentality" what do you mean? How do you understand these connections and the broader problems we have been discussing?
>
> *Olivia*: We just accept the fact that because we are all minorities and we live in this neighborhood that we're treated second rate. There are dirty rotten books and broken desks and graffiti everywhere. It just kind of adds to that. It's like you're looking for someone to blame and you can just go up the ladder but eventually you don't know who else to blame. You can blame your principal, but your principal has someone to blame because she's got a boss, and her boss's boss has a boss. So I don't know. It's a hierarchy. You just have to climb the ladder and ask who is ultimately to blame.

Olivia here broaches questions of racial inequality and responsibility. While she recognizes clearly the inequities that mark life in Ellison Square and CHS, she does not assign blame other than suggesting that "it's a hierarchy," where everyone is apparently implicated. I found that students in general reject the trope of victimization. However, a central problem that emerged again and again in my conversations with youth is that the realities of concentrated inequality so permeate life in the neighborhood and school they become normalized and, in turn, feed a kind of everyday acceptance and resignation. As Olivia put it in her comment above, "It's just the mentality that we bring in. I hear people say all the time, 'Well, it doesn't matter. It's just Ellison Square.' Well, that's just the culture of this school."

Forms of resignation often stem from, and translate into, the internalization of dominant neoliberal narratives of individual responsibility. Such narratives tend to frame the understanding of inequities in terms of private and personal failure detached from historical and social conditions. This contributes to feelings of stigma and shame.

> *Alex*: You just said something like, "We're thought of as second rate," or something like that. Could you explain that a little bit more?
>
> *Olivia*: I don't know—it's like, we are in this place for so long eventually you just embrace everything that it is. So if you have to deal with a book that has so much graffiti on it that you can't read the words or there are ripped out pages eventually you are like, "Oh, it's alright. It's Ellison Square." You don't worry about it. That's just kind of like the mentality that everyone has. And that probably comes from home too. Like if your parents are on welfare—I don't think that public aid is something you should necessarily be ashamed of but it's something you should work to get away from. You want to be able to stand on your own two feet but you see people that love LINK [Illinois food program], because you can go to the grocery store and get free food…you don't want to work for yourself or strive to be better.

Olivia doesn't reflect on why someone might be in the position of needing food assistance, but is more concerned to affirm the value of self-determination amid what she views as the tendency among students and their families to just accept the status quo and their place within it. These comments can be read as the reproduction of antiwelfare ideologies and tropes of "personal responsibility" that have become so prevalent in mainstream discourse concerning the poor. While Olivia states that public aid is not something to be ashamed of, I found that welfare carries profound stigma in the community and there is considerable shame that comes from having to rely on government assistance. The reality is, of course, that many families in the community have very little choice but to accept food assistance in an economic milieu where jobs are scarce and the ones that are available often do not pay enough to meet basic needs.[2] As Olivia's comments suggest, this can be stigmatizing and demoralizing for youth and their families. However, I want to suggest that there is more going on here than simply the internalization of dominant narratives and victim blaming. While there is an element of this operating at CHS among youth and adults, Olivia's avowal of self-determination cannot simply be reduced to the realization of narratives regarding the supposed culpability and pathology of the poor. As I come back to this below, it has as much to do with her belief in the talents and capacities of those around her as it does with their personal flaws and failures. Like many youth I spoke with, Olivia maintains a faith in the capacity of those around her to determine their own lives despite the obstacles they face.

Talking with Olivia about these matters was particularly enlightening because she embodied and clearly articulated many of the contradictions I found at CHS among youth and also among adults. These contradictions define attitudes not only toward inequality and everyday life in Ellison Square but also toward CHS as an institution and the value of education in the lives of young people in the community. When we first spoke in the hallway outside of her seventh period class, one the first things Olivia said to me was that she really enjoys school. She appreciates her teachers and, although she is often frustrated by her peers, she voiced a strong sense of loyalty and love for them. She likes coming to CHS every day because she values learning new things and interacting and taking part in what the school has to offer. She would like to attend art school after CHS but doubts that she or her struggling mother can afford it. Realistically, she thinks that she might be able to afford training as an auto mechanic and make a good living this way. While Olivia expresses strong affection for CHS, like other students and staff, she also expresses deep frustration with how the institution is organized.

> It's very reminiscent of a prison. Even though I've never been in prison but it is reminiscent. Like, "Why are we treated like this?" I haven't done anything bad but I kind of have to pay by having to be searched by the metal detectors or having to be caught in a hall sweep. It does make you feel—if you treat me like a dog I might want to react like a dog. It does explain why some of the students act the way they do. Like I said, it's bad energy that you're giving, and I'm gonna give it right back. That's just how people are. But the thing is you kind of learn to just take what you're given. We don't think about these things. When you're walking down the hallway it just kind of blends in to your everyday—it's like your mentality. You're like, "just take it" because it's where you are from and a lot of times you think it's just not gonna get any better. I mean, if you strive for better, you'll get better but a lot of people are like, "Well, if you can maintain then you can do it." This is not necessarily what I want for the rest of my life. I don't want to have to deal with just watching people fall. I don't think anyone should want that.

Contemporary educational policy and neoliberal reform discourse tends to frame equity and opportunity through the logic of market efficiencies, accountability, and testing. The stated goal is make sure that all children are learning what they need to make it to college. As I have discussed in the previous chapters, these goals are tied to a misguided policy web that subverts its own stated aims by marginalizing public schools like CHS via privatization and disinvestment while narrowing curriculum and deprofessionalizing teachers. This places limits on the intellectual development of youth and degrades connections between knowledge and learning, and cultural and everyday experience. Moreover, as Olivia describes above, this policy web has also been responsible for the punitive transformation of educational environment that creates spaces and cultures of insecurity and criminalization. Amid these conditions, youth at CHS articulate a variety of complex views regarding the role of education in their lives. Many, like Olivia, have conflicted feelings. They appreciate many aspects of school while they are profoundly critical of the punitive governmental structure. Many youth reject the culture of CHS outright. For instance, as with the description that Olivia voices above, the institutionalized prison aesthetics along with the dominant standardized test-based curriculum leave much to be desired in terms of inspiring youth to realize and fulfill their human potential. As a result of a complex mix of factors, many students simply do not view high school graduation and college as representing a pathway for a viable and secure future. They may not have role models who have been successful in the high school to college and career track, or they may know someone who graduated high school, and even invested in postsecondary schooling, only to remain unemployed and/or under-employed while being saddled with often crippling levels of student debt. Many young people recognize quite clearly the value of education within a world of constricting labor markets, but struggle to succeed amid multiple external bar-riers and limited choices. I broached some of these issues with Javier, a Latino junior at CHS.

> *Alex*: How do students view schooling and education at CHS?
>
> *Javier*: All of us know the value of education. All of us know that it's supposed to get us somewhere and that someday in life all of us know that we're going to need it for the future. The thing is, like I said, a lot of students don't really believe it. For a lot of us, we don't like school so they are not going to do it. They're going to care more about staying off the streets and doing whatever they can to survive.
>
> *Alex*: So even though students know the value of education many just don't care about school?
>
> *Javier*: They see how it is around here. How it is everywhere. We don't have as much chances as everybody else. Us blacks and Hispanics, we don't get as much as white people and all that. We can do it if we set our minds to it, but once we stop thinking something, we just stop caring. Like me, I used to be an A/B student. I stopped liking school, I stopped doing my work, I stopped going to class. I mean like Mr. B, he knows I'm smart and he knows that I can do it but the thing is…
>
> *Alex*: Why did you stop caring?
>
> *Javier*: A lot of stuff that goes around. I had some stuff going on at home. Everything just went crazy. I guess that's what it is with everybody. We all adapt to it differ-ently. The way I saw it was, I'm not gonna get a chance. The least I can do is help my siblings get a chance to do something. I mean, the way I see it, the only way I can get out of here is if I do my work and I pull up my grades, but how hard it is to pick up your pace after how I started, and the only way out of it is if I get some kind of athletic scholarship or something. Because basically, the only way we're gonna get out of here—I mean, education is only for people who haven't screwed up already. Everything else is down to athletic, entertainment and all those sorts of things like that.

Javier believes that education is a primary avenue for achieving economic security and legitimate social status. This certainly challenges assumptions that minority youth are failing because they do not understand the importance of education. However, Javier is not at all blind to the fact that opportunities are not evenly dis-tributed and that the odds are stacked against him. Javier said that he fell behind in school mostly due to issues at home. His mom has struggled financially and he has had a difficult time dealing with the stress. There were moments when food was scarce and bills piled up. He had a hard time concentrating on his school work and eventually he stopped caring about school altogether. After falling behind in his grades he now focuses his attention on his two younger brothers, helping them to stay focused on school and stay out of trouble. Javier has placed much of his hope now in making sure they succeed while placing hope for his own future in acquiring a football scholarship so he can attend college.

> *Alex*: Is part of the problem with school related to how you feel about your classes?
>
> *Javier*: Sometimes when they are reading or lecturing us, some of us get put to sleep. All we hear is them talking and we have to listen. Like, if they find activities that we can do that are—like group projects that we can do in the classroom. That's when I see that most kids actually do work. Because when it's mostly individual work, some do it and some don't. They do it when they want, some even copy. It's not really good. If we don't like it, we're not going to do it. I mean, I know they gotta keep up with their lesson plan and what the city wants them to do and what the city don't get is that if we don't like it we're not going to do it.
>
> *Alex*: So you think quite a few students just give up?
>
> *Javier*: That's what I did. I mean, I know it's not too late but I think it is. I have a 1.8 GPA. Out of high school all I can see myself is working and helping my brothers get to university so they can have a future.
>
> *Alex*: What kind of a job do you think you'll be able to get when you get out of here?
>
> *Javier*: I don't really know. If anything, I can try applying around. But mostly I can see myself working at a fast-food place or landscaping, shoveling snow and all of that.
>
> *Alex*: Have you thought about dropping out?
>
> *Javier*: I've thought about it. But something's always stopped me. I see how it is outside when you don't even get your high school diploma. My cousin didn't get it and now he's stuck working the graveyard shift for twelve hours, then he goes home and he's tired and he has nothing to do. I see that and the same motivation that I want to give my Mom the pleasure of seeing me walk across the stage—those two things combine together and that's why I am still in school today.
>
> *Alex*: Why have some of your friends dropped out?
>
> *Javier*: They didn't like school. They saw no point in it; they were failing. They gave up. A couple of them got involved in some stuff, a couple of them got arrested. A couple of my cousins dropped out and started working day-to-day jobs, not going anywhere. It's not like it's gonna be easy finding a good paying job—if you drop out, chances are of getting that are really slim. It's hard to know what to expect. I mean, things happen here. I think it's on the kids, if they want to drop out that's what they're gonna do. If they want to fight and they want to stay on the streets fighting and getting involved in gangs and all that, they're gonna do it. It's basically on us.

Javier finds the curriculum to be generally less than engaging, framing it in the terms of what Paulo Freire (2003) referred to as "banking education"—the dull transmission of information from teacher to student—*"all we hear is them talking and we have to listen."* He also understands that the creativity of teachers is limited by *"what the city wants them to do."* He suggests that perhaps project-based and problem-posing learning might be a more effective and engaging approach than the transmission-oriented standardized test pedagogies currently in place. Javier also recognizes that his future options are extremely limited despite the fact that he doesn't intend to drop out and would like to go to college. However, ultimately Javier appeals to individual responsibility and self-blame—"*It's basically on us.*" He doesn't see any real possibility for collective social change in the conditions that confront him. In the following comments, Olivia connects the resignation expressed by Javier to the failure of the school to provide the basis of student engagement and to foster an environment where they might discover and learn the tools to transform the conditions of their own lives and secure a different future.

> Like, most students see the fact that things aren't that great but they don't really connect the dots that there's a reason, that there's a cause and effect for everything. They just kind of take it as it is and go with it. I don't know, it's just—I guess I'm realizing it as I speak about it. We just don't do anything. And there is probably things we could do but then again we all are degraded sometimes. Like what I said about the prison aspect. You do have a voice and I think people know they have a voice but they don't use it and when they do use it they use it in a negative manner so it doesn't really do anything for them. Like, a lot of kids are probably really opinionated. They are opinionated because I see it all the time. But they're just opinionated about the wrong things I guess, in my definition anyway. I just feel like there is a lot of energy that can go into better stuff that we just don't—we just aren't given the basis to care. We're not even given the option. Because you can be given the key to a door, it's your choice to open it or not. But I think that we aren't given the key at all. Even though we have the ability to. I don't know, it's strange. We're just kind of lost.

We see in Olivia's comments that students want to assume responsibility for their own actions and their future. However, as Olivia articulates, they are denied the basic support necessary to make doing so a reality. Part of this denial is the fact that the feelings and perspectives of young people are simply not taken into substantive consideration in school governance, curriculum, and school organization. Students, for the most part, have very little recourse to affect change in their schools, and often this denial of student experience and agency, along with the emphasis on control and passivity in the curricula, translates into the kind of resignation that Javier and Olivia describe. This production of resignation can be thought of in terms of what Michelle Fine (1991) has referred to as "silencing" where disinvested urban public schools both overtly and tacitly undermine and fail to support and nurture the capacities, voices, hopes, and talents of young people due to unresponsive organizational structures, curricula, and policies. This "silencing" often translates into the channeling of what could be positive critical and transformative energies into ultimately destructive processes such as pushing students out of school altogether. For Olivia, and for other young people I spoke with, it appears that the impersonal and punitive culture of the school largely fails to provide either the substantive or the inspirational basis from which they can develop their full human, creative, and academic talents and their capacities as future adults and citizens. Many simply end up assuming a cynical distance to the dominant narrative that tells them that hard work in school will translate into a better life and successful future. For many, this narrative simply does not cohere with their experience.

> *Olivia*: I feel like CHS has so much potential because there are so many kids in here who can do really amazing things but maybe they aren't just facilitated in what it is they want to do or maybe they have bad direction. You know, maybe they have a great talent but aren't using it in a way that is beneficial to them or anyone around them. For the most part, if we were given the right something, the right one thing—I don't want to say it's money because I don't want to give that much power to money. But like, if we were given some money and it actually made things nice here it might put a better mentality on the kids and we would see the results. But I don't know if that's what would really happen, if the result would be a better school.

The work of establishing a more thriving, socially just, and attentive educative culture would necessarily involve multiple elements. One of those elements would be the need to rethink how public schools like CHS can tap into and harness the talents and creative energies that Olivia recognizes in herself and in her peers. As articulated by Olivia and Javier, students want to assume responsibility for their own lives. However, they generally do not view their school in terms of how it is currently organized as a reliable partner either in the affirmation of their humanity—*"we are all degraded sometimes"*—or in facilitating their educational engagement and potential. As a result, students are caught within a set of opposing tendencies and forces that delimit the conditions of possibility and capacity for social agency within the neoliberal school. As Olivia articulates above, there is a wealth of creativity, talent, and desire for direction and change among youth themselves. However, while Olivia and other youth demonstrate a degree of critical awareness of the sociopolitical forces that shape their lives and a desire for transformation, this critical energy is often left underdeveloped, lost, or subverted.

Teachers:
Struggling for Professional Autonomy

Like students at CHS, teachers are also caught within systems of enclosure and the search for meaningful engagement and change. It has been well-established that neoliberal policies have had a significant impact on teachers, extending to how teachers are understood and understand themselves as professionals and the vital work that they perform (Ball, 1993; Ingersoll, 2003; Luke, 2004). While there has been a historical tension between teachers' professional status and efforts to control their work, neoliberal governance attempts to refashion this struggle in specific ways. Under the social democratic paradigm of the 1960s and 1970s, institutional norms and policy objectives were rooted (at least formally) in norms of social accountability and professional ethics. Here, teachers were understood to be largely self-regulating actors within a system of professional knowledge and public responsibility. In contrast, under market governance, top-down centralized systems of management have sought to rationalize what teachers do within new schemas of performativity and accountability. Teachers are still required to regulate themselves under the ubiquitous mantra of "personal responsibility" but this self-regulation is rerouted through economic rationalities and enhanced external systems of discipline such as tying teacher pay to "value-added" performance and the proliferation of administrative tasks and performance targets and evaluations. Bronwyn Davies (2003) suggests that this means that "the locus of power is removed from the knowledge of practicing professionals to auditors, policy-makers, and statisticians, none of whom need know anything about the profession in question" (p. 91). This represents an attempt to make teachers accountable within a system ruled by "an almost subliminal anxiety and fear of surveillance rather than a sense of personal value within the social fabric" (p. 93).

This can be viewed as the turn to more explicit control of teacher labor via market rationalities or what Stephen Ball (1993) has referred to as the "overdetermined and over regulated situation of schoolteachers' work" (p. 106). The current proletarianization of teaching has included the intensification of teaching work through the growth of class sizes, top-down accountability mandates, and pressure to meet market driven norms of entrepreneurialism and service delivery of commercialized test-oriented curricula. It has also included shifting more of the burden for educational responsibility and achievement from society to teachers while simultaneously eroding their input in decisions regarding curriculum content and pedagogy. In this schema, measurement is everything. Those aspects of teaching and curriculum that cannot be measured and tested are devalued, if not eliminated, from the instructional clock altogether. Performance becomes less about content and achievement and more about simply making the numbers. This has coincided with attacks on the teaching profession in recent years. Allan Luke (2004) notes:

> The common discourse strategy of the political right is a shunting of responsibility for changes in youth culture, community demographics, and employment, and, indeed, moral stance to schooling as cause and concomitant of such changes. Teachers and teaching get blamed for everything from deteriorating physical plants and eroded funding of schools, changing family structure and community social relations, youth unemployment, to changes in identity and dominant technologies for intellectual formation and cultural expression. (p. 1424)

Blaming teachers and controlling their work has significant benefits for educational and political leaders. It presents a ready scapegoat for social and educational problems of all stripes and has also proven useful in undermining teachers' unions and building resentment against public sector work in general. Moreover, emphasis on accountability and testing presents a cheap and cost effective alternative to investing in proven measures such as lowering class sizes, providing equitable resources and support services, and promoting well-rounded and culturally relevant curriculum at schools like CHS.

In chapter 3, I outlined how the neoliberal management of curriculum at CHS has reflected many of these trends. It has been defined largely through efforts to control what and how teachers teach, particularly in the integration of commercialized and standardized test-based curricula. This has impacted the way teachers at CHS approach their work and, in turn, has significant impact on institutional and social life including how students relate to learning and the educational process. Mr. Wilson here reflects on how systems of control have served to limit creative teaching and how they inhibit student engagement:

> We drill these objectives and these units and stuff like that and it makes them [students] more institutionalized. In the sense that you need to do this and hit this number and if you don't then you need to come back and do it again. Would I rather teach math in a more investigative way like, "What's going on in the community." Like, "What are some social issues that we could look at and use math to analyze and even solve these problems?" I think that would be a better way of going about it. It would allow students to perhaps better comprehend the issues that are affecting them and teach them to express themselves about things that matter in their lives. Like our arts program is hugely popular with the students and I think they love it so much because they are actually allowed to express themselves, whereas in most of our other subjects that are so strict with testing schedules and things like that there is no expression. There's no imagination. There's nothing. It's a very rudimentary sort of education and so I think some shifts of emphasis within the curriculum would be greatly beneficial. I know that for instance the creative writing classes are very popular. And so when I see like creative writing and art and these other subject areas that kids absolutely love to go to and when you see them in class and they are so involved and attentive, even calm in a sense. Even those students who are often crazy in the hallways are often model students in those classes, so if we could somehow model our curriculum on those kinds of experiences for students and to allow the students more freedom I think it would make a huge difference.

Mr. Wilson's comments echo much of what I heard and observed in this study regarding the controls that are placed on teachers and the way that this impinges on their capacity to reach and engage students. Along with numerous other issues such as expanding class sizes and resource scarcity, the rigid rationalization of teachers' time and work functions as a barrier to promoting enriching learning opportunities. It is also indicative of the disempowerment of teachers and the frustrations that accompany it:

> *Mr. Wilson*: It's not about pushing teachers to expand their ideas of what teaching can be or what a classroom can look like. These are just not conversations I have ever had with the administration. It's always just, "Did you do these five things," and that's it. And this is what it's like throughout the CPS—just knowing teachers at other schools, it's the same throughout the system. I mean we receive very little respect or support. I had a student last year pass the AP calculus exam which is huge at a school like this and all I was told was that next year I need to have at least two to pass because I have to always improve my pass rate. If I don't I was told they would cut my class. So they didn't show any curiosity about how I was able to get a

student to pass. Or maybe, "Hey, great job." All they said was our AP numbers are low this year so we need to have more students pass next year. Because they said if our percentage doesn't go up (and percentage is such a terrible metric for judging this, I can't even believe they use it, but it's what they use from downtown) then my Calc class will be cut. So I have a success that could actually be used to terminate the entire class. So our knowledge is not respected and we have very little voice.

Research suggests that when teachers feel they are valued, their knowledge is respected, and their work as professionals is acknowledged in a supportive learning community, then academic instruction improves, expectations are raised, and students are more likely to feel that faculty care and support their well-being (Fine, 1991; McNeil, 2000). In short, it furthers community, learning, and security. Conversely, disempowered teachers are more likely to go through the motions, punch a clock, and experience burnout. Linda McNeil (2000) has referred to this as the "contradictions of control" where efforts to manage teachers and rationalize their work through authoritarian bureaucratic structures serves to undermine the depth and quality of education. She argues that this can lead to "defensive teaching," characterized by a shift in the focus of teachers' energy toward meeting minimal institutional requirements at the expense of engaged teaching (2003, pp. 11–12).

> They [students and teachers] fall into a ritual of teaching and learning that tends toward minimal standards and minimal effort. This sets off a vicious cycle. As students disengage from enthusiastic involvement in the learning process, administrators often see the disengagement as a control problem. They then increase their attention to managing students and teachers rather than supporting their instructional purpose. (p. 11)

The erosion of teaching and learning is not the only consequence of excessive efforts to control curriculum and manage teachers' work. It also contributes to strains on the foundation of all successful school communities—teacher-student relationships. Rigid and impersonal structures in urban schools tend to coincide with overworked teachers, scarce resources, larger class sizes, overcrowding, and institutional structures seemingly more invested in control of teachers and students than in creating uplift and community. Darling-Hammond (2010) notes:

> when teachers have little opportunity to come to know their students well, and students have little opportunity to relate to any adult in the school on an extended, personal level, it should not be surprising that factory model high schools create virtual chasms into which students can fall. (p. 64)

Ms. Gibbs, a special education teacher, expressed to me that, "they have us doing a whole lot of paper work about nothing, I feel like I don't have time to follow-up with a lot of my students. And our students have more problems than students at some suburban school...we all just do the best we can." Large class sizes and increased demands of teachers' time for administrative tasks presents a challenge to building substantive and supportive relationships. Teachers are thus torn between fulfilling what they perceive as their ethical obligations to their students and pressing administrative responsibilities to standardized mandates and commercial programming. As a result, many classes I observed at CHS could be classified as lifeless, transmission-oriented affairs, with teachers engaged in "defensive teaching." However, I also observed teachers routinely going far beyond the accountability and testing regime by organizing dynamic learning including student discussions, projects, and making essential connections between curriculum and students' life experiences. The formal curriculum is generally indifferent to such efforts, placing value largely on meeting measurable outcomes as opposed to the ethical content of teaching. Moreover, teachers face intensive and extensive forms of surveillance, where deviation from the script can translate into shaming and disciplinary sanction. Despite this, and due to their own sense of professional responsibility, teachers nonetheless work to create spaces for creative engagement within and beyond the official curriculum. Mr. Parks, for instance, graciously invited me into his English classes for group discussions with students on issues related to security and insecurity in their lives. This coincided with creative writing assignments where students reflected on the roots of conflict and the way these problems are currently managed by the school. Mr. Parks comments that many of his students are not used to such exploratory engagements as they have been acculturated at a young age into a regime of imaginative enclosure.

> My teaching style is very frustrating to the good students because they have been programmed and brainwashed by teachers over the years to get a cue of what I'm looking for and they'll give it to me: "Just tell me what you want." And the frustration of, "We don't have good students." My problem is no, I've got way too many good students but it's killed their imagination, creativity and their ability to be learners.

Struggles for meaningful and creative teaching also underscore how teachers in the building have attempted to carve out alternative spaces in the school beyond the official curriculum to address issues of immediate concern to students and to foster supportive relationships. This includes partnership programs such as Building with Books, Helping Hands Chicago, VOYCE, and various after-school clubs oriented to enhancing student engagement and literacy and for providing safe and alternative spaces for dialogue. For instance, in response to the violent death of one of her students in 2006, Ms. Lorrie started a student club called Peace Café as a safe space for students to discuss and reflect on issues of violence in their lives.

> *Ms. Lorrie*: We needed to have some place where we don't just have to keep going with the lesson. Some place where it's okay to just be and actually talk about it. That said, I know nothing about counseling or crisis intervention or anything, I just agreed that there needed to be a space to talk about violence in the community. Another teacher, one of the main founders of the group, also felt similarly. She is an art teacher so I feel like she at least, even if she doesn't have any formal training in that area, has a medium for getting feelings out on paper or by other means. And

then we had another gentleman who—I don't know if he has any formal training but he is just really good at that. He's a very spiritual person. So we and a couple of other teachers came together and nobody had any—it wasn't founded as a crisis intervention or anything like that but it kind of worked because it gave the kids options, whether it was through art or just talking about violence.

Despite her involvement in creating this space for educators and students to come together and reflect as a community in a safe and supportive setting, Ms. Lorrie, like other teachers I spoke with, does not feel like enough is being done to engage and serve youth in the school or to support teachers who are attempting to do so. While teachers often go beyond the official curriculum in order to address their students' varied social and emotional needs, due to the often overwhelming challenges of performing their formal duties, they may simply not have the time, energy, and resources needed to provide the kind of focused attention that students require. In sum, I found that teachers were placed in a position where they had to struggle between fulfilling what they believed were their professional and ethical obligations to students in ways not addressed in the official curriculum, and fulfilling their working obligations to the systems of accountability and control defining the official curriculum. This highlights two very different forms of accountability. On the one hand, an ethically driven form based on a sense of professional responsibility to young people, and on the other, an externally imposed form of responsibility rooted in threat of disciplinary sanction. One form of responsibility based in a moral and ethical register, the other in instrumental rationality and enclosure. Amid overbearing administrative demands and the realities of large class sizes and minimal external support for students, such as social-emotional services and counseling, teachers are placed in an exceedingly difficult position. In order for teachers to meet their professional obligations they are forced to individually carve out spaces within and outside an official curriculum that often operates to limit these aims. This contrasts sharply with having a curriculum responsive to the knowledge and judgment of teachers as a community of professionals. The development of such a curriculum and community of professional practice could not be more necessary and urgent.

Soldiers:
Exceptional Citizenship and the Desire for Service

"Class attention! Fall in line! Four squads people! Cover down!" I am in the CHS gym watching Sergeant Major Davis, head of the school's JROTC program, lead a group of rag-tag freshman "cadets" through a 20-point uniform inspection. The youth are all clad in the same light green army uniforms with shiny black patent leather shoes. Two Hispanic students, one male and the other female, are at the front of the formation. The female cadet is wearing a dark green coat with a US Army JROTC patch on the upper arm; the male cadet is wearing a light green shirt and black tie. The solid black bars patched on his shoulder signify his rank in the unit. Sergeant Major Davis explains that the boy is being trained for a "Cadet Captain" position. In his hand the boy has a folder with the slogan

"There's Strong, and Then There's Army Strong" emblazoned on its cover. I watch as the two budding commanders proceed to check each student in the formation for proper posture, stance, and uniform before engaging in a string of 16 separate drill commands that the youth perform in unison: "Ready, open rank, march!"

The JROTC was created in 1916 by Congress as a readiness program to inculcate martial and patriotic values and to facilitate the matriculation of young men into the US armed forces. Colin Powell is widely credited with overseeing the contemporary revitalization of JROTC. In the wake of the Los Angeles riots in 1992 when white middle class fears of urban chaos and black and brown youth reached a recent high water mark in US culture, Powell, as chairman of the joint chiefs of staff under George H. W. Bush, worked to double the size of the JROTC. Powell later wrote in his memoir, *My American Journey*, that JROTC represents a great "social bargain" where mostly "inner-city kids, many from broken homes, found stability and role models. They got a taste of discipline, the work ethic, and they experienced pride of membership in something healthier than a gang" (McDuffee, 2008). According to the JROTC, the program is not a recruitment tool. Rather, its stated mission is "to infuse in its student cadets" who are, as Powell noted, overwhelmingly urban youth from low-income and minority backgrounds, "a sense of discipline and order" through the "study of ethics, citizenship, communications, leadership, life skills and other subjects designed to prepare young men and woman to take their place in adult society" (JROTCweb).

The growth of JROTC programs can be understood as part a broader expansion of military education in Chicago and throughout the United States. Today, the Chicago Public Schools are widely considered the "most militarized in America." David Goodman (2002) notes that "Chicago is in the vanguard of a growing national movement that is responding to the problems of struggling inner-city schools by sending in the Marines and the Army, Navy, and Air Force." There are currently around 11,000 students participating in some type of military education program in Chicago. This includes those enrolled in JROTC at schools like CHS as well as students currently attending one of the city's 12 distinct military academies. These military academies are public schools of "choice" funded by a combination of Pentagon and Department of Defense money along with local tax revenue. Andy Kroll (2009) reports:

> Chicago has six military high schools run by a branch of the armed services. Six smaller military academies share buildings with existing high schools. Nearly three dozen JROTC programs exist in regular high schools, where students attend a daily JROTC class...and at the middle school level, there is a new JROTC program for sixth, seventh- and eighth-graders...[this] "Middle School Cadet Corps" program brings the JROTC's lockstep, uniformed culture to students as young as 11 or 12. Five hundred middle school students from more than 20 schools enrolled in the Cadet Corps in the 2008–2009 school year.

Military education in Chicago needs to be understood in the context of the broader military incursion into schools since September 11 and the War on

Terror. Falling explicitly under the Pentagon's $20 billion yearly recruitment budget, funding for military programming in schools rose from $76 million in 1992 to $210 million by 2002 (Schaeffer-Duffy, 2003). This has been directed, among other things, to creating military academies, the Troops to Teachers program, the training of former military officers as school leaders and superintendents, and the vast multiplication of JROTC programs across US school districts, particularly in urban areas (Saltman & Gabbard, 2010). For example, in 2009 the National Defense Authorization Act provided an additional $170 million explicitly to expand JROTC in schools nationwide with a goal of 3,700 programs by 2020 (Kroll, 2009). This expansion of military education has occurred primarily in struggling urban communities and traditionally underfunded and neglected public schools in cities like Chicago, Oakland, Los Angeles, Philadelphia, and New Orleans. This turn to military education in impoverished urban schools can be seen as a powerful symbolic and institutional infusion of military influence in education while framing the civic and social development of young people through prescriptive military values and service.

All incoming freshman at CHS have a choice between taking two years of traditional physical education or JROTC. However, in 2010, the school had to lay off two physical education teachers due to the austerity measures and budget cuts. As a result, the JROTC program swelled, turning what would be a choice into something more like conscription for many youth. The JROTC program at CHS is facilitated by two former army officers who I refer to as Sergeant Majors Davis and Lee. Like other JROTC instructors, they received their leadership training at the US military recruitment center at Fort Knox, Kentucky. Like all JROTC instructors, Sergeant Majors Davis and Lee receive half of their pay from the army and the other half from the school district. The US army directly provides educational resources and technology to the cash-strapped schools that adopt the program. This makes the JROTC classroom the best resourced classroom at CHS, complete with new state of the art Apple products and new textbooks and supplies. Davis and Lee oversee the JROTC curriculum at CHS which includes military formations, inspections, and drills along with classroom instruction in US military history and organization, military terminology and values, and the application of military principles to physical, moral, civic, and character development. JROTC students at CHS also participate in JROTC related service and events such as attending JROTC sponsored outdoor excursions where they receive leadership training and participate in activities such as orienteering and war game simulations.

After cadet formation and inspection in the gymnasium, Sergeant Major Davis and the cadets transition into an adjacent classroom. The room is plastered over with army iconography. There are multiple flags representing different branches of the armed forces and posters adorn the walls with recruitment slogans such as "Army of One." In one corner of the room there is a life-size cardboard cutout of a noble looking "storm-trooper" with weapon ready in full battle dress and desert camouflage, presumably of the type worn in Iraq and Afghanistan. The bulletin boards feature various JROTC codes, slogans, and procedures set against dark green army camouflage backdrops. Sergeant Major Davis calls the class to attention, "Class, on your feet, face the colors!" With hands over chests the students proceed to face the US flag and recite the JROTC creed:

> I am an Army Junior ROTC Cadet.
> I will always conduct myself to bring credit to my family, country, school and the Corps of Cadets.
> I am loyal and patriotic.
> I am the future of the United States of America.
> I do not lie, cheat or steal and will always be accountable for my actions and deeds.
> I will always practice good citizenship and patriotism.
> I will work hard to improve my mind and strengthen my body.
> I will seek the mantle of leadership and stand prepared to uphold the Constitution and the American way of life.
> May God grant me the strength to always live by this creed.

Next, Sergeant Major Davis asks the cadets to open their textbook *Citizenship in Action and Leadership*. They are going to review vocabulary terms for a section titled "The History of Drills." On his Department of Defense issued Mac laptop, Sergeant Major Davis brings up a colorful computer-generated version of hangman on the class smart board. The cadets are clearly familiar with the game. On the screen appear blank dashes above which hovers a hangman post. The students take turns guessing letters. After a few guesses, a young Latina cadet correctly identifies the word "discipline" after which the definition appears on the screen: *"Discipline: Orderly, obedient, or restrained conduct."* This is followed by several other words including "drill" and "precision." The remainder of the class is spent learning the proper military procedure for folding and carrying the American flag.

Sergeant Major Davis has been serving in the Army for over 25 years and has been working in Chicago schools for over a decade. Before joining JROTC, he served as a military recruiter and as a procurement officer for the Pentagon ("You've probably heard of the $10,000 toilet seat? That was me. That's what I did, I was a middle man between the Pentagon and defense contractors"). Sergeant Major Davis is a welcoming, congenial and talkative fellow who I believe sincerely loves his students and views his job largely in terms of community service and citizenship development.

> *Alex*: What would you say the goals are for JROTC?
> *Sergeant MajorDavis*: Our motto is to motivate young people to be better citizens so we try to establish a dual program. Not only do we have an academic curriculum but we also have a very competitive curriculum, which teaches them to be leaders and not just follow the group. So we're constantly putting them in situations where they have to stand up before the class and they might have to review a subject or give an impromptu speech or take control of a small unit of six or seven cadets, like you saw yesterday folding the flag.

Supporters argue that JROTC has little, if anything, to do with recruitment. For example, current secretary of Education, Arne Duncan, has argued that military education is about providing "options" and consumer "choice" to families along with the promotion of discipline in the lives of disadvantaged youth (something they are imagined as lacking in sufficient quantity). He has said: "I love the sense of leadership. I love the sense of discipline." I heard similar sentiments from students in the program at CHS. Rose, a freshman African American female cadet explains:

> I like that it gives you discipline and self-control. It's like, you have to act and remain a certain way, you have to represent them well.

Kristina suggests that part of the appeal of JROTC is that there aren't many other activities available for students.

> It's really a great opportunity. Here they promise you except it's not there. I'm asking a million people, "Where's acting class? Where's music class?" and they're like, "Oh, we don't have it right now." And if no one develops it you have no luck whatsoever. That's why I'm not really in any activities besides JROTC. It's just a class but with military basics. It's not like, if someone's goofing off they give them a hundred push-ups. That doesn't happen. I was expecting a little bit of that though.

Many parents have also expressed support for military education and each year applicants for the military academies far exceed the number of slots available (McDuffee, 2008). Critics of the program have argued, however, that JROTC is a blatant recruitment strategy that has no place in public schools. Sergeant Major Davis is insistent that the JROTC program at CHS is not a recruitment strategy. Although as a former army recruiter this does not mean that Sergeant Major Davis is against recruitment *per se*.

> *Sergeant MajorDavis*: Not everybody is gonna go to college and everybody that goes to college doesn't graduate. I made a living off of that, I was a recruiter and my market was college dropouts. They are smart enough to pass the test to get into the military and they don't want to tell Mom and Dad that they dropped out of college.
>
> *Alex*: So they go home with, "I've made the decision to join the army" as opposed to, "I've dropped out of college." How would you identify those kids? Did you work on a college campus?
>
> *Sergeant MajorDavis*: Yes. I was the commander for the city of Pittsburgh recruiting and the people before me were not successful and so when I looked at the demographics I found that there was a huge population of high school grads who only had one or two years of college and were just lingering around at home. And so I redirected our efforts into that market and I was very successful but it was because these guys go to Jr. college and they might at best get a job as a manager of a restaurant chain or something like that and they were kind of happy, but kind of disenchanted, too, at the same time, and so I worked on them and redirected their efforts. I got out of the high school and into the college market, the grad market and it really worked well.

Sergeant Major Davis claims that very few youth join the military directly from CHS. Similarly, the Department of Defense has estimated that around 10 percent of JROTC students enlist directly from high school. However, these numbers are highly misleading because they are based on surveys given to students long before they graduate. If the student has not enlisted at the time of the survey they are not considered to have enlisted. Official statistics kept by the Department of Defense indicate that between 45–55 percent of JROTC students later in enlist in the military—a far higher percentage than the general population. In Chicago the figures are estimated at 40–50 percent (thus almost half of JROTC cadets end up joining the military at some point after high school) (Goodman 2002, McDufee, 2008). It is well known that the US military has faced a recruitment crisis in the wake of 9/11 and has had to continually lower its own enlistment criteria in order to meet quotas—for instance, providing a path to citizenship for undocumented immigrant youth and adults if they join the military and allowing moral waivers to ex-felons so that they can join as well. Militarized education is inextricably tied to post-9/11 strategies of military recruitment in schools such as making federal education funding contingent upon allowing the military access to student information and allowing recruiters access to campuses through the No Child Left Behind Act. This coincides with military marketing promotions like the "Army Strong" and "Army of One" campaigns, military sponsored home and internet video games, and a more robust online presence with pro-army music videos and other interactive media meant to capture the imagination of young people and their desire for belonging, adventure, and educational and economic opportunity. The expansion of military education and JROTC in schools can hardly be viewed separately from these trends. As former secretary of Defense William Cohen stated to the House Armed Services Committee in February 2000, JROTC is "one of the best recruiting devices that we could have" (Shaefer-Duffy, 2003).

While the ethical implications of recruitment on campus are an important element in this story, I think that what is at stake here are deeper and more important questions regarding the pedagogical and structural relations embedded within and communicated through the expansion of military education. The majority of those who join the military out of JROTC programs are low-income urbanized African American and Hispanic youth from schools like CHS (Robbins, 2009). Marvin Berlowitz and Nathan Long (2010) state:

> Defense Department guidelines for JROTC specifically seek "the less affluent large urban school" and populations who are "at-risk." These children are trapped by a form of economic conscription referred to as the "push-pull phenomenon," in which they are pushed by poverty and the economics of racism and pulled by the promise of military benefits. (p. 185)

Military programs like JROTC tie acquisition of economic security and citizenship to military values and participation (Cowen & Siciliano, 2011b). Here, prescriptive military discipline is positioned as an exceptional form of civic development for "at-risk" and "troubled" young people. Participation in military learning and soldiering becomes a key "legitimate" avenue for racially marginalized students with few other options to acquire economic and educational opportunity along with the status accorded to full citizens. My position here should not be misinterpreted as a rejection of the need to provide young people with avenues for developing self-discipline and economic and civic participation. Rather, my intent is to raise fundamental questions about the underlying system of value and assumptions which animate military programs. Lost is any recognition of the violent and destructive realities of war, such as the human suffering and terror inflicted by American imperialism either historically or in the disastrous wars in Iraq, Afghanistan, and beyond. Lost too is recognition of the tragic realities facing veterans—many disabled, wounded, and/or suffering deep psychological trauma—as they are forced to wage shameful bureaucratic struggles in order to make good on the educational and medical benefits promised them. Most importantly perhaps, military learning favors prescriptive forms of knowledge over expansive and critical forms of learning and intellectual inquiry. Underlying this is an emphasis on the value of obedience over the intrinsic values of autonomy, questioning, and dissent within a democratic society. In this light, military education can be seen largely as another symptom of neoliberal enclosure rather than an opening of new horizons and possibilities for young people. Such questions about underlying values are necessary if we are to develop systems of student engagement and citizenship beyond encroaching militarization and the narrowing of security for young people. As articulated alongside other forms of neoliberal enclosure and violence, militarization in all its forms represents a threat to developing sustainable economic opportunity and cultures of collaboration and justice in cities, schools, and communities.

There is something more going on under the surface of military education that is crucial to note, however. Expansion of military schooling positions itself as a legitimate "way out" for disadvantaged kids, and its popularity with many students and parents speaks of something deeper about the desires of young people and their families that should not be ignored. In contrast to ideological tropes that position poor black and Latino youth as lacking the sufficient drive and desire for participation and achievement, the apparent popularity of military programs in schools speaks of a profound hunger for opportunity, belonging, and service. It is precisely this desire for participation and community that military education presupposes and seeks to capitalize on. For those like myself who oppose all forms of militarization and therefore do not support military education in public schools, we must recognize that the attraction to these programs is a symptom of a fragmented society and that military education promises a sense of belonging and community amid the broader erosion of the commonweal under neoliberalism. In an atomized culture where notions of the social good are increasingly privatized, military education becomes an exceptional site of civic development for young people, offering the promise of otherwise unavailable benefits, belonging, and security in exchange for service (Cowen & Siciliano, 2011b).[3] Any effort to critically rethink educational policy and practice has to take these forces and desires for participation and belonging seriously. We need to consider how educational environments and practices can work to promote and nurture holistic and vibrant senses and formations of community, service, and security in social democratic rather than militaristic terms. As I detail in the following section, there are already numerous community organizations and social collaborations throughout Chicago working toward these important goals.

Activists:
Learning as Liberation

On a cold and rainy evening in early November 2010, I attended a meeting at the Chicago Freedom School, an autonomous nonprofit organization dedicated to youth development and movement building. This particular meeting involved a small group of CPS students who were working on a project to pressure CHS to change their discipline policies in line with the principles of restorative justice.[4] Two of the youth in the group were students at CHS; the others came from schools and neighborhoods throughout Chicago. Brought together by their involvement in the Freedom School and broader youth activist networks in the city, the students had chosen to focus on disciplinary issues at CHS as part of a longer term strategy to challenge the school-to-prison pipeline in the Chicago schools. They identified CHS as a site to focus their work because they felt that the school is broadly representative of the larger demographics of the Chicago schools and it has a reputation for having a punitive culture. With support from their two adult allies at the meeting, the students developed a plan of action. This included holding workshops for students at CHS in order to build awareness and inform them about their civil rights and the school-to-prison pipeline, with the goal of encouraging CHS students to join them in pressuring administration to develop a peer jury and to have the security guards and Deans trained in conflict mediation and other restorative alternatives to suspensions, expulsions, and reliance on arrests. Eventually, due to the group's efforts, and the efforts of others in the school, the administration at CHS did agree to adopt a peer jury where students are afforded the opportunity to mediate and settle certain disciplinary matters through dialogue. Broader struggles over training and substantive alternatives to suspensions, expulsions, and arrests are ongoing.

The Chicago Freedom School is one of many nonprofit youth organizations in Chicago committed to popular education and to working with youth in order to develop their potential as activists and critical citizens. These groups include Voices of Youth in Chicago Education (VOYCE), Blocks Together, Gender Just, Project NIA, Community Renewal Society, Dignity in Schools, and many more. Youth in these programs develop their sense of agency and citizenship; they take part in community building; they learn movement history; they conduct participatory action research; they plan protests and rallies; they run workshops for their peers; and they engage in social justice organizing and activism through direct action and the arts. In recent years, blossoming networks of youth organizations and activism in Chicago have been at the forefront of challenging neoliberal educational policies such as school closures, teacher layoffs, and cutbacks while organizing movements around a host of issues of importance in the lives of young people such as zero tolerance policing and criminalization, bullying, violence, LGTBQ and immigration issues, and economic, racial, and ecological justice. One of the young people involved in the Freedom School project against zero tolerance policies at CHS was a senior African American student named Chris whom I interviewed for this research.

> *Alex*: Talk to me a little about the Freedom School. What motivates you to get involved like this?
>
> *Chris*: Because at the Freedom School I see more people that are like me that actually want to see change and pursue change for the better and they challenge me in a way so that I challenge myself. So it's like I find myself being attracted to the Freedom School because they bring a lot of the things out of me that I knew they were there and they help me understand the things that are inside of me that I couldn't understand by myself.
>
> *Alex*: Do you feel like you guys have a chance to change some things at CHS?
>
> *Chris*: Of course. As much that goes on at CHS, I can always see potential for change which is why I stayed all four years and which is why I love this school so much. I want to see change and I know I can make a change in this school. Chicago Freedom School will actually help me do that. Right now we are trying to introduce restorative justice to CHS and to open up a peer jury here that gives students a chance to be heard by other students.
>
> *Alex*: Do you think that will help improve life at CHS?
>
> *Chris*: Yeah, I think it will help to an extent. But we need to do more. We need to find things that will get the attention of students. Offer more programs. Allow students to be creative. Allow students to be students rather than prisoners of CPS and that's how it is at CHS. Students feel the need that they "have to" and we need to focus more on the "we want to." Find what's attractive to the students so they can find happiness within themselves. Every student here at CHS is different. Every student has their own feelings and every student is involved in their own situations and experiences and if we find these things then we get the attention of the students. I believe CHS can be one of the best schools in Chicago but if people continue to be afraid and fear themselves the school will only go in the direction it's been going for a while now.
>
> *Alex*: What would restorative justice ultimately mean here at CHS?
>
> *Chris*: It's important to give and show love to the students that may not have it at home or that they can't find on the streets. School is a big deal for children in my generation. School is a big percentage of what's going on in a kid's life. It's school, home and the in-between school and home, the travel, the streets, you know. School, like I said, you spend six hours in school so it ultimately has a big role in deciding what a student becomes. It's very important to understand that.

Social and community organizations like the Freedom School provide a crucial space for young people to engage with issues that matter to them in a safe and supportive environment. For Chris, his involvement with the program has tapped into and nurtured his own capacities for leadership, reflection, and action. It has given him a sense of hope that things can be otherwise and that his participation and ideas matter and can make a difference. As he articulates above, his involvement in activism with the Freedom School has opened his eyes to possibilities for positively impacting life at CHS. This not to say that all of this is free of tension—Chris, and other youth workers and youth activists also described the many barriers they confront from unresponsive administrators, bureaucratic hurdles, and from police and other adult authorities invested in maintaining the status quo. This is particularly pronounced in efforts to transform school cultures and curriculum in line with the principles of progressive and social democratic education.

In the course of this research, I interviewed one of the founders of the Freedom School, Ms. Roberts, who has worked with youth at CHS and throughout the city. A prominent figure in many different progressive youth organizations and movements, Ms. Roberts was an articulate adult voice in describing the many challenges confronting youth development work and what this work means for educational struggles.

> The biggest part of my work as an adult ally is and has been for years to run interference against the adults who attempt to crush these young people on a regular basis. They do it all the time. It's not so easy when you are fifteen years old and you want to change your community. In this day and age it's very hard to figure out where the points are where you can make a difference. It's very difficult to figure out how to navigate it. It's very complicated. These young people are not provided in this culture with a lot of places where they are seen as valuable and valued, where their voices are taken seriously ever. Most of them are super oppressed, living in very difficult circumstances and their resilience is remarkable. So for me, I always think about it as, the young people I have worked with I have always wanted to find a way for them to take control of their own circumstances and their own lives. It may not look like the activism that is prepackaged, but for some young people that is a huge activist life step, to start becoming conscious of your surroundings so that you don't fall into the trap of destroying yourself while the system is already trying to destroy you. I guess I think about it as having levels of activism and organizing defined by your circumstances, which looks different for every young person. I think the young people that come to the Freedom School feel that. They feel very much like it is a family space where they can figure out their own identities. We focus a lot on that. "Who are you and what are those identities about you like your race, your class, your gender—how do those play out for you? Your sexual orientation—is this the first time you've ever met an LGBTQ young person and talked with them. What is oppression, what does it look like, how does it work?" So providing them a space and a sense of history about what came before and then providing them the support they need to create their campaigns and make those work. I feel like if we can have more spaces like that around the city and the country. That would be a helpful thing. I think that's what it's going to take.

Ms. Roberts describes the core principle of her work with the Freedom School and other youth organizations in the terms of "education for liberation." Education for liberation has its roots in a variety of traditions ranging from the Enlightenment ideals of reason and autonomy articulated by Immanuel Kant; to the progressive pedagogy of John Dewey; to the tradition of popular education within the American labor, civil rights, feminist, and black freedom movements; to critical pedagogy developed by thinkers like Paulo Freire and Henry Giroux. All of these various strands of education for liberation, while bearing distinct histories, have in common the ethical faith that all human beings have the potential to understand and transform the conditions of their own lives in the interest of promoting greater human freedom and the common good.

> *Ms. Roberts*: Education liberation doesn't mean that you don't have the basic subjects, it just means that they have to be applied and relevant and make sense. You can still teach people how to read by reading a book that is interesting. The girls at the Chicago Freedom School hated me at first because I would do everything possible—every Thursday night we would all read together because it's important in order to survive in the world. You're not going make it through school or life. Those things are critical. You have to have basic computational skills. You can do that. I will never forget this example; I worked with this one young woman when I first started Rodgers Park Young Women's Action team seven years ago. She was one of the founding members of the organization and she came up to me one day early on, we had just met each other. She said, "I'm not going to college." And she was like fifteen at the time. I was like, "Why are you announcing that to me?" She was testing me and she was like, "I'm not interested in college" and I was like, "I don't care what you're interested in, you don't need to go to college," and she said, "I'm going do hair," and I said, "that's great. I'm glad you're going do hair." I knew what it was about because she knew that I had been to college and that I had gotten my Master's degree. Her notion was already that she was going be antagonistic with me because her idea was that I was doing this group so that they would all go to college when that wasn't it at all. I was like, "You do whatever you want to do. I don't care what you do." So then about a year later, she came up to me and she was like, "You never talk to us about going to college…all these programs I go to people go up there and start talking about how to get into college." So she is thinking, "Here is this black woman who is educated. Why isn't she doing the same thing?" I said, "Well, the reason I'm not talking to you about going to college is because I don't care whether or not you're going to college. I care whether or not you actually know how to understand stuff. I want to know whether or not you can look at a piece of paper and make sense of it. If you don't go to college but you can do that, I'm going to be really happy."
>
> *Alex*: That seems like almost the polar opposite of what the education system is geared towards right now particularly for working-class and racialized kids.
>
> *Ms. Roberts*: Right. So I said, "If you can understand what we are reading in our sessions, I am really happy. That's your college for me." She just graduated from college last year. She had decided to go, and it was a very difficult time and we had to do all these things to get her scholarship money and loans and her family was sabotaging her experience to go to college. She was the first one in her family to graduate from high school let alone go to college. So we went through this whole thing and I went to her graduation last year and she said to me, "Do you remember when I said to you that I wasn't going to college?" and I said, "Yes I do," and she said, "I felt like you were going tell us that this is what we needed to do because you think that you're better than us because you were educated. You would be telling us that we need to go in this direction. But I just watched you all those years and I thought to myself, she doesn't even push it. She just makes us learn stuff and learn how to do research and learn how to go out and write our own surveys and do interviews and focus groups for these projects we were doing, the participatory research projects." I'll never forget that she called me in November of her first year and she said, "Ms. Roberts, everything we did

we're doing here. I already know all of this stuff." Later on she said, "It's amazing because you taught us how to do all this stuff without it being school. We didn't even know we were learning how to do this stuff. We didn't know we were learning how to do research by doing it this way." Her senior thesis was easy for her because she had already learned how to do all that stuff. They knew that at sixteen. That's the point. That you can still teach basic knowledge and skills, you just have to apply it, it has to make sense to young people, and you have to be able to master it. That's what keeps them going. People always say to me, "How do these girls do all this stuff where they are creating all these things?" But it's like, "Because they care about the issue. They pick the topic, they want to do it." That's why. It's not magic.

I include this long excerpt from Ms. Roberts's interview because I think that it captures a number of important insights. To begin with, the point here is not that kids shouldn't be encouraged to go to college. I do not believe Ms. Roberts was at all indifferent to the further education of the young woman she mentored. Rather, Ms. Roberts is suggesting that authentic learning and the desire to learn does not emanate from external sources of authority or from coercion such as telling kids that the primary purpose of school (and, by extension, learning) is to pass standardized tests. In contrast, Ms. Roberts intimates that to substantively engage youth, especially youth living under various forms of oppression, learning has to be connected to both the internal curiosity and interests of young people and also to their historical and cultural locations. Crucially, Ms. Roberts's comments suggest that such approaches to learning are not at all incompatible with the educational skills required to survive in the current economic and political order. As Ms. Roberts articulates, young people cannot hope to meaningfully operate in the world without learning to read, to think analytically, and to have competence with math and science. However, progressive and critical models of education root the development of these skills within the internal motivation of the learner and their social reality as opposed to extrinsic authority such as the reductive technical calculations and curricular content privileged under the dominant emphasis on markets, testing, and workforce preparation. Moreover, progressive and critical approaches do not view learning as simply a means to accommodate oneself to the existing economic, social, and political order but to develop the capacities and intellectual tools to intervene in this order in the interest of deepening democratic social relations. This frames the pursuit of knowledge as an active and collective engagement with the world for human development and democratic understanding and transformation as opposed to a prescriptive set of discreet, privatized, and decontextualized skills transmitted to students to be mastered and tested. I would argue that such a reordering of educational values is precisely what is required for creating future citizens capable of redefining what human security and dignified work might mean beyond the present race to the bottom of wages, workers' rights, and environmental protections under globalized neoliberal capitalism.

My interest here is not to suggest that the Freedom School and other organizations that effectively engage youth in activism should simply be translated into another standardized model to be implemented into public schools like CHS.

Such a move runs counter to the logic of education liberation that views social organization and learning as part of a democratic process as opposed to a prescriptive and static method. Rather, I would argue that organizations like the Freedom School provide valuable lessons about how the real desires of youth for participation, service, social change, and authentic learning can be translated into engagement and action. Such insights are not only critical for building social movements capable of deconstructing the harmful assumptions and underlying systems of value that animate neoliberal educational policy and practice, including military education, but also provide real working alternative models of learning, hope, and youth engagement from which to draw valuable insights for rethinking our approaches to educational policy and practice on a broader scale.

In this chapter, I have explored different barriers and possibilities for the development of human security and engagement at CHS. I have highlighted tensions between various forms of enclosure and how students, educators, and youth workers at CHS imagine their own sense of social and ethical responsibility in relation to educational change. As the perspectives I have outlined throughout the chapter (students, teachers, soldiers, and activists) make clear, there is a wealth of creativity, talent, and intensive desire for direction, service, belonging, and change at schools like CHS, particularly among educators and the youth themselves. I would argue that reclaiming public schools as spaces of hope and possibility as opposed to spaces of enclosure for youth will require imagining ways in which educational institutions can unleash and redirect this energy toward expansion of broadly shared opportunities, meaningful work, human development, and democratic life. The privatize, test, control, and punish agenda will not ultimately uplift this generation of young people. We will have to rethink our approach to public education, particularly in its connection to the human and economic security of youth, along with a broader focus on developing critical public values and ethical cultures beyond narrow economic or militaristic imperatives and forms of enclosure and control. Importantly, this requires more than simply rejecting the values and destructive consequences of market governance. It will require fostering cultures of investment, solidarity, and collaboration, themes to which I return in the conclusion.

Conclusion: Public Schooling for a Common Security

Speaking to the Progressive Education Association in 1932 at the height of the Great Depression, renowned sociologist and radical educator George Counts observed a historical moment similar to our own that he described as "full of promise, as well as menace." In language as fresh and as relevant as anything written about education today, Counts observed that:

> there is no *good* education apart from some conception of the nature of the good society. Education is not some pure and mystical essence that remains unchanged from everlasting to everlasting. On the contrary, it is of the earth and must respond to every convulsion or tremor that shakes the planet. It must always be a function of time and circumstance.

Counts argued forcefully against the prevailing dogmas of his time. Rather than seeing a rational social order on a march toward infinite progress, he saw a society that was fundamentally irrational: where "mastery over the forces of nature, surpassing the wildest dreams of antiquity, is accompanied by extreme material insecurity," and where "dire poverty walks hand in hand with the most extravagant living that the world has ever known." Counts argued that for education to realize its promise as a truly progressive force, it must be connected to a transformative vision of society. On the one hand, this meant an educational project that directly addresses the contradictions in the economic sphere, where, he argued, "competition must be replaced by cooperation," and "the urge for profits by careful planning." On the other hand, it meant the cultivation of the moral, intellectual, and aesthetic capacities at the heart of any viable notion of democracy. "Life cannot be divided neatly into a number of separate compartments," he argued, and therefore "educational theory will have to embrace the entire range of life." This is the "great need of our age, both in the realm of education and in the sphere of public life."

In this book, I have argued that the problems confronting urban public education today can be traced largely to a failure of neoliberal culture and political economy that has generated a crisis of human security in schools and in the lives of young people. Foremost is an economic system that is not working for the vast majority. This has been highlighted by a global economic crisis that continues to undermine the livelihoods and dignities of millions of people across the world.

As David Harvey, Robert Brenner, David McNally, and others have noted, continuing instabilities in global markets, debt crises, and austerity can be understood as a historical turning point organizing new limitations and possibilities for the neoliberal project. As Harvey (2010) states, "financial crises serve to rationalize the irrationalities of capitalism. They typically lead to reconfigurations, new models of development, new spheres of investment, and new forms of class power" (p. 11). Additionally, with the triumph of market values and consumer identifications and three decades of persistent right-wing attacks on the public trust, US culture has become increasingly individualized and fragmented—a site where seemingly all aspects of contemporary life from policy, citizenship, art, sex, friendship, to ethical judgments are reduced to a permanent spectacle of commodification. This loss of noncommercial public values, formative democratic cultures, and sense of mutuality has meant that individuals have little recourse to translate private problems into social concerns (Giroux, 2012). The historian and political theorist Tony Judt (2009) has noted that the result is an "eviscerated society" where "the thick mesh of social interactions and public goods has been reduced to a minimum, with nothing except authority and obedience binding the citizen to the state" (p. 118). Any movement for educational and social justice will have to consider these economic and cultural dynamics and work to reimagine and transform the system of values and practices in which they are embedded.

The dominant narrative in educational reform asserts that access to an educational marketplace and "get tough" corporate management designed to hold schools and their teachers accountable for low test scores, combined with gritty individual determination, can lift people out of poverty and ensure material security and well-being. Such assertions have tended to transfer the blame for entrenched educational and social inequality from historical and structural considerations and political decisions onto the backs of public schools, teachers, and the students and communities that they serve. Rather than investing in universal public education, young people, and vibrant neighborhoods, neoliberal school reform punishes urban public schools and students for externally produced conditions such as concentrated poverty, food insecurity, homelessness, racial segregation, endemic unemployment and underemployment, and general lack of access to human resources and social services. As Jean Anyon (2005) has pointed out, urban public schools do not exist in a vacuum and are ultimately limited in what they can do. Particularly for communities at the margins of the postindustrial economic order, schools do not provide health care or other basic social protections that ensure healthy child development, nor do they create living-wage jobs for communities and students. She states that "we have been counting on education to solve the problems of unemployment, joblessness, and poverty for many years. But education did not cause these problems, and education cannot solve them. An economic [and political] system that chases profits and casts people aside (especially people of color) is culpable" (p. 3).

In my analysis of educational life in Ellison Square and CHS, I have argued that the current educational policy agenda is deeply misguided and is contributing to already shameful conditions of human insecurity, social abandonment, and precariousness in urban neighborhoods and public schools. While privatization,

testing, and accountability policies are intended to spark improvement and innovation, they have largely failed to improve public schooling in any meaningful
sense. In contrast, these policies have tended to extend and intensify the worst
aspects of industrial schooling, while pioneering new mechanisms of technocratic
management and repression. I have highlighted in this book how the emphasis
on privatization has led to the further marginalization and defunding of public
schools like CHS. I have shown that amid the drive to close public schools and
replace them with privately run charter and selective contract schools, public
schools like CHS have become warehouses for the most disadvantaged students
(those in poverty, those with low test scores, those for whom English is a second
language, and those with learning and other disabilities). This is heightening
race and class segregation in the educational system, undermining neighborhood
public schools like CHS, and paving the way for further school closures and privatization. Continued austerity measures and financial disinvestments are further
raising class sizes, reducing the teaching force, and destabilizing and stigmatizing public educational environments. Moreover, my analysis has pointed to how
the cult of measurement, competition, and standardized high-stakes testing in
the management of curriculum is eroding meaningful instruction and student
engagement, the professional discretion and autonomy of teachers, and commitment to broad emphasis on liberal arts, progressive and critical forms of teaching
and learning. Such a curriculum can hardly be seen as much more than sorting
youth in public schools like CHS into the lowest employment tracks and/or pushing them out of school and the labor market altogether. As I have shown, this is
exacerbated by the integration of law enforcement and punitive forms of social
control, which are eroding the educative and civic mission of educational environments by framing students as potential criminals as opposed to young citizens on the path to adulthood. Such policies tend to reinforce what Slavoj Žižek
(2008) has delineated as objective, symbolic, and subjective forms of violence that
are immanent to our economic and political systems.

Lastly, I have brought to light the lucid and often conflicted perspectives that
young people, their teachers, and other adults have about life in Ellison Square
and CHS as an institution. For teachers, their commitment to young people and
the institution is constrained by multiple pressures that include frustration over
class sizes, external control over curriculum, and their marginalization in decision making. This is combined with a general sense of being overextended due to
lack of time and resources to address the social, emotional, material, and intellectual needs of their students. As Mr. Charles puts it:

> It's unbelievable the things that teachers have to go through on a regular basis, that
> students have to go through. Literally you find yourself having to sift through so
> much more that's not really part of the curriculum. And you could heal more stu-
> dents and create more safety and security if you are able to address some of those
> things in your curriculum or classroom and give time to it. But you can't.

Despite their often insightful critiques of the systems of control, scarcity, and
authority that they work within, teachers often have little choice within the

institutional structure of CHS but to become active agents of neoliberal policy. This creates a conflicted reality for teachers. On the one hand, under the threat of sanction and almost constant surveillance, teachers must expend a great deal of time and energy meeting the expectations and putting into practice mandates stemming from the external control of their curriculum. Further, while teachers are denied a meaningful democratic voice in key decision making, responsibility has largely been framed in private terms. What this means is that teachers are no longer primarily held accountable within a system of professional norms and social responsibility, but are subject to and become agents of a regime of "personal responsibility" defined narrowly by their willingness and success in implementing the narrow and reductive forms of curriculum and pedagogy that the system demands of them. On the other hand, teachers do often seek to actively perform another type of social and ethical responsibility whereby they go beyond the official curriculum in an attempt to meet the diverse needs of their students. This includes often ignoring and/or subverting the official test-based curriculum in favor of more exploratory and culturally relevant learning. It also includes things that do not fall under the structured curriculum such as helping students cope with family problems and personal issues and creating alternative learning spaces in the school through after school programs and other measures to address issues of immediate social and emotional import to students. Thus, despite the difficulties and challenges of schooling within the neoliberal age, there are incalculable moments of inspired teaching, learning, and programming that take place at CHS both within and beyond the official curriculum.

Students also inhabit a conflicted reality at CHS. For many students, there is a broad recognition that education can and should be a vehicle for a better life and future. They have been told from an early age that education is the only legitimate avenue for making it in the broader society. Unfortunately, many do not view CHS as a reliable or sufficient partner in making this a viable option. The impersonal and socially decontextualized nature of much of the curriculum alongside the punitive culture of the school elicits for many a sense of disillusionment, alienation, and/or cynicism. This opens a space where interpersonal dramas, conflicts, violence, and oppositional behavior against school authority often become more important than academic pursuits and investments. These conflicts reflect and contribute to a milieu where students are viewed and treated more as potential criminals than as future citizens worthy of compassion and investment. Not only does this betray the democratic promise of public schooling, it also functions to push many students out of school altogether and thus aggravates a cycle of gangs, violence, joblessness, hopelessness, and mass incarceration. As Olivia suggested, "We just aren't given the basis to care. We're not even given the option. Because you can be given the key to a door, it's your choice to open it or not. But I think that we aren't given the key at all." This sense of abandonment reflects a more general state of precariousness that marks educational life for students. For many, dire economic conditions and lack of access to employment and social services combined with ubiquitous criminalization renders hope in a different and brighter future, fleeting if not inoperable. In line with the dominant narrative and against the trope of victimization, some youth place responsibility and blame for their circumstances largely on themselves and/or on their community. As I have argued, however, neoliberal schooling more often than not serves to intensify rather than ameliorate or transform these structures of insecurity and exclusion. Coming of age and living in a moment of austerity and uncertainty, young people are actively being failed by the very institutions that purportedly aim to serve, guide, and protect them.

Despite the entrenched problems and dysfunctions, many of the young people and teachers I spoke with maintain a love and commitment toward their school. This sense of loyalty and faith in the community provides hints toward positive institutional and social change. Again in Olivia's words, "I feel like CHS has so much potential because there are so many kids in here who can do really amazing things but maybe they aren't just facilitated in what it is they want to do or maybe they have bad direction." Students are broadly not satisfied with the status quo at CHS. Some channel their desire for service and belonging into the deeply problematic form of martial discipline and future opportunity promised by military education at CHS. Others have joined organizations such as the Chicago Freedom School that seek to develop the potential of youth for activism and for pursuing transformative change in their schools and communities. Such examples point to a strong current of desire among students for more opportunities to develop their sense of leadership and voice in an institutional structure that too often simply ignores or subverts it. As I have argued, efforts to transform educational environments like CHS from spaces of enclosure to spaces of hope and possibility will require tapping into and providing more opportunities for students to become involved and facilitated in decision making regarding their school and their own learning. The question, however, remains: Where do we go from here?

*   *   *

In the years and decades that followed George Counts's lecture to the Progressive Education Association in 1932, the United States entered the New Deal era which culminated in the social democratic reforms of the 1960s that included Lyndon Johnson's Great Society initiatives, landmark civil rights legislation, and the war on poverty. These reforms were the direct result of decades of intensive labor activism and civil rights struggles by working people, women, students, and racially oppressed and marginalized groups who put their lives on the line in the service of creating a better and more just world.[1] The policies and social reforms adopted during this era contributed to dramatically reducing poverty in rural and urban America; promoted employment, stable wages, rights to organize, and social benefits for many working people; and supported large-scale investment in public education and social infrastructure at all levels. This worked to ameliorate deep historical inequalities while providing a foundation for the advancement of millions of young people and their families. There is much to be learned from this social democratic tradition. While it fell short in fundamentally transforming the structural relations of race, class, and gender inequality at the heart of the US capitalist system, it does provide an important set of historical and ethical referents from which to advocate for substantive reform of public policy as well as strategies to greatly expand equity and human security in education and the broader society. With this being said, such models of social democratic reform cannot be viewed as adequate to the task of ensuring a just and sustainable future in light of the looming economic, social, political, and ecological challenges facing the twenty-first century.

With these concerns in mind, in recent years, scholars in the social sciences and humanities along with activists of all stripes have sought to rejuvenate a discourse of the *commons* as both a critique of the neoliberal drive toward the enclosure and expropriation of public wealth and natural resources and also as a rallying cry for a different kind of politics suitable to the unique challenges of the contemporary moment. The various movements associated with Occupy Wall Street are only one instantiation of broader global movements that have flourished under a call to reclaim a sense of the commons for the collective good. Michael Hardt and Antonio Negri (2009) have offered a useful definition of the commons, or what they simply refer to as the common, that encompasses both the totality of the public goods and natural resources that we all share as well as the world of immaterial production and culture—language, ideas, values, affects, knowledge, and social relations. Educational spheres are firmly grounded on both sides of this equation. They represent not only vital public goods beneficial to all, but are also key sites for the production of knowledge, ideas, and social relationships vital to the common good and democratic life.

The common school movement that began under Horace Mann in the nineteenth century is an important referent in the history of public schooling. However, by and large, educational advocates haven't thought much about the common lately. I read present concerns over the commons and the common as providing a language and a set of creative and ethical referents not only for thinking substantive educational reforms in the social democratic tradition but as a means to think creatively and critically beyond this tradition as well. Perhaps most significantly, the commons provides a frame for thinking past stale impasses dominating educational politics today. One of the consequences of the neoliberal turn in education has been to put progressive and critical educators on the defensive. Suddenly, the forces of conservative reaction have become the "progressive innovators" by promoting "choice" and "competition" in educational spheres while framing the democratic purpose of education within the language of the market and the values and private concerns of business. Conversely, those traditionally critical of the status quo in public schooling have become the conservatives, left to defend a public educational system that continues to spectacularly fail the most disadvantaged young people. Imagining public schooling as a commons is one way of avoiding this dilemma, that I refer to as the "blackmail" of neoliberalism, which paints our only options as those between a business agenda of deregulated market sovereignty, an outmoded image of unresponsive state domination of the public, and uncritical liberal accommodation to the existing economic and political order. I want to suggest that the common is a concept that opens a different space for critically rethinking a public outside this false choice between either market imperatives or state domination and instead locates questions of educational value and organization within the values and principles of radical democracy. What this means, simply put, is reclaiming an open commitment to the common governance of common wealth and labor for the democratic good of society and all its members.[2] In what follows, I want to suggest several areas of reform conducive to reclaiming public schooling as a commons. I do not claim to be offering a prescriptive program, merely some suggestions that would not only provide a set of concrete ways to improve public schooling in the inner-city and beyond, but also potentially open education and educational values toward a broader vision of justice, reciprocity, and democratic possibility in public life. Given the polarization and corruption that presently define the US political system, these areas of reform may seem rather farfetched at the moment. I would only offer that historical change is often rapid and unpredictable. It is typically carried out by ordinary people, often spurred by deep frustrations and profound contradictions. I remain, therefore, guardedly optimistic.

1. *Democratization of Human Security*: For public schooling to serve as a force for promoting shared prosperity, opportunity, and equality for all young people, its reform will have to be connected to greater equity in the distribution of wealth and security. Beyond the long-term social and ecological necessity of developing viable democratic alternatives to an endless growth model of political economy, one approach for reclaiming a social contract and for creating a strong public commons and promoting human security might be to revive a second Bill of Rights similar to the one proposed by Franklin D. Roosevelt in his 1944 State of the Union address. In this speech, Roosevelt stated that "we cannot be content, no matter how high the general standard of living may be, if some fraction of our people—whether it be one-third or one-fifth or one-tenth—is ill-fed, ill-clothed, ill-housed, and insecure." He proceeded to outline a series of goals where "a new basis of security and prosperity can be established for all—regardless of station, race, or creed." At the core of his proposal was a series of public rights and protections including the right to dignified work and a guaranteed basic income; the right to a decent and affordable home; the right to medical and health care; the right to protection against economic dislocation, old age, and sickness; and the right to a free, equitable, and enriching public education. These rights are crucial to promoting security and societal well-being. As Roosevelt put it, "unless there is security here at home there cannot be lasting peace in the world." *Reviving, renewing, reimagining, and agitating* for such a bill of rights and protections would give progressive educators and citizens something concrete to rally around and would also work as a useful intervention into transforming some of the most immediate and pressing issues facing working people and marginalized populations in the inner-city and beyond.

2. *Progressive Reclamation of Public Schools*: Schools are common public resources and should be treated as such. Charter and contract schools and other small school experiments have generated an important discussion about the need for opening up and modernizing public school bureaucracy and creating spaces for creativity and innovation in curriculum. In some

cases, they have even provided opportunities for progressive organizations in partnership with communities to have a direct positive impact on schools including opening spaces for critical and progressive learning environments. However, the charter school movement has diverted resources away from traditional public schools, while the research shows that they are typically of no better quality than their public school counterparts. Most significantly, the charter movement has been broadly co-opted by a neoliberal agenda invested in moving the public system toward a private corporate-run system. I believe that the evidence suggests that this would only aggravate many of the problems I have outlined throughout this book concerning equity, the professional role of teachers, and the engagement of young people. Not to mention, it would deeply pervert the ideal of a universal and democratically operated public education system. The leading advocates for charter schools today are not progressive nonprofit organizations and communities, many of which have become utterly disillusioned with the movement, but educational corporations, Wall Street financiers, and other prominent figures from the business world, many of whom know nothing about education or about young people in communities like Ellison Square, and whose ultimate aim is the conversion of the public system into a cheap, union free, and for-profit system. For those who doubt this claim, one need only peruse the publications of the market reformers themselves (Brill, 2009; Chubb & Moe, 2009). Lastly, despite their claim to efficiency and innovation, neoliberal school reforms have only added to dysfunctional bureaucracy in the public system through the top-down management of decision-making and curriculum while limiting the input of educators, parents, students, and communities over school organization. Demands for a moratorium on privatization should thus be combined with a path toward equity and opening up flexibility and democracy in the public system in order to spur progressive innovation, enrichment, and creativity.

3. *Public Investment in Communities, Youth, and Schools*: Transforming schools like CHS would require substantial investment. Closing such schools, firing the staff, and reopening as a "turnaround" school or as a charter will not alter the fundamental problems. This should be viewed as an opportunity and not as an insurmountable obstacle. We could create millions of stable jobs by substantially investing in public infrastructure in low-income communities. This could include early childhood education and human services for young people and families; the modernization of school buildings; the rehiring, hiring, and investment in the retention of high quality teachers in disadvantaged schools and communities that will lower class sizes and improve instruction; and the creation of new positions in schools for college and career coaches, counselors, nurses, and social workers that provide key "wrap-around" services for youth. How do you pay for it, one might be reasonably expected to ask? Current budget realities can in fact be brought into alignment with such a program of public and social investment. First, we need to close corporate tax loopholes; end

corporate welfare, personhood, and subsidies; raise taxes on corporations and the wealthy while lowering tax rates on small businesses. This would dramatically increase revenue, encourage locally-owned business, and generate public investment and employment. Second, we could generate hundreds of billions of dollars in additional revenue by dismantling the military and prison industrial complexes; ending the war on drugs (which is a public health problem, not a crime problem); raising the capital gains tax rate and implementing a financial transactions tax (FST) on Wall Street. According to the Economic Policy Institute (2012), combined with strong new financial regulation to reign in the too-big-to-fail casino, such an FST tax would raise tens of billions of dollars per year while tempering down on the activities that led to the last financial crisis.[3] These measures would not only spur job creation and economic development but also free up significant revenue streams that could be used to square the long-term federal debt, shore up social benefits like social security, and provide investment in public infrastructure, job training, rebuilding communities, and in public schools and, thus, in the future of young people.

4. *Shifting Practices and Values in Curriculum:* The creation of successful urban schools will require a shift in curriculum. Too much of our educational discourse and policy is rooted in the reductive logics of economic and individual competition as opposed to social development and cooperation. This is a degraded and atomizing vision of education in a democratic society. John Dewey (1944) reminds us that democracy is "more than a form of government; it is primarily a form of associated living, of conjoint communicated experience" (p. 87). The incessant calls to make public schools accountable to economic imperatives and the reduction of learning to test scores lies at the root of many of the problems in schools today. It is mistakenly assumed that the reason why people teach and learn is only either economic self-interest or fear. Like other urban schools, key decisions affecting teaching and learning at CHS are made by reformers from the business world and business-minded politicians who often know little, if anything, about education and are miles removed, both physically and culturally, from the "on the ground" dynamics of schools and communities. This has led to the commercial standardization of curriculum and a focus on testing that is doing little to engage youth and to prepare them adequately for the world. Here, I would refer back to my conversation with Ms. Roberts at the Chicago Freedom School, in which she eloquently spoke of making education meaningful to the cultural experiences, histories, and everyday lives of students. This is not to discourage mastery of such core skills as reading and mathematics—on the contrary, it is to suggest that these skills are best learned through broad exposure to liberal arts and progressive and critical approaches to learning that have relevance to the lives of young people and that reflect their interests and desires. Such a shift would require the professional empowerment of those closest to youth, namely their teachers, and a commitment to engage parents and youth themselves in decision making. This would have the added benefit

of developing and supporting a notion of accountability based not on test scores, labeling, and punishments, but on professional and social norms of cooperation and reciprocity, which would certainly be more humane, if not also far more efficacious and effective in promoting responsibility and trust.

5. *Community Schools and Transformative School Environments:* Public schools have the potential to be exciting and transformative places. Catalyst Chicago, an independent journal that reports on education in the city has suggested that public schools need to be *community schools* that are open well into the evening and provide learning and services for whole families. Such community schools, "must be planned and run with deep and democratic involvement by parents and others, and must be welcoming learning communities responsive to community needs and cultures." Based upon years of extensive research, they make a number of critical suggestions for improving the quality and efficacy of public schools. This includes investing in smaller class sizes and high quality teachers in order to facilitate academic excellence and the conditions for supportive relationships among faculty, students, and parents to take root and flourish; developing college and career services and counseling in order to help lower dropout rates and enable youth to make a successful transition from high school to the next stage in their life; investing in students' overall health and wellness including access to health care, counseling, physical activity, and healthy food; and working to build real working forms of leadership and governance that involve and empower all members of the community. Lastly, it includes replacing harsh criminalizing discipline policies with restorative approaches that eliminate the corrosive impact of punitive forms of surveillance and policing of students at their schools and that work toward building safe and nurturing learning environments. Such a restorative approach recognizes that student misbehavior and conflict in school is often an understandable reaction to physically, psychically, and spiritually adverse conditions. As such, it would concern itself with teaching and healing as opposed to punishment and containment in matters of school safety and discipline.

These five areas of reform are, of course, incomplete and open-ended. Ultimately, I believe that it will be up to educators, students, parents, and communities to agitate for educational and democratic change. This may take many different forms depending on the geographical, social, and political context. In Chicago, there has been a groundswell of educational activism in recent years. This has included high-profile protests, hunger strikes, and occupations, such as in 2010 when parents in Chicago's Pilsen neighborhood took over a local public high school field house for 43 days in order to push the city to provide a working library for the school. It has also included the development of community organizations like the Chicago Freedom School, VOYCE, Teachers for Social Justice, Project NIA and many others designed to engage youth and communities and to press for change. What has united these actions and organizations is a broad dissatisfaction with the direction toward neoliberal governance in education and a strong desire for public schooling to become more responsive to the complex needs of young people and communities—in short, to function as a commons. There is certainly no shortage of this sentiment in schools and neighborhoods like Ellison Square and CHS where the general sense is that the status quo is intolerable. The translation of this dissatisfaction into viable social movements and alternative public models of educational policy and governance remains undecided. The philosopher Hannah Arendt (1961) perhaps put it most eloquently by suggesting that the sphere of "education is where we decide whether we love our children enough not to expel them from our world and leave them to their own devices, nor to strike from their hands their chance of undertaking something new, something unforeseen by us, but to prepare them in advance for the task of renewing a common world" (pp. 174–175). This is, and remains, our fundamental educational challenge.

Notes

Introduction: Schooling in a Time of Crisis and Austerity

1. This quote can be found on page xii in the Preface to the 2011 edition of Bowles and Gintis's *Schooling in Capitalist America*.

2. Studies consistently show, however, that average Americans tend to think quite highly of their own local public schools and teachers. It is only when asked about the system as a whole that they express a concern that public education is failing. Further, US youth in the upper middle class and elite continue to place near the top in the international rankings of student achievement. They only begin to fall behind as one travels down the socioeconomic spectrum. Youth in high poverty communities fare the worst (Ravitch, 2010). While the quality of individual public schools and teachers is indeed a crucial factor in promoting educational success, longstanding research indicates that achievement gaps have more to do with class disparities and social disadvantages than with differences between schools (Coleman, 1966; Rothstein, 2004). In short, the blame lies not in public schools but in deepening poverty and social fragmentation.

3. For further elaboration on this paradox see Christopher Newfield's (2008) *Unmaking the Public University* and Alex Means's (2011) "Creativity as an Educational Problematic in the Biopolitical Economy" in Michael Peters and Ergin Bulut's (eds) *Cognitive Capitalism, Education, and Digital Labor*. Here I argue that neoliberal systems of knowledge management and reform in secondary and higher education represent a distinct struggle over the global educational commons that opens up new challenges and possibilities for democratic resistance and development. For further analysis and the most comprehensive and acute examination of the failures of neoliberal schooling see Kenneth J. Saltman's (2012) *The Failure of Corporate School Reform*. Saltman systematically deconstructs how corporate reform in US secondary education has failed as a movement—functioning largely as a means for dismantling public schooling through privatization in the interest of short-term profits and long-term management of staggering inequalities and systemic contradictions.

4. While Canada has fared much better overall than the United States and countries in Western Europe in the wake of the crisis, the Canadian Broadcasting Corporation (CBC, 2011) reports a series of disturbing statistics concerning the effects of the recession on Canada: "In March 2010, 867,948 Canadians (38% of them children) turned to food banks for food support—a 28% increase over March 2008 and the highest level of food bank use ever; In 2010, 150,000 to 300,000 persons were visibly homeless, another 450,000 to 900,000 were "hidden" homeless, 1.5 million households were in "core housing need", and 3.1 million households were in unaffordable housing. In 2010, 59% of Canadian workers lived paycheque to paycheque, saying they would be in financial difficulty if their paycheque was delayed by a week. In 2009,

per capita household debt, at $41,740, was 2.5 times higher than in 1989; in 2010, 20% of Canadians reported they had too much debt and trouble managing it. In 2009, the average annual income ($6.6 million) of Canada's best-paid CEOs was 155 times higher than the average worker's income ($42,988); a third of all income growth in Canada over the past two decades has gone to the richest one percent of Canadians. At the end of 2009, 3.8% of Canadian households controlled 67% of total household wealth."

5. Chicago's homicide rate peaked in the wake of crack epidemic in 1994 at 929. In contrast, there were 440 homicides in Chicago in 2011. The majority of these were the result of firearms violence. In 2008, there were 510 homicides in Chicago, 80% of these were due to firearms violence, nearly half the victims were between the ages of 10–25, and the vast majority of the victims were male. Chicago has seen a 40% jump in firearms-related homicides in early 2012. Reasons often cited for this increase in 2012 are a fragmentation of the gang structure, as gang leaders have been arrested, splintering gangs into smaller rival sets. Another prominent reason for the spike in violence is traced to the effects of high unemployment and the economic crisis.

6. All proper names in this study including street names and the names of individuals are pseudonyms. Ellison Square and CHS are also pseudonyms. I have not identified the race or ethnicity of most of the adults at CHS as I am concerned that doing so could result in their identification. I have included the race and ethnicity of the students in the study.

7. Along with McNally, I understand the 2008 economic crisis as symptomatic of more general crisis tendencies in global capitalism. See also David Harvey's (2010) *The Enigma of Capital*. In this book, Harvey locates the global economic crisis as indicative of the long-term structural barriers to continued economic expansion in the neoliberal era. He argues that while the extension of easy credit to consumers combined with semiotic manipulations in finance offered one avenue of continued capitalist growth in the 1990s and 2000s, the failure of deregulated finance capital in 2008 signals broader problems and limits for an accumulation paradigm beset by tensions between, on the one hand, finding new exploitable markets and opportunities for profitable investment, on the other hand, encroaching environmental depletion and resource scarcity.

8. I frequently make reference to "social disinvestment" throughout this book. I want to be clear that by social disinvestment I mean not only cuts in social spending, but also to a shift in cultural attitudes toward the public. In this latter sense, by social disinvestment I refer to the ways we have lost a sense of social and collective responsibility toward the public sphere and the public values which sustain it.

9. Harper's magazine reported that in 2007 there was $78 billion in venture capital invested in US education startups. In 2011, it was $452 billion (Harpers Index, 2012). For an analysis of the influence of educational corporations on US education policy see Lee Fang's (2011) "How online learning companies bought America's schools" published in *The Nation*, Saltman's (2012) *The Failure of Corporate School Reform*, and in a global context see Stephen Ball's (2012) *Global Education Inc: New Policy Networks and the Neoliberal Imaginary*.

1   Securing Precarious Urban Futures

1. I take this to signal the abstract intensification of what Jurgen Habermas (1987) once referred to as "colonization of the life world" by expansionary market and state systems.

2. Quote from Foucault (2008) page 131.

3. Linebaugh (2008), Harvey (2003), Federici (2004) and others have observed that movements to enclose the commons through privatization have been a long-standing and ongoing process of capitalist development. Updating Marx's concept of "primitive accumulation," Harvey (2003) has called this "accumulation by dispossession" to signal how capital seeks to commodify sites previously held in common. Today, we have seen a global movement to expropriate land and resources and a wave of privatization across the Global North and South. The movement to privatize public schools and to make them commercially viable has to be understood within these trends.

4. My view is that despite epistemological incongruities, a Foucauldian governmentality approach broadly compliments a Marxian political economy perspective, particularly in understanding the mutually inflected relationships between the operations of global capitalism, the state, and subjectivity from the macrological to the micropolitical levels. Thomas Lemke (2001) notes: "the analysis of governmentality focuses not only on the integral link between micro- and macro-political levels (e.g. globalization or competition for 'attractive' sites for companies and personal imperatives as regards beauty or a regimented diet), it also highlights the intimate relationship between 'ideological' and 'political-economic' agencies (e.g. the semantics of flexibility and the introduction of new structures of production)" (p. 13).

5. Foucault (2003) positions biopolitics as a historical development in modern rationalities and technologies of power and social regulation that emerges out of and compliments two other modalities—sovereignty and discipline. Whereas sovereignty refers to control over the legitimate use of violence within a distinct territory under the law, discipline refers to investments in the individual body—its spatial distribution, serialization, training, and surveillance. Biopolitics, in contrast, concerns itself with the regulation of "man as a multiplicity"; that is, as a "global mass that is affected by overall processes characteristic of birth, death, production, illness, and so on" (p. 243). The target of biopolitics is thus naturalization and regularization of particular frames of economic and political life. Biopolitics thus describe the always-contested dynamics of the political in its most basic sense—the antagonistic economic and social processes where some lives and forms of life are made more or less valuable than others. These dividing practices between deserving and undeserving lives, is a crucial axis upon which notions of security operate.

6. Women, particularly immigrant women and women of color, occupy positions at the bottom of the wage scale and in the informal sector of work in far greater numbers, and, along with their children, also bear the primary brunt of the effects of poverty (Goldberg, 2010). While women and children are overrepresented among the working poor, men are far more likely to face chronic unemployment coupled with higher rates of imprisonment. Here "workfare" directed predominantly at exploiting low-wage female labor and "prisonfare" aimed at managing unemployed men emerge as dominant race- and gender-coded class strategies for managing dispossessed and alienated populations in the neoliberal city (Wacquant, 2009).

7. According to a research study by the Pew center (2009), as of 2008, 1 in 31 adults in America was in prison or jail, or on probation or parole. It is observed that 25 years ago, the rate was 1 in 77. These numbers are highly concentrated by race and geography: 1 in 11 black adults (9.2 percent) versus 1 in 27 Hispanic adults (3.7 percent) and 1 in 45 white adults (2.2 percent); 1 in 18 men (5.5 percent) versus 1 in 89 women (1.1 percent). Loïc Wacquant (2009), Michelle Alexander (2010), Paul Street (2007), and Ruth Gilmore (2009) among others, have argued that soaring rates of

incarceration in the United States are largely unrelated to actual crime rates. For instance, Alexander points out that between 1970 and 1990 the crime rates of Finland and Germany were roughly identical to the United States, yet the US incarceration rate quadrupled during the same period while the Finish rate declined by 60 percent and Germany's stayed about the same. Since 1990, the US crime rate has slightly dipped below the international average while its rate of incarceration has continued to rise 6–10 times faster than any other industrialized country. These statistics and their deep racial characteristics suggest that the imprisonment binge has more to do with extrinsic factors than with crime rates—factors such as institutional and cultural racism; turning profits and providing a tax base and jobs to rural white communities; the gutting of the social state; and the need to exert direct social control of populations dislocated by the global economy.

8. According to Smith (2002): "communications and financial deregulation have expanded the geographical mobility of capital; unprecedented labor migrations have distanced local economies from *automatic dependency on home grown labor*; national and local states (including city governments) have responded by offering carrots to capital while applying the stick to labor and *dismantling previous supports for social reproduction*; and finally, class and race based struggles have broadly receded, giving local and national governments increased leeway to *abandon that sector of the population surplused by both the restructuring of the economy and the gutting of social services*. The mass incarceration of working-class and minority populations, especially in the US, is the national analogue of the emerging revanchist city" (p. 433, my emphasis).

9. Darling-Hammond's (2010) book *The Flat World and Education*, offers a rational defense of liberal and social democratic approaches to educational policy and public schooling. However, while arguing for educational investments and liberal commitments to fairness and equity, Darling-Hammond largely reproduces the neoliberal viewpoint that education is or should be valued primarily according to its capacity to serve economic ends. In contrast, I subscribe to the values articulated within progressive and critical traditions articulated by the likes of John Dewey (1944), Paulo Freire (1998), and Henry Giroux (1983) that situate the purpose of education within the terms of human development, social transformation, and democracy as opposed to the reductive logic of global economic competition.

10. Neoliberals like Eric Hanushuk, Paul T. Hill, Stephen Brill, and others roundly reject the notion that school funding and socioeconomic condition have anything to do with educational performance. They cite statistics indicating that the United States has one of the highest per pupil expenditures. Deceptively, however, they do not acknowledge two key determinates in promoting educational success (narrowly measured here in terms of test scores). First, the United States spends a significantly lower percentage of GPD on education and other social services than other developed nations (Sachs, 2011). This means that the poor receive far less support in matters like health care for mothers and children and early childhood education—things that are consistently cited as key factors in child development and whether or not young people enter school ready to learn (Anyon, 2005; Ravitch, 2010). Second, the reformers also deny the impact of poverty on school performance, however, the research is overwhelmingly clear that socioeconomic status is the single greatest determinate in predicting educational achievement (Rothstein, 2004). In short, as the vast majority of educational research has concluded (which the market reformers roundly ignore), poverty and inequality matter, while investments in social provision and educational

services (or the lack thereof) are central factors in the relative success of individual students and schools.

11. Qoute from Giroux (2009) page 78.

2   Chicago and the Management of Social Research

1. Quote on page 19 of Horkheimer & Adorno (2002).
2. Student quoted in 2011 Report on Illinois Poverty (Heartland Alliance, 2011).
3. The restrictions placed on the research inhibited a more immersive approach to the data collection. For instance, with only one semester, I simply did not have as much time to develop longer term relationships with staff and students and to become more deeply acculturated into everyday life at CHS. Despite the fact that I have taught in the Chicago schools, my presence as a white male researcher decidedly mark me as an outsider at CHS and in the Ellison Square community. However, the limitations on time may also contain some potential positive value. While I was afforded less physical time in the field, my outsider perspective could theoretically be productive in maintaining a fresh and critical distance to everyday realities. Another consequence of the time restrictions placed on the research was that I ended up relying perhaps more heavily on my formal and informal interviews. In theory, this has the value of letting the young people, educators, and others in the community speak largely for themselves. Such an approach enables a rich picture to develop through the actual voices and points of view of those living and working in Ellison Square and at CHS, particularly when balanced out against city and neighborhood data, media reports, CPS policy analysis, and my observations from the field. However, this too has its own ethical and theoretical problems. We cannot simply assume that the educators and young people that speak in the following chapters do so unproblematically. Rather, their perspectives along with those of the researcher are situated within and inflected by particular histories and cultural locations. This situated character of knowledge marks the ethically fraught terrain of relations to truth, to power, and to authority. I have attempted, where possible, to highlight productive contradictions and moments of slippage in the narratives that I think provide vivid insight into the inner tensions and the often conflicted nature of the reflections. However, I also recognize that my own social location has both informed the dialogic specificity of the narratives as they unfolded in real time as well as how I have represented them here. I do not claim to speak either for or on behalf of the participants nor am I naïve enough to think I am simply and unproblematically "representing" their voices. Rather, I view the narratives as well as their representation here as part of a dialogic process and the shared construction of knowledge between researcher, reader, and the researched. I think that when viewed in this light we get a much richer and more deeply empirical view of the narratives that appear in this text.

   On a further note on methods, interview subjects for this study were selected using a "snowball" sampling approach, meaning that I selected interview subjects as I began to meet teachers, staff, and students and make connections with them. In some cases, teachers whose classes I was observing recommended particular students to interview and made introductions for me. Throughout the research process, I attempted to select interview subjects in a way that would ultimately reflect the gender and racial diversity of the staff and student body at CHS. For instance, I tried to pick students from across the various grade levels and achieve a close balance of male and female, African American and Latino students. Formal interviews followed a semi-structured format whereby I utilized question guides for teachers, students, staff, and others with pre-determined questions concerning issues of economic, social, political, and human security at HS. However, these question guides provided only a loose framework. I was careful in the interviews to allow for flexibility in order to be able to further explore in the moment the often unexpected pathways that open-up in human conversation. For the analysis, I used NVIVO research software which enabled me to develop a set of themes and codes from my interview and observational data that logically followed from my research questions concerning how notions of security are imagined, lived, and practiced at CHS. I made every attempt to allow the codes and themes to develop organically from the data in contrast to imposing a pre-determined schema onto the analysis. Quotes were selected on the basis of how they contributed to elaborating the patterns, connections, conflicts, contradictions, and themes that emerged during the research and in the analysis. In many instances, I have chosen to focus on one or more interview subjects in depth as opposed to cluttering the text with quotes from multiple subjects. I think that this is a valuable way of humanizing the narratives and a tool for delving deeper into particular points of view.

4. This is a point that Lather (2010) has also made.

3   Learning by Dispossession: Objective Violence and Educational Failure

1. For more on the practice and effects of predatory mortgage lending in minority communities see Matt Taibbi's (2010) *Griftopia*, David Harvey's (2010) *The Enigma of Capital,* and David McNally's (2011) *Global Slump.*
2. See the database of articles by Jon Conroy on Chicago police brutality in the Chicago Reader via: http://www.chicagoreader.com/chicago/police-torture-in-chicago-jon-burge-scandal-articles-by-john-conroy/Content?oid=1210030

4   Criminality or Sociality: A Zero Sum Game?

1. These figures do not count the youth who do not attend CPS schools killed by gunfire in Chicago each year. See footnote 5 in the introduction for more on this.

5   Searching for Human Security and Citizenship

1. Quote from Freire (1998), p. 58.
2. As of 2011, 45.8 million Americans were receiving some form of food assistance.
3. For a broader historical analysis of this phenomena see Deborah Cowen (2008) *Military Workfare: The Soldier and Social Citizenship in Canada.*
4. Restorative justice is a philosophical and practical alternative to punitive forms of discipline rooted in aboriginal traditions and principles of dialogue, peer mediation, and community reparation and accountability.

Conclusion: Public Schooling for a Common Security

1. A useful text to explore this history is Howard Zinn's (2003) *A Peoples History of the United States.*

2. I owe Ken Saltman (2012) for this phrasing from his *The Failure of Corporate School Reform*. Ken Saltman, Noah de Lissovoy, and I further develop these ideas concerning the educational commons in a forthcoming book to be published on Paradigm Press.

3. An FST tax has broad support even among hard core neoliberals like Lawrence Summers; only the most regressive factions of the conservative and libertarian right oppose such a measure.

Bibliography

Advancement Project (AP). (2005). Education on Lockdown: The schoolhouse to jail-house track. Retrieved from http://www.advancementproject.org/digital library/publications/education-on-lockdown-the-schoolhouse-to-jailhouse-track

———. (2010). Test, punish, and push out: How zero tolerance and high stakes testing funnel youth into the school to prison pipeline. Retrieved from http://www.advancementproject.org/digital-library/publications/test punish and-pushout-how-zero-tolerance-and-high-stakes-testing-fu

Agamben, G. (2002). Security and terror. *Theory and Event*, 5(4).

Alexander, M. (2010). *The New Jim Crow: Mass incarceration in the age of colorblindness*. New York: The New Press.

Anderson, G. (1989). Critical ethnography in education: Origins, current status, and new directions. *Review of Educational Research*, 59(3), 249–270.

Anyon, J. (2005). *Radical possibilities: Public policy, urban education, and a new social movement*. New York: Routledge.

Apple, M. (2005). Education, markets, and an audit culture. *Critical Quarterly*, 47(12), 11–29.

———. (2006). *Educating the "right" way: Markets, standards, god, and inequality*. 2nd ed. New York: Routledge.

Arendt, H. (1961). The crisis in education. *Between Past and Future*. New York: Viking.

Aronowitz, S. (2008). *Against Schooling: For an Education that Matters*. New York: Paradigm.

Associated Press. (2010). Chicago most closely watched U.S. city. Retrieved from http://www.cbsnews.com/2100–201_162–6367705.html

Baez, B., & Boyles, D. (2009). *The politics of inquiry: Education research and the "culture of science."* New York: State University of New York Press.

Ball, S. (1993). Educational policy, power relations, and teachers' work. *British Journal of Educational Studies*, xxxxi(2), 106–121.

———. (2003). *Class strategies and the education market: the middle classes and social advantage*. New York: Routledge.

———. (2012). *Global education inc.: New policy networks and the neoliberal imaginary*. New York: Routledge.

Bauman, Z. (1998). *Globalization: The human consequences*. New York: Columbia University Press.

———. (1999). *In search of politics*. Palo Alto, CA: Stanford University Press.

———. (2001). *The individualized society*. New York: Polity.

———. (2011). Interview—On the U.K. riots. *Social Europe Journal*. Retrieved from http://www.social-europe.eu/2011/08/interview-zygmunt-bauman-on-the uk-riots/

Beck, U. (1991). *The risk society.* London: Sage Publications.

Beckett, K., & Herbert, S. (2008). Dealing with disorder: Social control in the postindustrial city. *Theoretical Criminology,* 12(1), 5–30.

Bellamy Foster, J. (2011). Education and the structural crisis of capital. *Monthly Review.* Retrieved from http://monthlyreview.org/2011/07/01/education-and-the structural-crisis-of-capital

Berlowitz, M., & Long, N. (2010). The proliferation of JROTC: Educational reform or militarization. In K. J. Saltman, & D. Gabbard. (Eds.), *Education as enforcement: The militarization and corporatization of schools.* 2nd ed. New York: Routledge.

Bogira, S. (2011). Separate, unequal, and ignored: Racial segregation remains Chicago's most fundamental problem. Why isn't it an issue in the mayor's race? *The Chicago Reader.* Retrieved from http://www.chicagoreader.com/chicago/chicago-politics seg-regation african-american-black-white-hispanic-latino-population censuscommunity /Content?oid=3221712

Bourdieu, P. (1999). *Acts of resistance: Against the tyranny of the market.* New York: New Press.

Bourdieu, P., & Passeron, J. C. (1977). *Reproduction in education, society and culture.* Beverly Hills, CA: Sage Publications.

Bowles, S., & Gintis, H. (2011). *Schooling in capitalist America: Educational reform and the contradictions of economic life.* 3rd ed. Chicago, IL: Haymarket Books.

Brenner, N., & Theodore, N. (2002). Cities and geographies of "actually existing neoliberalism." In N. Brenner, & N. Theodore. (Eds.), *Spaces of neoliberalism: Urban restructuring in North America and Western Europe.* Oxford, UK: Blackwell.

Brill, S. (2011). *Class warfare: Inside the fight to fix America's schools.* New York: Simon & Shuster.

Brown, W. (2005). *Edgework: Critical essays on knowledge and politics.* Princeton, NJ: Princeton University Press.

Brown, E. (2010). Freedom for some, discipline for "others": The structure of inequity in education. In K. J. Saltman, & D. Gabbard. (Eds.), *Education as enforcement: The militarization and corporatization of schools.* 2nd ed. New York: Routledge.

Bryant, J. (2011). Starving America's schools. *National Education Association.* Retrieved from http://www.ourfuture.org/files/documents/starving-schools-report.pdf

Bureau of Labor Statistics (BLS). (2012). Occupations with the largest growth. *Monthly Labor Review.* Retrieved from http://www.bls.gov/emp/ep_table_104.htm

Burch, P. (2009). *Hidden markets: The new education privatization.* New York: Routledge.

Calm Classroom. (2012). Retrieved from http://calmclassroom.com/

Canadian Broadcasting Corporation (CBC). (2011). *The Current.* Retrieved from http:// www.cbc.ca/thecurrent/books/2011/12/08/fast facts-about-poverty-in canada/

Catalyst. (2009). Reaching black boys. *Catalyst,* xx(5). Retrieved from http://www .catalystchicago.org/issues/2009/06/reaching-black-boys

———. (2010). Renaissance 2010. *Catalyst.* xxi(4). Retrieved from http://www.catalyst chicago .org/sites/catalyst- chicago.org/files/assets/20100803/catsummer2010.pdf

Clifford, J. (1983). On ethnographic inquiry. *Representations,* 1(2), 118–146.

Coleman, J. S., Campbell, E. Q., Hobson, C. J., McPartland, J., Mood, A. M., Weinfield, F. D., & York, R. L. (1966). *Equality of educational opportunity.* Washington, DC: U.S. Government Printing Office.

Counts, G. (1932). Dare progressive education be progressive? Retrieved from http:// courses.wccnet.edu/~palay/cls2002/counts.htm

Cowen, D. (2008). *Military workfare: The soldier and social citizenship in Canada.* Toronto: University of Toronto Press.

Cowen, D., & Siciliano, A. (2011a). Surplus masculinities and security. *Antipode*, 43(5). 1516–1541.

———. (2011b). Schooled in/security: Surplus subjects, racialized masculinity, and citizenship. In S. Feldman, R. Geislor, & G. Menon. (Eds.), *Accumulating insecurity: violence and dispossession in everyday life*. Athens, GA: The University of Georgia Press.

CREDO at Stanford University. (2009). National charter school study. Retrieved from http://credo.stanford.edu/research-reports.html

Cronin, A., & Hetherington, K. (2008). *Consuming the entrepreneurial city: Image, memory, spectacle*. New York: Routledge.

Center for Tax and Budget Accountability. (2012). Ramifications of state budget cuts to human services: Increase job loss, decreases economic activity, harms vulnerable populations. Retrieved from http://www.ctbaonline.org/New_Folder/Human%20 Services/IPHS_Private_Imp ct_Public_Cuts_Full_FINAL_revised.pdf

Darling-Hammond, L. (2010). *The flat world and education: How America's commitment to equity will determine our future*. New York: Teachers College Press.

———. (2011). The service of democratic education. *The Nation*. Retrieved from http://www.thenation.com/article/160850/service-democratic education

Davis, A. Y. (2005). *Abolition democracy: Beyond empire, prisons, and torture*. 1st ed. New York: Seven Stories Press.

Davies, B. (2003). Death to critique? The policies and practices of new managerialism and of "evidence-based practice." *Gender and Education*, 15(2), 91–103.

Davis, M. (1990). *City of quartz: Excavating the future in Los Angeles*. London: Verso.

Dean, M. (2007). *Governing societies: Political perspectives on domestic and international rule*. New York: Open University Press.

Deleuze, Gilles. (1995). *Postscript on the society of control, October* 59, 2–7.

Denzin, N. K., & Lincoln, Y. (2005). Introduction: The discipline and practice of qualitative research. In N. K. Denzin, & Y. Lincoln. (Eds.), *The Sage Handbook of Qualitative Research*, Thousand Oaks, CA: Sage Publications.

d'Eramo, M. (2002). *The pig and the skyscraper: Chicago, a history of our future*. New York: Verso.

Devine, J. (1996). *Maximum security: The culture of violence in inner-city schools*. Chicago: University of Chicago Press.

Dewey, J. (1944). *Democracy and education*. New York: The Free Press.

Dickar, M. (2008). *Corridor cultures: Mapping student resistance at an urban school*. New York: New York University Press.

Dignity in Schools. (2010). Illinois Fact Sheet (IFS). Retrieved from http://www .suspensionstories.com/research/illinois-fact-sheet/

Duminél, G., & Lévy, D. (2004).*Capital resurgent: Roots of the neoliberal revolution*. Cambridge, MA: Harvard University Press.

———. (2011). *The crisis of neoliberalism*. Cambridge, MA: Harvard University Press.

Durkheim, E. (1961). *Moral Education*. New York: The Free Press.

Economic Policy Institute. (2012). Facts and myths about a financial speculation tax. Retrieved from http://www.cepr.net/documents/fst-facts-myths-12–10.pdf

Fang, L. (2011). How online learning companies bought America's schools. *The Nation*. Retrieved from http://www.thenation.com/article/164651/how-online-learning companies-bought America's schools

Federici, S. (2004) *Caliban and the witch: Women the body, and primitive accumulation*. Brooklyn: Autonomedia

Feldman, S., Geisler, R., & Menon, G. (2011). Introduction: A new politics of containment. In S. Feldman, R. Geisler, & G. Menon. (Eds.), *Accumulating insecurity: violence and dispossession in everyday life*. Athens, GA: The University of Georgia Press.

Fine, M. (1991). *Framing dropouts: Notes on the politics of an urban public high school.* New York: State University of New York Press.

Fine, M., & Weis, L. (Eds.). (2005). *Beyond silenced voices: Class, race, and gender in United States schools.* New York: State University of New York Press.

Fisher, M. (2009). *Capitalist Realism: Is there no alternative?* New York: Zero Books.

———. (2011). Questioning capitalist realism: An interview with Mark Fisher. *Ready Steady Book.* Retrieved from http://www.readysteadybook.com/Article.aspx?page=markfisher

Foucault, M. (1977). *Discipline and punish: The birth of the prison.* New York: Random House.

———. (1994). What is enlightenment? In P. Rabinow, & N. Rose. (Eds.), *The essential Foucault.* New York: The New Press.

———. (2003). Society must be defended. *Lectures at the Collège de France,1975–1976.* New York: Palgrave Macmillan.

———. (2007). Security, territory, population. *Lectures at the Collège de France, 1977–1978.* New York: Palgrave Macmillan.

———. (2008). The birth of biopolitics. *Lectures at the Collège de France, 1978–1979.* New York: Palgrave Macmillan.

Fraser, N. (2003). From discipline to flexibilization? Rereading Foucault in the shadow of globalization. *Constellations,* 10(2), 160–171.

Fraser, N., & Gordon, L. (1996). A genealogy of dependency: Tracing a keyword of the U.S. welfare state. *Signs,* 19(2), 309–336.

Freire, P. (1998). *Pedagogy of Freedom.* Lanham: Rowman and Littlefield.

———. (2003). *Pedagogy of the oppressed.* New York: Continuum.

Gallagher, K. (2007). *The theatre of urban: Youth and schooling in dangerous times.* Toronto: University of Toronto Press.

Gallagher, K., & Fusco, C. (2006). I.D.ology and the technologies of public (school) space: An ethnographic inquiry into the neo-liberal tactics of social (re) production. *Ethnography and Education,* 1(3), 301–318.

Garland, D. (2001). *The culture of control: Crime and social order in contemporary society.* Chicago: University of Chicago Press.

Gerwitz, S., Ball, S., & Bowe, R. (1995). *Markets, choice, and equity in education.* Philadelphia, PA: Open University Press.

Gilligan, J. (2003). Shame, guilt, and violence. *Social Research: An International Quarterly,* 70(4), 1149–1180.

Gilmore, R. W. (2009). *Golden gulag: Prisons, surplus, crisis, and opposition in globalizing California.* Berkeley, CA: Berkeley University Press.

Giroux, H. (1983). Theory and resistance in education: Towards a pedagogy for the opposition. Westport: Bergin and Garvey

———. (2003). *The abandoned generation: Democracy beyond the culture of fear.* New York: Palgrave.

———. (2009). *Youth in a suspect society.* New York: Palgrave Macmillan.

———. (2012). *Twilight of the Social: Resurgent Publics in the Age of Disposability.* Boulder, CO: Paradigm.

Goldberg, D. T. (2002). *The racial state.* Oxford, UK: Blackwell.

Goldberg, G. S. (2010). *Poor women in rich countries: the feminization of poverty over the life course.* Oxford, UK: Oxford University Press.

Goodman, D. (2002). Recruiting the class of 2005. *Mother Jones.* Retrieved from http://motherjones.com/politics/2002/01/recruiting-class-2005

Graham, S. (2010). *Cities under siege.* London: Verso.

Grossberg, L. (2005). *Caught in the crossfire: Kids, politics, and America's future*. Boulder: Paradigm.

Gwynne, J., & de la Torre, M. (2009). When schools close: Effects on displaced students in Chicago Public Schools. *Consortium on Chicago School Research at the University of Chicago*. Retrieved from http://ccsr.uchicago.edu/content/publications.php?pub_id=136

Habermas, J. (1987). *Theory of communicative action*. Volume 2. Boston, MA: Beacon Press.

Hacking, I. (1986). *Representing and intervening: Introductory topics in the philosophy of natural science*. Cambridge, MA: Cambridge University Press.

Hagedorn, J. (2008). *A world of gangs: Armed young men and gangsta culture*. Minneapolis, MN: University of Minnesota Press.

Hagen, J., Hirschfield, P. J., & Shedd, C. (2003). Shooting at Tilden High School: Causes and consequences. In M. H. Moore, C. V. Petrie, A. A. Braga, & McLaughlin. (Eds.), *Deadly lessons: Understanding lethal school violence*. National Research Council. Retrieved from http://books.nap.edu/catalog.php?record_id=10370

Haggerty, K., & Eriscson, R. (Eds.). (2006). *The new politics of surveillance and visibility*. Toronto, ON: University of Toronto Press.

Harding, S. (1986). *The science question in feminism*. Ithaca, NY: Cornell University Press.

Hardt, M., & Negri, A. (2001). *Empire*. Cambridge, MA: Harvard University Press.

———. *Commonwealth*. Cambridge, MA: Harvard University Press.

Harper's Index. (2012). *Harper's Magazine*. (April).

Harrar, A. (2011). Revisiting the cost of the Bush tax cuts. *The Washington Post*. Retrieved from http://www.washingtonpost.com/blogs/fact-]checker/post/revisiting-the-cost-of-the-bush-taxcuts/2011/05/09/AFxTFtbG_blog.html

Harvey, D. (1990). *The condition of postmodernity*. Malden, MA: Blackwell.

———. (2003). *The new imperialism*. New York: Verso.

———. (2005). *A brief history of neoliberalism*. Oxford, UK: Oxford University Press.

———. (2006). *Spaces of global capitalism*. New York: Verso.

———. (2010). *The enigma of capital*. New York: Profile Books.

Heartland Alliance. (2010). 2010 Report on Illinois poverty. Retrieved from http://www.heartlandalliance.org/whatwedo/advocacy/reports/2010-report-onillinois poverty.html

———. (2011). 2011 Report on Illinois poverty. Retrieved from http://www.heartlandalliance.org/research/annual-povertyreport/pr11_report_final.pdf

Hellman, C., & Kramer, M. (2012). Our insanely big $1 trillion national security budget. *Mother Jones*. Retrieved from http://www.motherjones.com/politics/2012/05/national-security budget-1-trillion congress.

High Hopes Campaign. (2012). From policy to standard practices: Restorative justice in the Chicago public schools. Retrieved from http://www.communityrenewalsociety.org/civicactionnetwork/issues/high-hopescampaign

Hirschfield, P. J. (2008). Preparing for prison? The criminalization of school discipline in the USA. *Theoretical Criminology*, 12(1), 79–101.

———. (2010). School surveillance in America: Disparate and unequal. In T. Monahan, & R. D. Torres. (Eds.), *Schools under surveillance*. New Brunswick, NJ: Rutgers University Press.

Horkheimer, M., & Adorno, T. (2002). *The dialectic of enlightenment*. Stanford: CA: Stanford University Press.

Hulchanski, D. (2008). Violent schools in divided city: School board has little real power to overcome social divisions based on economic inequality. *Toronto Star*. Retrieved from http://www.urbancentre.utoronto.ca/pdfs/gtuo/Violent_Schools_Toronto_2008

Ingersoll, R. M. (2003). *Who controls teacher's work: power and accountability in America's schools.* Cambridge, MA: Harvard University Press.

Isin, E. (Ed.). (2000). *Democracy, citizenship, and the global city.* New York: Routledge.

Johnson, T., Boyden, J. E., & Pittz, W. J. (2001). *Racial profiling and punishment in U.S. public schools: How zero tolerance policies and high stakes testing subvert academic excellence and racial equity.* Oakland, CA: Applied Research Center.

JROTC. https://www.usarmyjrotc.com/

Judt, T. (2009). *Ill fares the land.* New York: Penguin.

Justice Policy Institute. (2007). Gang wars. Retrieved from http://www.justicepolicy.org /research/1961

Kantor, H. & Lowe, R. (2006). From New Deal to no deal: No Child Left Behind and the devolution of responsibility for educational opportunity. *Harvard Educational Review,* 76 (4), 474–502

Karp, S. (2009). Chicago schools plan to combat violence: kinder gentler security guards, disciplinarians. *Catalyst.* Retrieved from http://www.catalyst chicago.org/notebook /2009/10/27/chicago-schools-plan-combat-violence-kinder gentler security-guards

———. (2010). Huberman claims progress in creating "culture of calm" in schools. *Catalyst.* Retrieved from http://www.catalystchicago.org/notebook/2010/05/26 /huberman-claims progress-in-creating-culturecalm-in-schools

———. (2011). Youth murders up, money for school violence prevention in doubt. *Catalyst.* Retrieved from http://www.catalyst chicago.org/news/2011/01/28/youth-murders -money school-violence-prevention in-doubt

Kelly, P. (2003). Growing up as risky business? Risks, surveillance, and the institutional-ized mistrust of youth. *Journal of Youth Studies,* 6(2), 165–180.

Klein, N. (2007). *The shock doctrine.* New York: Picador.

Kochhar, R., Fry, R., & Taylor, P. (2011). Wealth gaps rise to record highs between whites, blacks and hispanics. *Pew Research Center's Social & Demographic Trends.* Retrieved from: http://pewresearch.org/pubs/2069/housing-bubble sub-prime-mortgages-hispanics blacks-household-wealth-disparity

Koval, J. P. (2006). An overview and a point of view. In J. P. Koval, L. Bennet, M. I. J. Bennet, F. Demissie, R. Garner, & K. Kim. (Eds.), *The new Chicago: A social and cultural analysis.* Philadelphia: Temple University Press.

Kozol, J. (2005). *The shame of the nation.* New York: Three Rivers Press.

Kroll, A. (2009). Fast times at recruitment high. *Mother Jones.* Retrieved from http:// motherjones.com/politics/2009/08/fast-times-recruitment-high

Kupchik. A. (2010). *Homeroom security: School discipline in an age of fear.* New York: New York University Press.

Kupchik, A., & Monahan, T. (2006). The new American school: Preparation for postin-dustrial discipline. *British Journal of Sociology of Education,* 27(5), 617–631.

Land, K. C. (2010). 2010 Child well-being index. Retrieved from http://fcd us.org /resources/2010-child-well-being-index-cwi?doc_id=4642

Lareau, A. (2003). *Unequal childhoods: class, race, and family life.* Berkeley, CA: University of California Press.

Lather, P. (2010). *Engaging science policy: From the side of the messy.* New York: Peter Lang.

Latour, B. (1987). *Science in action: How to follow scientists and engineers through society.* Cambridge, MA: Harvard University Press.

Leitner, H., Sheppard, E., Sziato, K., & Maringanti, A. (2007). Contesting urban futures: Decentering neoliberalism. In H. Leitner, J. Peck, & E. S. Sheppard. (Eds.), *Contesting neoliberalism, urban frontiers.* London: The Guilford Press.

Lemke, T. (2001). The birth of bio-politics—Michel Foucault's lecture at the Collège de France on neoliberal governmentlity. *Economy & Society,* 30(2), 190–207.

Lesko, N. (2001). *Act your age! : A cultural construction of adolescence*. New York: Routledge.

Lipman, L. (2007). Students as collateral damage? *Substance Magazine*. Retrieved from http://www.uic.edu/educ/ceje/articles/midsouth%20initial%20report%201-3107.pdf

Lipman, P. (2003). *High stakes education: Inequality, globalization, and urban school reform*. New York: Routledge.

———. (2011). *The new political economy of urban education: Neoliberalism, race, and the right to the city*. New York: Routledge.

Linebaugh, P. (2008) *The Magna Carta manifesto*. Berkely: University of California Press

Luke, A. (2004). Teaching after the market: from commodity to cosmopolitan. *Teachers College Record*, 106(7), 1422–1443.

Lyons, W., & Drew, J. (2006). *Punishing schools: Fear and citizenship in American public education*. Ann Arbor: University of Michigan Press.

Macek, S. (2006). *Urban nightmares: The media, the Right, and the moral panic over the city*. Minneapolis, MN: University of Minnesota Press.

Madison, S. D. (2012). *Critical ethnography: Methods, ethics, and performance*. Thousand Oaks, CA: Sage Publications.

Magdoff, F. (2011). The jobs disaster in the United States. *Monthly Review*, 63(2). Retrieved from http://monthlyreview.org/2011/06/01/the-jobs-disaster-in-the united-states

Mansfield, B. (Ed.). (2008). *Privatization and the re-making of nature society relations*. Malden, MA: Blackwell Publishing.

Marx, K. (1977). *Capital volume 1*. New York: Vintage Books.

Massey, D. (2005). *For space*. Thousand Oaks, CA: Sage Publications.

Massey, D. S., & Denton, N. A. (1993). *American apartheid: Segregation and the making of the underclass*. Cambridge, MA: Harvard University Press.

McCormick, J. (2003). "Drag me to the asylum": Disguising and asserting identities in an urban school. *The Urban Review*, 35(2), 11–128.

McDuffee, A. (2008). No JROTC left behind. *In These Times*. Retrieved from http://www .inthesetimes.com/article/3855/

McNally, D. (2011). *Global slump: the economic and politics of crisis and resistance*. Oakland, CA: Spectre PM.

———. (2012). Slump, austerity and resistance. *Socialist Register*, 48, 36–63.

McNeil, L. (2000). *Contradictions of school reform: educational costs of standardized testing*. New York: Routledge.

McRobbie, A. (1978). Working class girls and the culture of femininity. In Women's Studies Group, Centre for Contemporary Cultural Studies, *Women Take Issue*. Birmingham: University of Birmingham. 96–108.

Means, A. (2011). Creativity as an educational problematic in the biopolitical economy. In M. A. Peters, & E. Bulut. (Eds.), *Cognitive capitalism, education, and digital labor*. New York: Peter Lang.

Mishel, L., Bernstein, J., & Shierholz, H. (2009). *State of working America*. Ithaca, NY: Cornel University Press.

Moe, T. M., & Chubb, J. E. (2009). *Liberating learning: technology, politics, and the future of American education*. San Francisco, CA: Jossey-Bass.

Mohanty, C. T. (2003). *Feminism without borders: decolonizing theory, practicing solidarity*. Durham, NC: Duke University Press.

Mojab, S., & Carpenter, S. (2011). Learning by dispossession: democracy promotion and civic engagement in Iraq and the United States. *International Journal of Lifelong Learning*, 30(4), 549–563.

Moynihan, D. P. (1965). *The Negro family: The case for national action*. Washington DC: Office of Planning and Research, United States Department of Labor.

NBC. (2009). Derrion Albert's death may be rooted in school closures. Retrieved from http://www.nbcchicago.com/news/local/holder-arne-duncan-fenger-city-hall`daley -63642507.html

Newfield, C. (2008). *Unmaking the public university: The forty year assault on the middle class*. Cambridge, MA: Harvard University Press.

Newman, O. (1972). *Defensible space: Crime prevention through urban design*. New York: Macmillan.

New York Civil Liberties Union (NCLU). School to prison pipeline: A look at New York City school safety. Retrieved from http://www.nyclu.org/node/1454

Nogeura, P. (2003). Schools, prisons, and social implications of punishment: Rethinking disciplinary practices. *Theory in Practice*, 42(4), 341–350.

Nolan, K. (2011). *Police in the hallways*. Minneapolis, MN: University of Minnesota Press.

Olssen, M., Codd, J., & O'Neil, A. M. (2004). *Education policy: globalization, citizenship, and democracy*. Thousand Oaks, CA: Sage Publications.

Parenti, C. (1999). *Lockdown America*. New York: Verso.

———. (2003). *The soft cage: Surveillance in America from slavery to the war on terror*. New York: Basic Books.

Patterson, O. (1982). *Slavery and social death: A comparative study*. Cambridge, MA: Harvard University Press.

Peck, J., & Tickel, A. (2002). Neoliberalizing space. In N. Brenner, & N. Theodore. (Eds.), *Spaces of neoliberalism: urban restructuring in North America and Western Europe*. Oxford, UK: Blackwell.

Pedroni, T. (2007). *Market movements: African American involvement in school voucher reform*. New York: Routledge.

PEW. (2009). One in 31 U.S. adults are behind bars, on parole or probation. Retrieved from http://www.pewcenteronthestates.org/news_room_detail.aspx?id=49398

Project NIA. (2010). Chicago youth justice data project. Retrieved from http://www .chicagoyouthjustice.com/Project_NIA_Arrests_page_v2.html

Raey, D., & Helen, L. (2003). The limits of "choice": Children and inner city schooling. *Sociology*, 37(1), 121–142.

Ravitch, D. (2010). *The life and death of the great American school system: How testing and choice are undermining education*. New York: Basic Books.

Rizvi, R., & Lingard, B. (2009). *Globalizing education policy*. New York: Routledge.

Robbins, C. (2009). *Expelling hope: The assault on youth and the militarization of schooling*. New York: State University of New York Press.

Rose. N. (1996). The death of the social: Re-figuring the territory of government. *Economy and Society*, 25(3), 327–356.

Rothstein, R. (2004). *Class and schools: Using social, economic and educational reform to close the Black White achievement gap*. Washington, DC: Economic Policy Institute.

Ruddick, S. (2006). Abnormal, the "new normal," and destabilizing discourses of rights. *Public Culture*, 18(1), 53–77.

Sachs. J. (2011). *The price of civilization: Reawakening American virtue and prosperity*. New York: Random House.

Said, E. (1989). Representing the colonized: Anthropology's interlocutors. *Critical Inquiry*, 15, 205–225.

Salter, M. (2004). Passports, mobility, and security: How smart can the border be?" *International Studies Perspectives*, 5(1), 71–91.

Saltman, K. J. (2007). *Capitalizing on disaster*. Boulder, CO: Paradigm.

——. (2009). *The Gift of Education*. New York: Palgrave Macmillan.

——. (2010). *Facing corporatization and the myths of charter schools*. Unpublished paper presented at the 2010 American Educational Studies Association Conference. Denver, CO.

——. (2012). *The failure of corporate school reform*. Boulder, CO: Paradigm.

Saltman, K. J., & Gabbard, D. (Eds.). (2010). *Education as enforcement: The militarization and corporatization of schools*. 2nd ed. New York: Routledge.

Sassen, S. (2006). *Cities in a world economy*. 3rd ed. Thousand Oaks, CA: Pine Forge Press.

Shaefer-Duffy, C. (2003). Feeding the military machine. *National Catholic Reporter*. Retrieved from http://www.natcath.org/NCR_Online/archives/032803/032803a.htm

Shipps, D. (2006). School reform, corporate style: Chicago 1880–2000. Lawrence: University of Kansas Press

Simon, J. (2007). *Governing through Crime*. Oxford, UK: Oxford University Press.

Smith, L. T. (2005). On tricky ground: Researching the native in the age of uncertainty. In N. K. Denzin, & Y. Lincoln. (Eds.). *The Sage Handbook of Qualitative Research*, Thousand Oaks, CA: Sage Publications.

Smith, N. (1996). *The new urban frontier: Gentrification and the revanchist city*. London: Routledge.

——. (2002). "New globalism, new urbanism: Gentrificaiton as global urban strategy." In N. Brenner, & N. Theodore. (Eds.), *Spaces of neoliberalism: Urban restructuring in North America and Western Europe*. Oxford: Blackwell.

——. (2008). *Uneven development. Nature, capital, and the production of space*. 3rd ed. Athens, GA: University of Georgia Press.

Stiglitz, J. (2012). *The price of inequality*. New York: Norton & Company.

Street, P. (2002). The vicious circle: Race, prisons, jobs, and community in Chicago, Illinois and the nation. Retrieved from http://www.prisonpolicy.org/scans/theviciouscircle.pdf

——. (2007). *Racial oppression in the global metropolis: A living black Chicago history*. New York: Rowman and Littlefield.

Sugrue, T. J. (1996). *The origins of the urban crisis: race and inequality in postwar Detroit*. Princeton, NJ: Princeton University Press.

Taibbi, M. (2010). *Griftopia: Bubble machines, vampire squids, and the long con that is breaking America*. New York: Spiegel & Grau.

Thomson, P. (2002). *Schooling the rustbelt kids: Making the difference in changing times*. Melbourne, AU: Allen and Unwin.

Tilton, J. (2010). *Dangerous or endangered: Race and the politics of youth in urban America*. New York: New York University Press.

Tyack, D. (1974). *The one best system: A history of American urban education*. Cambridge, MA: Harvard University Press.

UNICEF. (2012). Measuring child poverty. Retrieved from http://www.unicef irc.org/publications/pdf/rc10_eng.pdf

Voices of Youth in Chicago (VOYCE). (2011). Failed policies, broken futures: The true cost of zero tolerance in Chicago. Retrieved from http://www.publicinterestprojects.org/wp content/uploads/downloads/2011/08/VOYCE-report-2011.pdf

Wacquant, L. (2008). *Urban outcasts: A comparative sociology of advanced marginality*. Malden, MA: Polity.

——. (2009). *Punishing the poor: The neoliberal government of social insecurity*. Durham, NC: Duke University Press.

Weber, M. (1964). *The theory of social and economic organization*. New York: The Free Press.

Weisberg, B. (2010). On solutions to urban violence. Retrieved from http://www.wbez
.org/episode-segments/barry-weisberg-solutions-urban-violence

Wilkinson, R., & Picket, K. (2009). *The spirit level: why greater equality makes societies stronger*. New York: Bloomsbury Press.

Williams, R. (1977). *Marxism and literature*. Oxford: Oxford University Press.

Williams, T. (2011). As public sector sheds jobs, Blacks are hit the hardest. *New York Times*. Retrieved from http://www.nytimes.com/2011/11/29/us/as-public-sectorsheds-jobs-black-americans-are-hit-hard.html

Willis, P. (1977). Learning to labor: How working class kids get working class jobs. New York: Columbia University Press.

Wilson, W. J. (1996). *When work disappears: The new world of the urban poor*. New York: Vintage Books.

Wotherspoon, T. (2004). *The sociology of education in Canada*. Oxford, UK: Oxford University Press.

Yen, H. (2011). Census shows 1 in 2 people are poor or low-income. *Associated Press*. Retrieved from http://www.salon.com/2011/12/15/census_shows_1_in_2_people_are_poor _or_l w_income

Yon, D. (2003). Highlights and overview of the history of educational ethnography. *Annual Review of Anthropology*, 32, 411–429.

Zinn, H. (2003). *A People's History of the United States*. New York: Harper Perenial.

Žižek, S. (2008). *Violence*. New York: Picador.

Index